NEW ORLEANS

DK

NEW ORLEANS

CONTENTS

DISCOVER 6

EXPERIENCE 56

NEED TO KNOW 200

Left: Brass band performing at a parade
Previous page: City skyline seen from the Mississippi
Front cover: French Quarter balconies adorned with
festive decorations

DISCOVER

WELCOME TO
NEW ORLEANS

Nowhere in the United States is quite like New Orleans. Known as the "Crescent City," NOLA is set in a gentle curve of the Mississippi River, where a history of strong European, Caribbean, and African influences have shaped a local culture like no other. This heady mix results in a daily celebration of life, reflected in the city's food, music, and traditions. Whatever your dream trip to New Orleans includes, this DK travel guide is the perfect companion.

① A red streetcar clattering along Canal Street.

② Admiring a mansion in the leafy Garden District.

③ Fresh boiled crawfish, a Louisiana specialty.

④ Gathering around a brass band on Frenchmen Street.

Trundle through town aboard the famous streetcar and watch 300 years of history unfurl. From Gothic mansions, through colorful Creole cottages, to the elegant wrought-iron galleries of the French Quarter, the city's historic architecture creates a stunning cinematic backdrop.

Immerse yourself in Louisiana's finest art at the Ogden Museum of Southern Art, or get lost among the New Orleans Museum of Art's (NOMA's) array of international treasures. The food scene is equally enticing, with dishes like Cajun crawfish and Vietnamese bánh mì on the menu, accompanied by a classic cocktail.

This generous party city is also known as the "Big Easy," and its Mardi Gras spirit lives on year-round in jubilant daily celebrations and raucous nightly revelry on Bourbon Street. And don't forget, this is the home of jazz. Streets resound with a cacophony of music, from the buzz of cool clubs on Frenchmen Street, to the brassy bursts of second lines marching through Treme.

If it all gets too much, head to the river and catch a breeze cruising along on a paddle steamer. Outside the city, the landscape unfolds into watery swamps and bayous, where boat trips drift through mossy stands of cypress.

So, where to start? We've broken the city down into easily navigable chapters, with detailed itineraries, expert local knowledge, and colorful, comprehensive maps to help you plan the perfect visit. Whether you're staying for a weekend, a week, or longer, this DK travel guide will ensure that you see the very best New Orleans has to offer. Enjoy the book, and enjoy New Orleans.

REASONS TO LOVE
NEW ORLEANS

Infectious music, irresistible food, the beauty of the Mississippi, historic neighborhoods, and the world's biggest free party, Mardi Gras. There are endless reasons to love New Orleans, but here are some of our favorites.

1 LIVE JAZZ

This is the birthplace of jazz, and you can't leave the city without experiencing the scene (p28). Preservation Hall is the spot to hear traditional bands play every night (p77).

GREEN PARKS 2

With vast City Park in the north (p166), riverside Crescent Park in the east (p119), and bucolic Audubon Park to the west (p156), New Orleans is a truly green and pleasant city.

3 SIPPING ON CLASSIC COCKTAILS

A special kind of alchemy gives rise to the city's classic tipples. Brandy milk punch at brunch, or a sazerac at sundown, any time is the right time to savor a classic New Orleans cocktail.

LGBTQ+ CULTURE 4

NOLA is a liberal island in the state of Louisiana, with LGBTQ+ bars and clubs filling the French Quarter, and Pride and Southern Decadence festivals dominating the calendar (p46).

THE FESTIVALS 5

New Orleans' calendar is packed with celebrations (p46). Joining Mardi Gras are legendary music festivals like Jazz Fest (p174) and regular jubilant parades (p114).

DIVERSE CULTURES 6

A gumbo of international influences are evident in the culture of this eclectic place, from its colorful Creole cottages to the ubiquitous Italian-inspired muffuletta sandwich.

MARDI GRAS 7

New Orleans comes alive during a month of parades and parties. This culminates on Mardi Gras day, when the entire city dons fancy dress in a cacophony of revelry (*p66*).

WANDERING THE FRENCH QUARTER 8

The city's 300-year-old heart will awaken your inner *flaneur* (*p58*). Here, elegant ironwork-galleried streets are lined with antique stores, lively, storied bars, and Creole dining rooms.

9 THE ST. CHARLES AVENUE STREETCAR

Hop on the iconic green streetcar and trundle slowly uptown, past university campuses and opulent mansions along one of the city's most beautiful avenues (*p142*).

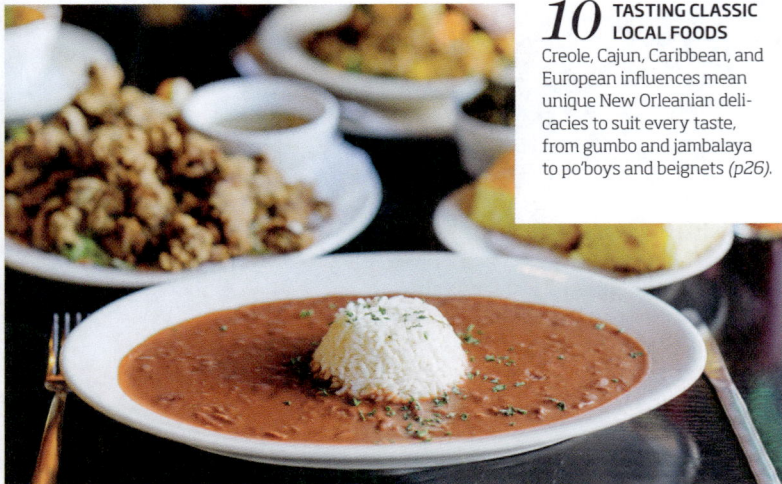

10 TASTING CLASSIC LOCAL FOODS

Creole, Cajun, Caribbean, and European influences mean unique New Orleanian delicacies to suit every taste, from gumbo and jambalaya to po'boys and beignets *(p26)*.

THE MISSISSIPPI 11

The river is a symbol of the city, and the source of its identity. Steamboat *Natchez* offers gentle jazz cruises *(p74)*, and Moon Walk is perfect for waterside strolling *(p99)*.

FABULOUS SHOPPING 12

Window shoppers and big spenders rejoice *(p38)*. Try Royal Street for antiques, Magazine Street for boutiques, or the Warehouse District for unbeatable fine art.

EXPLORE
NEW ORLEANS

This guide divides New Orleans into
six color-coded sightseeing areas,
as shown on this map. Find out more
about each area on the following
pages. For sights beyond the city
center, see p180.

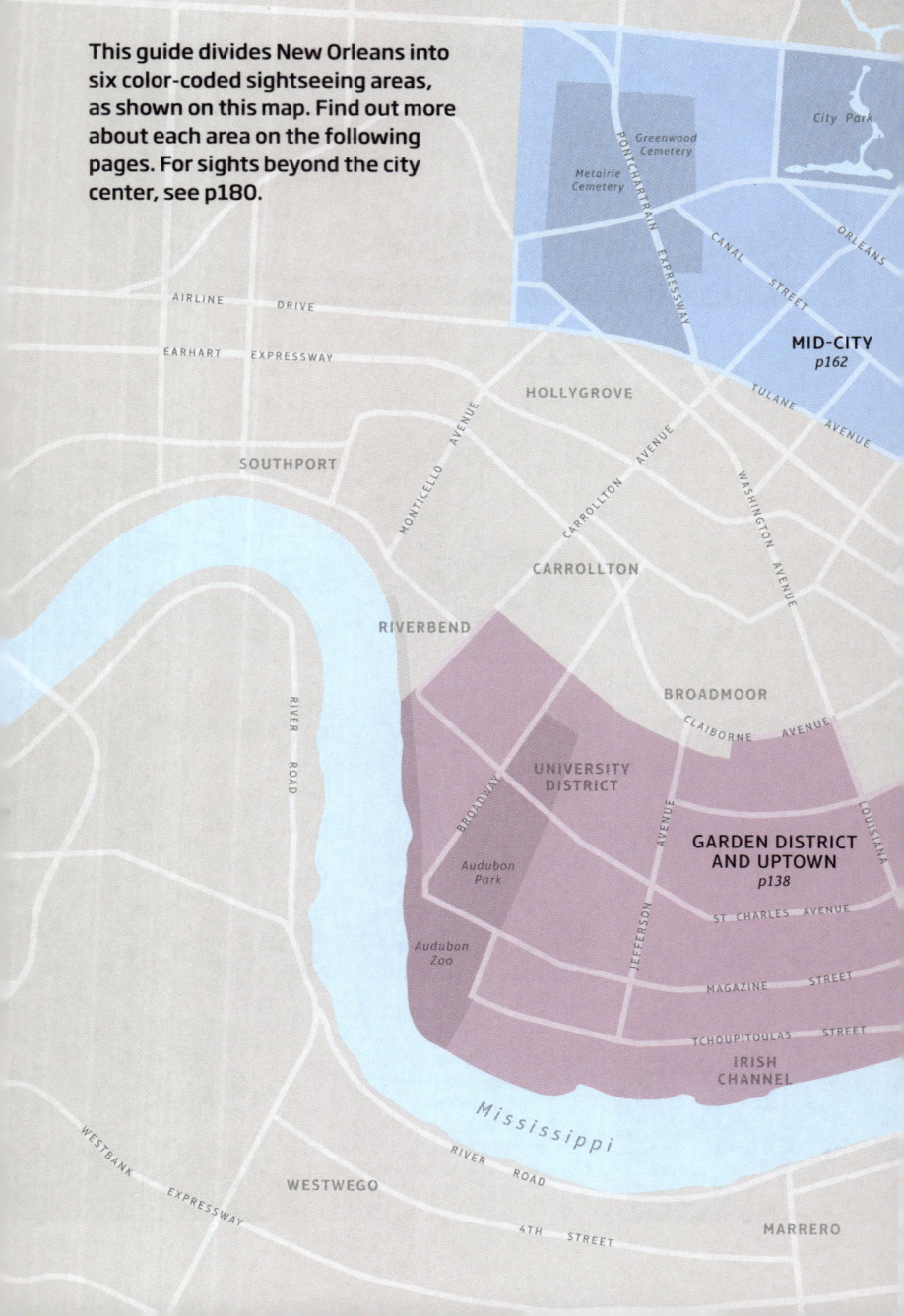

AIRLINE   DRIVE

EARHART   EXPRESSWAY

Greenwood
Cemetery

City Park

Metairie
Cemetery

PONCHARTRAIN EXPRESSWAY

CANAL   STREET

ORLEANS

MID-CITY
p162

HOLLYGROVE

TULANE   AVENUE

SOUTHPORT

MONTICELLO   AVENUE

CARROLLTON   AVENUE

WASHINGTON   AVENUE

CARROLLTON

RIVERBEND

RIVER   ROAD

BROADMOOR

CLAIBORNE   AVENUE

UNIVERSITY
DISTRICT

BROADWAY

Audubon
Park

AVENUE

LOUISIANA

**GARDEN DISTRICT
AND UPTOWN**
p138

Audubon
Zoo

JEFFERSON

ST. CHARLES   AVENUE

MAGAZINE   STREET

TCHOUPITOULAS   STREET

**IRISH
CHANNEL**

Mississippi

WESTBANK

EXPRESSWAY

WESTWEGO

RIVER   ROAD

4TH   STREET

MARRERO

NORTH AMERICA

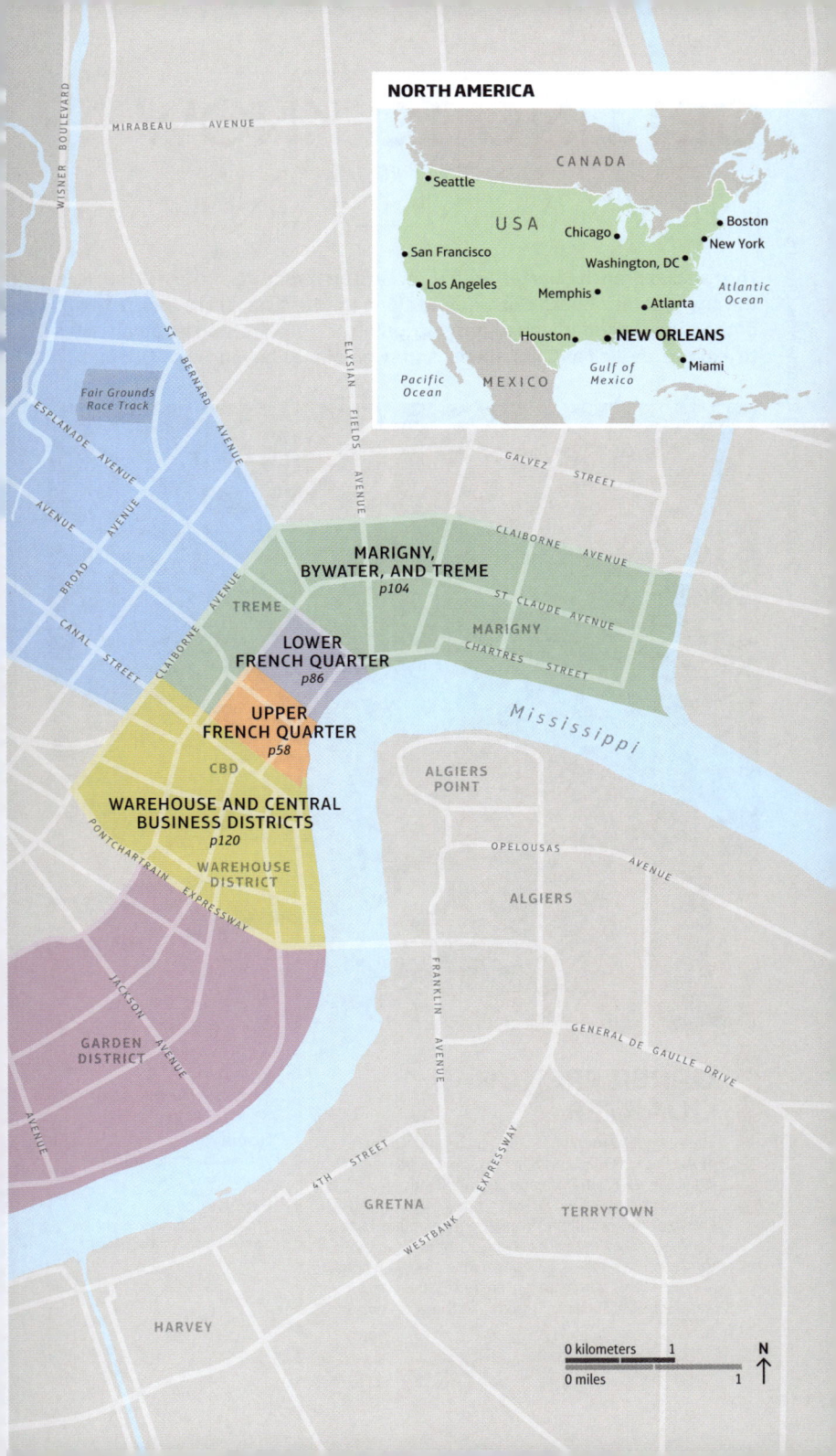

CANADA

USA

- Seattle
- San Francisco
- Los Angeles
- Chicago
- Boston
- New York
- Washington, DC
- Memphis
- Atlanta
- Houston
- **NEW ORLEANS**
- Miami

Atlantic Ocean

Pacific Ocean

MEXICO

Gulf of Mexico

WISNER BOULEVARD

MIRABEAU AVENUE

ST BERNARD AVENUE

ELYSIAN FIELDS AVENUE

GALVEZ STREET

ESPLANADE AVENUE

Fair Grounds Race Track

AVENUE

BROAD AVENUE

CLAIBORNE AVENUE

CANAL STREET

CLAIBORNE AVENUE

TREME

CLAIBORNE AVENUE

ST CLAUDE AVENUE

MARIGNY, BYWATER, AND TREME
p104

MARIGNY

CHARTRES STREET

LOWER FRENCH QUARTER
p86

UPPER FRENCH QUARTER
p58

Mississippi

CBD

WAREHOUSE AND CENTRAL BUSINESS DISTRICTS
p120

WAREHOUSE DISTRICT

ALGIERS POINT

OPELOUSAS AVENUE

ALGIERS

PONTCHARTRAIN EXPRESSWAY

FRANKLIN AVENUE

GENERAL DE GAULLE DRIVE

JACKSON AVENUE

GARDEN DISTRICT

AVENUE

4TH STREET

WESTBANK EXPRESSWAY

GRETNA

TERRYTOWN

HARVEY

0 kilometers 1

0 miles 1

N

GETTING TO KNOW
NEW ORLEANS

The famous French Quarter, with its ornate architecture and joyful music, is the city's historic heart. But winding along the Mississippi are colorful neighborhoods with superb museums, intriguing cemeteries, and landmark sites to explore, as well as Cajun towns and swamplands beyond New Orleans.

UPPER FRENCH QUARTER

PAGE 58

The city grew around Jackson Square, and this part of the French Quarter is home to some of its most iconic sights. From Dixieland jazz ringing out from street corners to the delicious aromas of Cajun and Creole dishes wafting from cafés and restaurants, this densely packed network of historic streets is a feast for the senses. Take a walk down Royal Street, where antique stores glow with glittering treasures, and wander along Bourbon Street to let the good times roll.

Best for
Sightseeing, fine dining, and strolling along the river

Home to
St. Louis Cathedral, The Historic New Orleans Collection

Experience
A cruise along the Mississippi aboard the Steamboat Natchez

PAGE 86

LOWER FRENCH QUARTER

The bustling French Market aside, this is the quieter end of the French Quarter, where relatively tranquil streets offer an escape from the crowds. Here, classic New Orleans architecture of Creole cottages sits neatly alongside some of the city's oldest buildings like the Old Ursuline Convent. Historic mansions such as Gallier House now hold museums offering an insight into what life was like in times gone by.

Best for
Admiring ironwork architecture and historic houses

Home to
The French Market

Experience
Tasting sugar-dusted beignets with coffee at Café du Monde

PAGE 104

MARIGNY, BYWATER, AND TREME

Treme is the country's oldest African American neighborhood, and its spirit and culture bubble up from the streets, with jubilant brass bands marching through the district. Downriver, Marigny and Bywater are peppered with colorful shotgun houses and Creole cottages, as well as spectacular street murals. Linger and soak up the atmosphere of second-hand stores, art galleries, and hip cafés, and cycle along the serene riverfront in Crescent Park. These quarters come alive at night, as trendy Bywater restaurants throng with diners, and revelers spill out from the jazz clubs of the cool musical enclave of Frenchmen Street.

Best for
Jazz clubs, African American history

Home to
St. Louis Cemetery #1, Louis Armstrong Park

Experience
Jazz bar-hopping on Frenchmen Street

→

PAGE 120

WAREHOUSE AND CENTRAL BUSINESS DISTRICTS

The broad thoroughfare of Canal Street marks the start of the city's commercial center. But the Central Business District (CBD) is much more than a corporate corridor. Beneath the bright lights of the Superdome, sophisticated bars and restaurants vie with landmark theaters and luxury shopping spots. The adjoining Warehouse District has been reborn as the city's Arts District, the SoHo of the South. This area glows with lively creativity, with its clutch of galleries, most found on Julia Street, and outstanding museums.

Best for
Museums and art galleries, shopping

Home to
Audubon Aquarium

Experience
Discovering Louisiana's art at the Ogden Museum of Southern Art

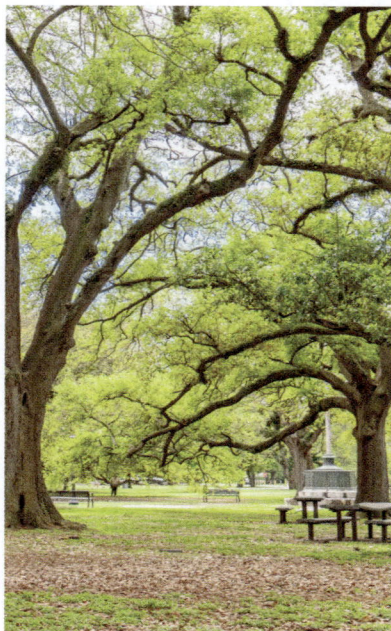

PAGE 138

GARDEN DISTRICT AND UPTOWN

A ride on the clattering St. Charles Avenue Streetcar transports you to the city's leafiest district. Wander past grand, eclectic mansions and explore tranquil Lafayette Cemetery No. 1; a stroll here seems a world away from the bustling city center. Uptown you'll find prestigious universities and family fun in Audubon Park, along with trendy Magazine Street, home to independent boutiques and cool cafés.

Best for
Grand historic homes, ornate cemeteries

Home to
St. Charles Avenue Streetcar, Audubon Park

Experience
Riding the streetcar along St. Charles Avenue

MID-CITY

PAGE 162

Dominating this district is City Park, a vast oasis of parkland cut through by a tangle of bayous and lagoons. Ride the classic wooden carousel in Storyland, or wander the lush grounds of the New Orleans Botanical Garden. The park is also home to the outstanding New Orleans Museum of Art (NOMA) and the expansive Besthoff Sculpture Garden. Along the park's eastern edge is Bayou St. John, an inner-city creek that winds northwards to Lake Pontchartrain. The bayou's grassy banks provide a picturesque spot for picnics, parties, and the occasional crawfish boil.

Best for
Local bars and restaurants, and picnic spots

Home to
New Orleans Museum of Art

Experience
Relaxing beneath the live oaks in City Park

BEYOND NEW ORLEANS

PAGE 180

New Orleans' surroundings provide a stark contrast to its compact city center. Just a few hours' drive away is the River Road, where former plantation mansions, now museums, teach visitors about the complicated history of the area's plantation economy. Further west lie the massive Atchafalaya Swamp and sprawling Cajun Country, where Francophone culture awaits in Lafayette's robust, spicy cuisine and lively music scene. Meanwhile, to the north, the Louisiana state capital of Baton Rouge is a thriving metropolis, with a vibrant nightlife and historic attractions.

Best for
Museums, Cajun culture

Home to
The Whitney Plantation, Lafayette, Baton Rouge

Experience
Spotting alligators on a swamp tour

←

1 Admiring artworks in Jackson Square.

2 Café du Monde.

3 Cruising along the river aboard Steamboat *Natchez*.

4 The neon lights of busy Bourbon Street.

With its romantic architecture, delectable cuisine, and vibrant array of live music and entertainment, New Orleans is a treasure trove for travelers. These itineraries will help you make the most of your visit.

24 HOURS
in New Orleans

Morning

Start by snagging an outdoor table at Café du Monde (p96), New Orleans' landmark coffeehouse. Sink your teeth into soft, powdery beignets and sip hot chicory coffee as you watch the world go by. Set up for the day, climb the steps to the adjoining Washington Artillery Park for a splendid panoramic view over Jackson Square (p76), flanked by the impressive trio from the early French and Spanish colony: St. Louis Cathedral (p62), the Presbytère (p64), and the Cabildo (p68). Wander the lively square, enjoying the tunes of jazz musicians, and watch artists displaying their colorful paintings on the perimeter fence. Head over to the Toulouse tram stop and enjoy a short ride on the historic Riverfront Line. Get off at Canal at St. Charles, wander up Royal Street (p70) to the Historic New Orleans Collection and spend an hour here inspecting the paintings and decorative arts (p72). Then stroll back along Royal Street to admire beautifully preserved period architecture, and pop into art galleries and antique shops filled with glittering treasures.

Afternoon

By now you'll have worked up an appetite, so wander along Decatur Street to reach the Central Grocery (p96). Indulge in a classic muffuletta sandwich stuffed with tasty Italian deli meats, cheese, and olive salad – you can take it away to eat at the little park across the street beneath a golden Joan of Arc statue. Stomach full, head to the riverfront to board the iconic Steamboat *Natchez* – you'll recognize the peals of the boat's calliope organ from a mile away (p74). Put your feet up on a relaxing two-hour river cruise (departing at 2:30pm), accompanied by live jazz, fascinating narratives on the city, and breezy views of the busy waterway.

Evening

Back on dry land, it's nearly cocktail time, so make your way to Bourbon Street, where there are lively bars to suit every style (p77). Start at the Old Absinthe House (p81). Oozing historic atmosphere, this has been a French Quarter watering hole since 1807. Then sip a sundowner at the elegant Arnaud's French 75 Bar, named after its classy champagne cocktail (p81). For fans of Tennessee Williams' play *A Streetcar Named Desire*, Galatoire's makes the perfect choice for dinner, with its delicious traditional Creole cuisine (p77). Your last port of call is Frenchmen Street, to party the night away in local jazz clubs (p117).

←

1 The French Market.

2 An elegant lunch at Ralph's on the Park.

3 Live music at the Spotted Cat on Frenchmen Street.

4 Bright lights of the grand Saenger Theatre.

3 DAYS

in New Orleans

Day 1

Morning Beat the crowds with an early start at the French Market (p90). Breakfast is coffee and a pastry from the food stalls, followed by a wander through the busy flea market. When you've picked up some souvenirs, aim for Jackson Square (p76), where you'll peak inside St. Louis Cathedral to glimpse the beautifully carved Baroque altar (p62).

Afternoon For lunch, head to Clover Grill (p93) for eggs, burger, or any diner fare you fancy. Refreshed, hop on the Esplanade Avenue bus to Mid-City for a walk along the tranquil Bayou St. John (p175). Cross Magnolia Bridge to reach the New Orleans Museum of Art, and the vast Besthoff Sculpture Gardens surrounding the museum (p169).

Evening Enjoy a light supper of fresh, farm-to-table fare at Ralph's on the Park (ralphsonthepark.com). Take the Canal Streetcar back to your hotel, the chic Audubon Cottages (p78), to freshen up for the evening. Then head to the plush Sazerac Bar (p135) for a nightcap of New Orleans' signature rye whiskey cocktail.

Day 2

Morning After breakfast at your hotel, ride the St. Charles Avenue Streetcar to the Garden District (p142). Stroll the leafy streets and admire grand mansions such as Gothic Revival Briggs-Staub House and Greek-columned Robinson House (p145), before exploring the Benjamin Button

House and the former home of renowned author Anne Rice (p144).

Afternoon Take a walk down Magazine Street and dip into trendy boutiques (p39), before stopping in at Joey K's for a taste of homestyle Creole cooking (joeyks restaurant.com). Reboard the streetcar and continue uptown to Audubon Zoo, home to rare and endangered creatures from around the globe (p157).

Evening Ride the streetcar back to the Warehouse District in time for a contemporary Caribbean dinner at Compère Lapin (p129). Take a cab to the Spotted Cat on Frenchmen Street for late-night jazz (p117).

Day 3

Morning Start the day with a bang-up breakfast at the Ruby Slipper Cafe (ruby brunch.com), before spending a few hours in the huge National WWII Museum touring numerous impressive military displays (p126). Grab a light lunch at the museum café, Jeri Nims Soda Shop.

Afternoon Catch a fresh breeze by taking a ferry across to Algiers, enjoying scenic views of the city. Stroll along the Jazz Walk of Fame and snap a photo with the grand statue of Louis Armstrong.

Evening Suitably chilled out, take the ferry back downtown and head to the modern Cajun restaurant Cochon for an early dinner of fine charcuterie and a glass or two of old-world wine (p129). Then make for the beautiful Italianate Saenger Theatre and end your day with a spectacular Broadway show (p133).

5 DAYS

Day 1

Morning Set out first thing for a wander of Jackson Square (p76) – you'll beat the crowds, and catch the morning light accenting the square's lacy ironwork. Peek into the Presbytère (p64), where you can browse a range of exhibits on topics such as Mardi Gras and Hurricane Katrina (p69).

Afternoon Begin an afternoon of French Quarter strolling with lunch at Coop's Place (p93). Then pay a visit to nearby Gallier Historic House museum for a glimpse of 19th-century life (p94).

Evening Have dinner in the courtyard of a charming Creole cottage at Bayona, before catching a show at Bourbon Street jazz club Fritzel's (p77). Stay up late at nearby Old Absinthe House (p81).

Day 2

Morning Make your way to Treme to immerse yourself in the rich African American history of this district. Meander through Louis Armstrong Park (p108), taking in the sculptures of Congo Square, before lingering in the Backstreet Cultural Museum to learn about Mardi Gras traditions (p115).

Afternoon Dip into Schooner Saloon (schoonersaloon.com) for a lunch of Cajun and Creole fare, then spend the afternoon wandering along the alleyways of St. Louis Cemetery #1 (p112) on a guided tour.

Evening For dinner, make for famed Dooky Chase and savor classic Creole dishes of gumbo and shrimp clemenceau (p176). Return to the French Quarter, and while the night away listening to impeccable trad jazz at Preservation Hall (p77).

Day 3

Morning Have a hearty breakfast at Buffa's (buffasbar.com), ready for a day of cycling. Rent a Blue Bike (p207) and ride through Marigny and Bywater, past colorful Creole cottages and shotgun houses. Continue along the river through Crescent Park (p119), and stop at Pizza Delicious for the best slice in town (p118).

① Historic French Quarter buildings.

② Trad jazz performance at legendary Preservation Hall.

③ Entrance to the historic Dooky Chase's.

④ Cocktail at Hot Tin rooftop bar.

⑤ Cycling through City Park.

⑥ The Audubon Aquarium.

Afternoon Head north to roll along the Lafitte Greenway and continue on up to City Park, where you'll wheel past lagoons and groves of oak trees (*p172*).

Evening After leaving your bike at one of the many Blue Bike stands across the city, head to Magazine Street. Take it easy with a cold beer or two at the Bulldog (*thebulldog.bar*), then hop in a cab to Saba for a dinner of modern Israeli cuisine (*p145*).

Day 4

Morning Start early and hit the espresso bar at Tout La, in the lobby of the Old 77 Hotel (*p133*). After coffee and pastries, head over to the Audubon Aquarium, where astonishing displays of underwater worlds await (*p135*).

Afternoon Amble along the riverfront to the Riverwalk Outlets for souvenirs and lunch inside the mall (*p129*). Ride the ferry across the river to Algiers Point and back, taking in the sparkling city vistas (*p128*).

Evening After a luxurious Cajun Creole dinner at Emeril's (*p129*), spend the evening dipping in and out of the dozens of art galleries along Julia Street (*p136*).

Day 5

Morning Rise early to get to the New Orleans Jazz National Historical Park Visitor Center in time for the 10am ranger talk (*p81*). After delving into the rich cultural history of the city, drop into Verti Marte and pick up a lunchtime po'boy sandwich (*p93*).

Afternoon Head back to your hotel in time for the afternoon pick-up for a Barataria Preserve swamp tour (*p194*). Out in the reserve, you'll spot alligators, turtles, and pelicans as you glide through a lattice of cypress-lined bayous by boat.

Evening Shake off the swamp and head to The Joint for a supper of slow-cooked barbecue (*p118*). Take a cab across town to the Pontchartrain Hotel (*p146*), where you'll savor cocktails and superb skyline vistas at the Hot Tin rooftop bar.

Sweet Treats

Indulge your sweet tooth with New Orleans' decadent desserts. The beignet – a sugar-dusted choux pastry doughnut – is a sweet staple, best savored with coffee at the legendary Café du Monde *(p96)*. During Mardi Gras *(p66)*, try the iconic king cake, a huge cinnamon roll with carnival-colored frosting, which will transport you straight to the heart of the celebration.

←

Café du Monde's famous beignets with hot chicory coffee

NEW ORLEANS FOR
FOODIES

New Orleanians have a generous appetite and a varied palate, and there is a dizzying array of dining options in this city. Cajun and Creole menus dominate, and though New Orleans is marinated in its own gastronomic traditions, there's innovation to explore beyond the classics.

Fine Dining

There are plenty of opulent spots here to satisfy discerning gourmands. Try Galatoire's for turtle soup and duck *andouille (p77)*, or Commander's Palace for its elegant Jazz Brunch and famous 25 cent Martini *(p145)*. Look beyond tradition to the city's cool contemporary spots: Compère Lapin brings a modern twist to Creole and Caribbean cuisine *(p129)*, and new-wave Restaurant R'evolution breathes new life into the classics with its unique dishes like deconstructed gumbo *(revolutionnola.com)*.

→

Innovative upscale dining at acclaimed Compère Lapin

Comfort Food

From silky Creole gumbo to sustaining Vietnamese pho (noodle soup), New Orleans' comfort food soothes the soul and sates the stomach. Dive into classic Creole cuisine at the city's must-stop soul-food spots. At the legendary Dooky Chase, savor plates of the most unctuous fried chicken and rich traditional gumbo *(p176)*, or at Coop's Place try the delicately spiced jambalaya *(p93)*. Contemporary Vietnamese restaurant Pho Tau *(pho taubayrestaurant.com)* is the place to slurp on a steaming bowl of pho.

A bowl of rich Creole gumbo, with shrimp, sausage, and okra

Slices of Life

New Orleans is a city of three sandwiches. At Parkway Tavern *(parkwaypoorboys.com)* the homegrown specialty, the mighty po'boy, comes laden with Gulf oyster, shrimp, or roast beef and gravy. Meanwhile, the pillowy Italian-inspired muffuletta is best sampled at Central Grocery *(p96)*. The crisp bánh mì completes the trio – make for Banh Mi Boys to taste this Vietnamese delicacy *(bmbsandwiches.com)*.

Local specialty, the muffuletta, filled with cheese and sliced meats

Stuck in Your Craw

A Louisiana specialty, crayfish, crawfish, or mudbugs are lobster-like critters that thrive in freshwater bayous surrounding the city. They're cooked up in a spicy Cajun seasoning with sausages, potatoes, and corn at huge communal "boils" – the perfect occasion to tuck in and socialize. Spots like Royal Street's R Bar *(royalstreet inn.com)* run one boil a week during peak season (March to June). Make sure to seek out this spicy seafood at festivals like Jazz Fest *(p174)*.

Enjoying spicy Cajun crawfish at a communal boil

Best of the Fests

Mardi Gras promises the city's biggest knees-up (*p66*), but there are parties here all year. In spring, Jazz Fest celebrates jazz, food, and culture (*p174*), and French Quarter Fest turns the Vieux Carré into a block party showcasing Louisiana's musical heritage (*frenchquarterfest.org*). Summer's Essence Fest celebrates African American culture with stellar lineups of R&B and soul artists (*essence.com*).

→

Mary J. Blige performing at Essence Fest

NEW ORLEANS FOR
MUSIC

New Orleans is the birthplace of jazz, but here all genres thrive, with live music suffusing the city with blues, bounce, hip-hop, and soul. From late-night brass band joints to uproarious festivals – in the Big Easy, music lovers are spoilt for choice.

All That Jazz

Think of New Orleans' music, and jazz is the first thing that comes to mind (*p110*). The city's musical heritage is kept alive at a host of venerable venues. Make for Preservation Hall to enjoy live trad jazz performances every evening (*p77*). Idle away a night on Bourbon Street at Fritzel's – the city's oldest club – and Jazz Playhouse, which showcases up-and-coming acts (*thejazzplayhouse.com*). Just a few blocks east, wander along club-lined Frenchmen Street and take in a show for the price of a drink at the bar (*p117*).

↑ Listening to a trumpet solo in cozy club Fritzel's

Let's Dance

Folk-heavy stylings of Cajun and Zydeco (p189) are played around the city, with groups like the Lost Bayou Ramblers packing out venues. It's hard not to join in the dancing, so brush up on your two- and three-step, and away you go! Tipitina's hosts a Zydeco night on alternate Sundays (tipitinas.com), or for a Cajun dance party, make for Mulates (mulates.com). For jazzy swing dance lessons, both the Spotted Cat (p117) and AllWays Lounge (p45) host low-key swing nights, on Wednesdays and Sundays respectively.

← Taking a swing dance lesson at Frenchmen Street institution, the Spotted Cat

TOP 4 **NEW ORLEANS MUSICIANS**

Trombone Shorty
Taking the sounds of brass bands into the modern scene with exciting collaborations.

Irma Thomas
The Soul Queen of New Orleans, in the style of Aretha Franklin and Etta James.

Big Freedia
At the vanguard of the "bounce" scene and beloved by Beyoncé.

Tank and the Bangas
A female-fronted band that blends styles to lead the future of New Orleans' music.

Bold As Brass

The hubbub of trumpets, saxophones, and trombones is the all-pervading soundtrack to the city. Wander the streets and you'll likely catch second lines parading downtown neighborhoods (p114), and brass bands playing swing jazz on the corner of Frenchmen Street. Make for the Maple Leaf Bar, a regular venue for grammy-winning brass stars Rebirth (mapleleafbar.com), or swing by the Candlelight Lounge in the Treme, a dark little dive that's popular with brass bands, and a neighborhood mainstay (925 North Robertson St).

→ Musicians performing on the street in the heart of the French Quarter

INSIDER TIP
Music Guide

To keep up-to-date with the wide range of exciting music events happening across New Orleans, check out the regularly updated Live Music Calendar at neworleans.com/events/livemusic-calendar.

The French Connection

The French colony of La Nouvelle-Orléans was founded in 1718, on land long occupied by the Chitimacha. French words and phrases pepper the city's language and place names: the French Quarter is known as the Vieux Carré ("old square"). Tour the quarter with Friends of the Cabildo (p69) and you'll pass Napoleon house, intended as a residence for the emperor in exile (p81), and the Ursuline Convent, built in 1734 – the Mississippi Valley's oldest building (p92). And you can't miss St. Louis Cathedral, proclaiming the faith of the first Catholic French settlers (p62).

↑ The 18th-century Napoleon House, now a restaurant

NEW ORLEANS FOR
HISTORY BUFFS

New Orleans has a 300-year rich and colorful recorded history of French, Spanish, African, and Cajun cultures. Numerous reminders of these influences remain, from old churches and crumbling cemeteries to historic houses and a host of specialist museums.

TOP 3
MUSEUMS OF NEW ORLEANS HISTORY

The Historic New Orleans Collection
Delve deep into the city's history at this museum with its extensive array of maps and artifacts (p72).

The Presbytère
Exhibits focus on Mardi Gras and Hurricane Katrina in this former courthouse on Jackson Square (p64).

The Whitney Plantation
Guided tours and detailed exhibits at this former River Road plantation house (p184) explore Louisiana's plantation history.

20th Century

During World War II, New Orleans' shipyards built thousands of the boats used by Allied troops: explore this legacy at the National World War II Museum (p126). In 2005, Hurricane Katrina swept through the city (p54). Pay homage to those who lost their lives in the disaster with a visit to Mid-City's memorial in St. Patrick's Cemetery #1, and in the Warehouse District (p120), see the striking Scrap House sculpture in Mississippi River Heritage Park.

African American Heritage

The city owes much of its unique cultural heritage to the enslaved African peoples brought here in colonial times. This legacy is preserved in Congo Square (p108), where festivals like Jazz Fest (p174) celebrate African American culture. Make sure to visit the Backstreet Cultural Museum to learn about the carnival traditions of Mardi Gras Indians (p115). Beyond the city, the Whitney explores the history of Louisiana plantations from the perspective of those enslaved (p184).

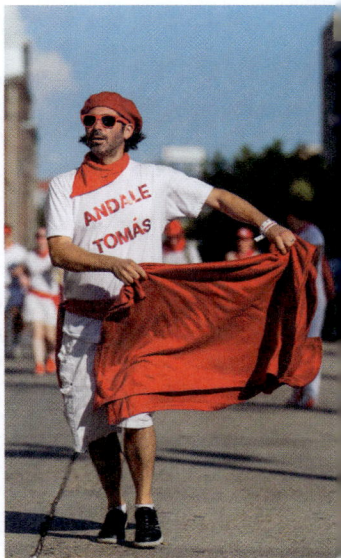

↑ Musicians performing in Congo Square during Jazz Fest

Streets of History

Stroll into the past in New Orleans' historic neighborhoods (p100). In Faubourg, Marigny and Bywater (p104), admire colorful Creole cottages and shotgun houses, home to French Creoles, German immigrants, and African Americans from the early 19th century. In the Garden District (p138), eclectic mansions hold stories of the bankers, planters, and merchants who lived here.

← Colorful shotgun house in Bywater

Signs of Spain

New Orleans was colonized by Spain from 1763 until 1803, and the country left its traces in the brightly painted buildings and ornate ironwork galleries in the French Quarter. Look out for the special tiled street signs hinting at the city's Iberian influence – Calle de Borbon for Bourbon Street, Calle Real for Royal Street, and Calle de San Luis for St. Louis Street. The Spanish spirit is kept alive with the Running of the Bull, which replaces the bulls with roller-derby skaters armed with plastic bats, and Mardi Gras - festivals that both originated under Spanish rule.

→ Celebrating the Running of the Bull festival

↑ The Hurricane Katrina Memorial, St. Patrick's Cemetery

Spiritual Homes

The sazerac is a New Orleanian whiskey cocktail that dates back to the mid-19th century, and there's no finer place to drink one than at its namesake bar at the Roosevelt *(p133)*. This is also the home of the Ramos gin fizz, an effervescent citrusy creation. The grasshopper was invented by Tujague's bartenders in 1918, and you can still enjoy this minty tipple at the iconic spot *(tujague srestaurant.com)*.

←

Sazeracs served straight up, without ice, at the Roosevelt

NEW ORLEANS
COCKTAIL
HOUR

A long tradition of good drinking is one of New Orleans' trademarks, so it's no surprise that the sazerac, Ramos gin fizz, and the grasshopper were all invented here. Concoct your own cocktail tour, toast a host of historic venues, and explore the unique mixology of the Crescent City.

Get Schooled

Cocktail connoisseurs and aspiring masters of mixology can dive into the history of the South's cocktail culture at the Museum of the American Cocktail, part of the Southern Food and Beverage Museum *(p146)*. Along with antique items of bar kit, the museum showcases cultural influences of the cocktail with regular seminars. To really get into the spirit of things, catch the Tales of the Cocktail Festival in July, a week-long event that takes over the city's bars with mixing lessons and tastings *(talesofthecocktail.org)*.

→

Cocktail bar party and tastings during Tales of the Cocktail Festival

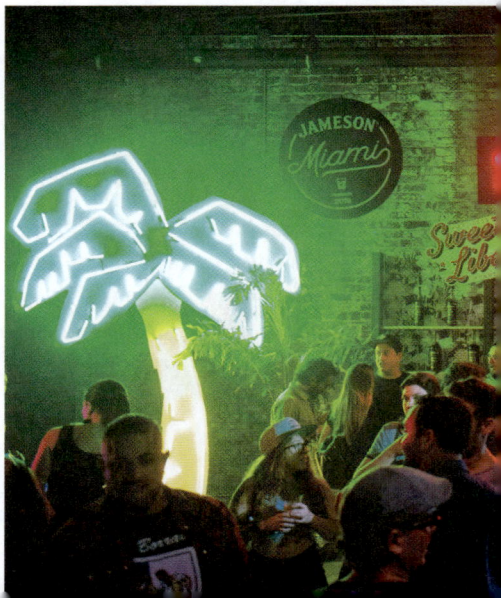

Drink Up

Cocktails always taste better with a view, so head up to the city's cool rooftop bars for fresher air and a scenic skyline. Downtown, the CBD is the place to be, with hotel bars often the swankiest option. Ingenue at the Troubadour Hotel has a relaxed vibe and a casual kitchen *(1111 Gravier St)*, while Rosie's on the Roof, the Irish rooftop bar at the Higgins Hotel, offers fresh seafood and lovely vistas *(higginshotelnola.com)*. In the Garden District, head up to the Pontchartrain Hotel's rooftop spot, Hot Tin, for scenic sundowners overlooking the Mississippi River *(hottinbar.com)*.

→

Enjoy drinks with city views from the serene rooftop at Hot Tin

A bartender serving an icy absinthe-based cocktail

←

TOP 5 LOCAL COCKTAILS

Sazerac
Rye whiskey, absinthe, and Peychaud bitters combine in this classic.

Ramos Gin Fizz
Two separate shaking processes create a fluffy, sweet-tasting brunch delight.

Grasshopper
Crème de menthe lends this after-dinner favorite its bright green color and minty flavor.

Brandy Milk Punch
Vanilla, nutmeg, brandy, and cream combine in this brunch-time cocktail.

Hurricane
The signature sweet rum cocktail at French Quarter stalwart, Pat O'Brien's.

Swamp Thing

New Orleans is surrounded by dense swamps and bayous, best investigated on a boat tour. Head for Honey Island Swamp and glide through the backwaters in a flat-bottomed boat with Cajun Encounters *(cajunencounters.com)*. Drift along channels lined with gnarly cypress trees, and look out for wildlife like turtles, pelicans, snakes, and alligators. If you prefer to stay on dry land, head to Barataria Preserve, and soak up the reserve's mysterious beauty as you wander the network of boardwalk trails *(p194)*.

↑ Swamp alligator relaxing on a log

NEW ORLEANS FOR
THE GREAT OUTDOORS

Though it's best known for its historic urban quarters, New Orleans has plenty of broad green parks and leafy streets where you can beat the heat and escape the city buzz. And the mighty Mississippi offers more outdoor pursuits, from riverside strolls to exciting swamp tours.

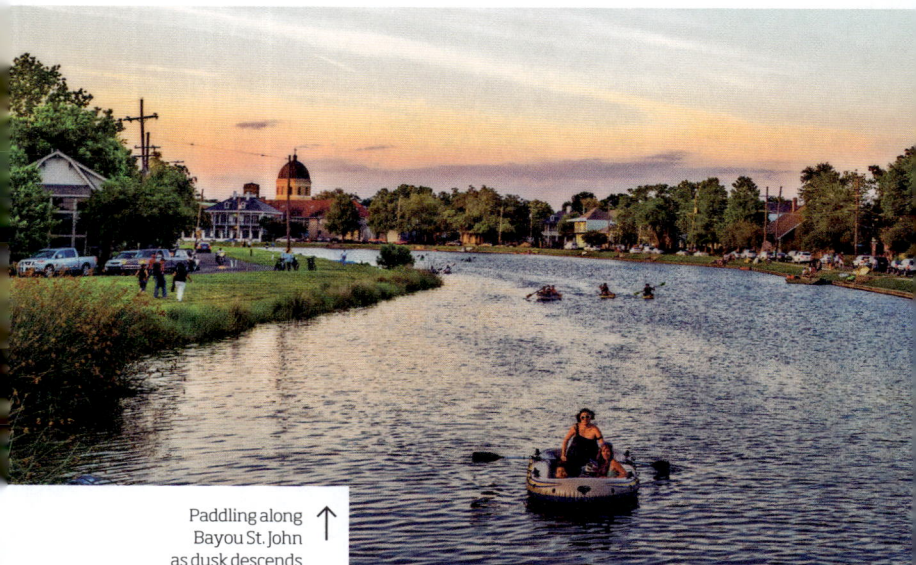

↑ Paddling along Bayou St. John as dusk descends

Let It Roll

With over 100 miles (160 km) of designated bike trails and flat streets laid out on a grid plan, New Orleans is a bike-friendly city. Cycle scheme Blue Bike has dozens of stations across the city, and American Bicycle Rental Co offers guided tours (p207). Hitch a ride and pedal the French Quarter, roll along the riverfront, or wheel to City Park along the Lafitte Greenway.

→

Wheeling through the city on Blue Bikes

Cool Off in the Park

City Park makes a refreshing escape from the heat, with its paths shaded by Spanish moss and the largest grove of mature live oaks in the world, and lagoons to explore by paddle boat (p166). Audubon Park is another great green space, with a golf course and recreation areas (p156). In Bywater, Crescent Park runs along the river, offering meandering bike trails and waterside picnic spots (p119).

←

Fountains and bright tropical borders in Audubon Park

A City On the Water

Whether you're gliding through the waters on a gleaming paddlewheeler or strolling a riverfront path, the mighty Mississippi is a thrill. The Steamboat *Natchez* has plied these waters for nearly 100 years, and a river cruise on this old steamer is a must (p74). In Mid-City, Bayou St. John is a peaceful spot for kayaking or a picnic along the banks (p175). Anglers can cast their lines into the vast Lake Pontchartrain at the city's northern end, and there are charter fishing tours into the coastal waterways with Salty Dog Charters (saltydogchartersllc.com) or the Redfish Charter Company (redfishcharterco.com).

HIDDEN GEM
Picnic on the Fly

At the southernmost riverfront end of Audubon Park (p156), Butterfly Riverview Park is a great chill-out spot. Locals call it "the Fly" and come here to soak up the sun, for picnics and parties, or to watch the sun set over the Mississippi.

World-Class Museums

Fine-art connoisseurs won't be disappointed here, with a host of grand museums to explore. The New Orleans Museum of Art (NOMA) holds a vast collection of international masterpieces (p168), and beside it, the Besthoff Sculpture Garden makes for dreamy strolling in the open air (p169). Housed in a futuristic glass and steel building, the Ogden Museum of Southern Art's wide-ranging collections cover works by Louisiana artists (p124). Across the street, at the Contemporary Arts Center, New Orleans, you'll find everything from paintings to installations and performance art (p134).

NEW ORLEANS FOR
ART LOVERS

With its sultry setting, laid-back atmosphere, and vibrant history, it's easy to see why this city has long been a haven for artists. New Orleans makes for an ever-changing canvas of world-class fine art, colorful street murals, and whimsical folk art creations.

Striking Street Art

Adding to the city's eclectic art scene are a host of startling and thought-provoking street murals. The best places to see these are in Marigny and Bywater (p104), where colorful works adorn the walls of second-hand shops and trendy cafés. Wander St. Claude Avenue, sometimes called the "Mural Mile," to spot several colorful works, including a huge painting, *Third Line*, by Henry Lipkis, which depicts the city's second line parades. Head to Studio BE warehouse, which showcases the work of celebrated New Orleans artist and activist Brandon Odums (p118).

←

Cycling past jazz-funeral-inspired street art in Bywater

←

Stormy (2015) by local artist MaPo Kinnord, exhibited at NOMA

Local Treasures

This creative city has an impressive lineup of venues exhibiting home-grown talent. In the heart of the Warehouse (or Arts) District, LeMieux Galleries champions emerging and established names *(lemieuxgalleries.com)*. In the French Quarter, George Rodrigue Studio exhibits distinctive Blue Dog paintings by the late Cajun artist *(george rodrigue.com)*, and in the CBD the Stella Jones Gallery showcases modern African American artists *(stellajonesgallery.com)*.

←

David Lambert's *Corner Bar* at LeMieux Galleries

Be Part of the Art

Unsurprisingly, this party city holds arts festivals through the year. Two of the biggest are the Arts District's White Linen Night *(artsdistrictneworleans.com/ events/fidelity-bank-white-linen-night)* and Art for Art's Sake, on Magazine Street. Both are joyful street parties with gallery openings, music, food, and more. Outside festival season, you can watch highly skilled artists blow glass during free daily demonstrations at the New Orleans Glassworks and Printmaking Studio, and even blow your own glass during workshops *(new orleansglassworks.com)*.

→

Glassblowing workshop at New Orleans Glassworks and Printmaking Studio

Wander the Markets

Make for the famous French Market to shop for souvenirs in the city's most historic retail setting (p90). At the adjoining French Quarter Flea Market, you'll find vendors selling everything from wood carvings to colorful woven bags. Meanwhile, the nightly market at the Frenchmen Art Bazaar (p117) is held in a lively outdoor lot amid clubs and bars – this is the city's best spot for sourcing unique local works of art.

←

Shoppers browsing the French Quarter Flea Market

NEW ORLEANS FOR
SHOPPERS

Whether it's hunting for outlet mall bargains, wandering bustling markets, or browsing unique boutiques for art, music, and fashion, New Orleans offers plenty for keen shoppers. This city is so full of irresistible treasures, you might want to bring an extra suitcase.

Meander Through Malls

Stretching out alongside the Mississippi, the Riverwalk Outlets is the country's first downtown outlet center (p129). Browse through this huge department store for bargains on both local and classic American brands. For upscale shopping, Canal Place (p130) houses designer fashion at Saks Fifth Avenue and Tory Burch, and jewelry at Tiffany & Co. In the French Quarter, Shops at Jax Brewery on Decatur Street is set in a former beer factory – today it makes for a pleasant spot to seek out clothing and souvenirs with a New Orleans flair.

→

The city's most upmarket shopping mall, Canal Place, also home to a hotel and cinema

Wandering Magazine Street, and *(inset)* hunting for antique jewelry ↑

Magazine Street

For leisurely shopping, take a stroll along Magazine Street. This 6-mile (9.5-km) stretch of the Garden District *(p138)* features clothing and home decor boutiques, antique dealers and independent bookstores, delightful restaurants, and historic homes. Browse vintage fashion at Funky Monkey *(funkymonkeynola.com)* or peruse gilded treasures at Antiques on Jackson *(antiquesonjackson.com)*.

SHOPS

Louisiana Music Factory
Renowned indie record store specializing in local music.

📍 421 Frenchmen St
🌐 louisianamusic factory.com

Maskerade
Buy artisanal Mardi Gras masks all year round.

📍 805 Royal St
🌐 themaskstore.com

Garden District Book Shop
Specializes in books and gifts featuring New Orleans and Louisiana.

📍 2727 Prytania St (Rink Shopping Center)
🌐 gardendistrict bookshop.com

An antique lamp store in New Orleans' French Quarter ↑

Quest for Antiques

Since its earliest days, New Orleans has been a repository for rare and remarkable collectibles. The city is studded with antique dealers, with some of the finest to be found on Royal Street *(p70)*: Keil's glitters with crystal chandeliers and French enamel jewelry *(p71)*, while M. S. Rau brims with elaborate silverware and objets d'art *(p71)*. Beyond the French Quarter, Magazine Antique Mall is a horde of heirlooms and vintage pieces *(magazinestreet.com)*.

Water-based fun at Cool Zoo in Audubon Zoo ↑

NEW ORLEANS FOR
FAMILIES

With a multitude of open-air and indoor attractions on offer, New Orleans is a superb city to explore if you're visiting with children. From hands-on museums and carnival exhibits to expansive green spaces and lush nature preserves, the Crescent City has something for kids of all ages.

Outdoor Fun

This city is peppered with green spaces, and spots like Audubon Park *(p156)* and vast City Park *(p166)* are perfect for when kids need to let off steam. In City Park's fairy-tale playground, Storyland, little ones can clamber aboard Captain Hook's ship, climb inside Cinderella's pumpkin carriage, or take a spin on an antique merry-go-round in the Carousel Gardens. Meanwhile riverside Crescent Park offers grassy stretches for picnicking, and meandering bike paths for cycling *(p119)*.

→

A tree-lined avenue in verdant Audubon Park

Explore the Natural World

Aspiring naturalists will delight in citywide attractions of the world-renowned Audubon Nature Institute. Creatures from around the globe roam their natural habitats at the 58-acre (23-hectare) Audubon Zoo (p157), which is known for its conservation efforts and is ranked among the best in the country. Visitors can also explore the underwater worlds of nearly 500 species of aquatic animals such as mesmerizing jellyfish, rare seahorses, and playful otters at the vast Audubon Aquarium (p135). Outside the city, intrepid explorers might enjoy a boat tour of Barataria Preserve's steamy green swampland (p194) – just watch out for the 'gators!

← Enjoying the wetlands in a bayou ride at Barataria Preserve

EAT

Reginelli's Pizzeria
Kids can create their own pizza at this casual establishment, while adults enjoy the range of delicious toppings, salads, and wines by the glass.

🏠 5961 Magazine St
🌐 reginellis.com

$ $ $

Muriels
A great children's menu and crayons keep the kids content at this fine-dining restaurant in the French Quarter.

🏠 801 Chartres St
🌐 muriels.com

$ $ $

Rainy-Day Favorites

If the sun doesn't shine (or indeed if it's too hot outside) there's still plenty to entertain young minds. Get stuck into hands-on exhibits and games at the Louisiana Children's Museum (p167) or head to the New Orleans Museum of Art (p168), which keeps kids entertained with story time, art workshops, and child-focused tours. Another good indoor option is Mardi Gras World (p147), where you can wander among giant characters in a warehouse of carnival floats and dress up in krewe costumes.

→ Throwing goodies from a float at Mardi Gras World

🔍 HIDDEN GEM
On Track

In a quiet corner of the New Orleans Botanical Garden (p167), the Historic Train Garden features mini replicas of the city's trains and streetcars. On weekends the carriages run through a model of the city (10am–4:30pm).

Literary Events

The city's best-known literary happening is the Tennessee Williams & New Orleans Literary Festival, held around the playwright's birthday on March 26 (tennesseewilliams.net). The five-day event features talks by authors, workshops, and writing contests. Also in March, the Saints and Sinners Literary Festival focuses on works by LGBTQ+ authors (sasfest.org). November sees the Faulkner Society's Words and Music Festival (wordsandmusic.org).

←

Literary talk at the Tennessee Williams & New Orleans Festival

NEW ORLEANS FOR
BOOKWORMS

With its lush setting, eccentric cast of characters, and fascinating history, it's no surprise that New Orleans has inspired an impressive list of writers. Their legacy can be found in a trail of literary landmarks, bookstores, festivals, and a wealth of prize-winning novels that bring the city to life.

Resident Writers

From William Faulkner to Tennessee Williams, New Orleans has been home to many world-famous authors and playwrights. Wander through the characterful French Quarter, and you will pass 711 Royal Street, where NOLA-born Truman Capote wrote his first novel *Other Voices, Other Rooms*; and 722 Toulouse Street, where playwright Tennessee Williams drafted his famous drama *A Streetcar Named Desire*. Today these buildings form part of the Historic New Orleans Collection *(p72)*, which explores the lives of Capote and Williams in its exhibits. Make sure to visit the Historic BK House & Gardens *(p93)* to pay homage to Frances Parkinson Keyes, who penned many of her novels here during the 1950s, and pick up a good read at Faulkner House Books *(p79)* – William Faulkner lived at this address while writing his first novel, *Soldier's Pay*.

← Truman Capote, one of the city's numerous literary luminaries

← Faulkner House Books, one-time home of William Faulkner

Follow the Plot

New Orleans is filled with sights immortalized in works of fiction. Trace the plot of Tennessee Williams' *A Streetcar Named Desire* and grab a bite at traditional French-Creole haunt Galatoire's *(p77)* – this is where Blanche and Stella DuBois dine at the start of the play. Or, catch a ride on the St. Charles Streetcar *(p142)*, which inspired the play's title. At 819 Canal Street, a bronze statue depicts Ignatius J. Reilly, the main character in John Kennedy Toole's *A Confederacy of Dunces*. Fans of Anne Rice's *Interview with a Vampire* should take a tour around St. Louis Cemetery #1 *(p112)*.

← New Orleans' famous St. Charles Avenue Streetcar, trundling along as it has done for more than 150 years

TOP 5 | **BOOKS SET IN NEW ORLEANS**

Interview with a Vampire (1976)
The first in the *Vampire Chronicles* series by Anne Rice.

A Confederacy of Dunces (1980)
Published after the author John Kennedy Toole's suicide; won the Pulitzer Prize for Fiction.

Why New Orleans Matters (2005)
A post-Katrina memoir by Tom Piazza.

What Went Missing and What Got Found (2015)
Evocative contemporary short stories from Fatima Shaik.

Those Who Don't Say They Love You (2021)
A collection of short stories by local author Maurice Ruffins.

Bourbon Street

This legendary street never sleeps. Spend a night dipping in and out of the bars and restaurants lining the strip, or linger in one of the famous jazz bars (p77). This is the heartland of the "go-cup" (most places will serve your drink in a plastic cup to go) – so you can wander along, cocktail in hand, and soak up the party atmosphere.

↑ People strolling along the neon-lit streets of the French Quarter

> **INSIDER TIP**
> ### Late-Night Haunts
>
> For nighttime chills, follow French Quarter Phantoms on a walking tour of the Vieux Carré. Their Ghost and Vampire trail leads you through the quarter's spookiest spots (frenchquarter phantoms.com).

NEW ORLEANS FOR
NIGHTLIFE

Mardi Gras might be this party city's biggest shindig, but there are *bons temps* to be had here all year round. With late-night shows and comedy gigs, burlesque and drag shows, 24-hour diners, and even nighttime ghost tours, you're sure to have a good time after dark.

Laughing Matters

Comedy-lovers are sure to get their funny fix here, with the city's lively stand-up scene and big-name hows to enjoy. Without a dedicated comedy club, open-mic nights take place in bars around the city, and almost all are free. Head to St. Claude for a clutch of venues with comic credentials, including AllWays Lounge and Cabaret and No Dice. For famous comics and standout shows, make for the Saenger (p133) and Joy theaters (thejoytheater.com).

↑ Stand-up comedian performing at No Dice in St. Claude

Late-Night Patty People

In need of a midnight feast? New Orleans has a good range of nocturnal snack spots to sate your hunger. Make Port of Call your first stop – this late-night dive delivers juicy burgers and a jukebox *(port ofcallnola.com)*. Meanwhile, local favorite Clover Grill serves its burgers cooked under a Cadillac wheel cap *(p93)*, and neighborhood joint Buffa's is known for its late plates and live music *(buffas bar.com)*. If you're craving something sweet, there's no line at the typically teeming Café du Monde at 11pm *(p96)*.

← Enjoying late-night beignets at Café du Monde

Venerable Venues

The city's grandest venues have been the seat of the performing arts for well over a century. The luxurious Saenger *(p133)* and neighboring Joy theaters both host broadway productions, live music, and comedy shows. Across Canal Street, the Orpheum has impeccable acoustics, and often hosts the Louisiana Philharmonic Orchestra *(orpheumnola.com)*.

→ Watching a concert at the Saenger Theatre

High Tease

Cabaret's proud history stretches back to the golden era of Bourbon Street, but these days, the best burlesque, drag, and cabaret shows can be found elsewhere too. St. Claude's charmingly louche AllWays Lounge and Cabaret holds sequin-spangled drag nights, and outlandish peep shows *(theallwayslounge.net)*. Fleur de Tease remains one of New Orleans's classic burlesque acts; catch performances at venues throughout the city *(fleurdetease.com)*.

← Glamorous show at the AllWays Lounge and Cabaret

A YEAR IN
NEW ORLEANS

JANUARY

Twelfth Night *(Jan 5)*. Joyous parades mark the official start of Carnival season and the build-up to Mardi Gras.

△ **King Cake Festival** *(late Jan, early Feb)*. Local bakeries compete in Champions Square to win the title of best king cake in the city.

FEBRUARY

△ **Mardi Gras** *(Feb, sometimes early Mar)*. After a month of celebrating, the city gears up for Lundi Gras and Fat Tuesday with more parties.

Tet Fest *(late Jan, Feb)*. Vietnamese New Year is honored with traditional music, food, and dancing at Mary Queen of Vietnam church.

MAY

△ **Bayou Boogaloo** *(mid-May)*. A three-day music festival celebrates a mix of local bands on the bayou waterfront in Mid-City.

Treme/7th Ward Arts and Culture Fest *(late May)*. Food, activities, and music in this historic African American neighborhood.

JUNE

△ **Creole Tomato Festival** *(early Jun)*. The French Market is filled with local vendors selling everything from Bloody Marys to tomato ice cream.

Pride *(mid-Jun)*. A huge weekend for the LGBTQ+ community, with a downtown Saturday evening parade and parties across various venues.

Tulane University Shakespeare Festival *(Jun)*. The university theatre company hosts classical performances of Shakespearean plays.

SEPTEMBER

△ **Football Season** *(early Sep)*. Sundays become football days as the New Orleans Saints begin their regular season games at the Superdome.

Hispanic Heritage Month *(mid-Sep to mid-Oct)*. Celebrate NOLA's Hispanic roots and community with special events at restaurants across the city.

OCTOBER

△ **Halloween** *(late Oct)*. The city dresses up and parades – see dazzling costumes as people wander up and down Frenchmen Street.

Po-Boy Fest *(early Nov)*. Sandwich makers vie for prizes in this hotly contested festival celebrating the city's favorite dish.

MARCH

△ **The Tennessee Williams Festival** *(Mar)*. The region's biggest literary event takes over the Monteleone Hotel and other city venues with panels, readings, and theatrical productions.

St. Patrick's Day *(mid-Mar)*. Various events take place as the city's American-Irish population celebrate with Mardi Gras-style parades.

APRIL

Ponchatoula Strawberry Festival *(Apr)*. Enjoy music, games, strawberry-eating, and cooking contests at this Ponchatoula festival.

△ **French Quarter Fest** *(Apr)*. A free festival in the French Quarter with a diverse mix of music and local food vendors across three days.

Jazz Fest *(late Apr, early May)*. The city's biggest music festival stretches over two weekends, with jazz, blues, rock, and pop music, and tasty food too.

JULY

Essence Festival *(early Jul)*. A huge festival held at the Superdome and around the city featuring soul, R&B, and hip-hop artists.

Running of the Bulls *(Jul 12)*. New Orleans' version of Spain's famous San Fermín event, with roller-derby skaters taking the place of bulls, and chasing participants through town.

△ **Tales of the Cocktail** *(mid-late Jul)*. Alcohol brands from across the globe host demonstrations and special events at all the city's major cocktail and hotel bars.

AUGUST

Satchmo SummerFest *(early Aug)*. A weekend of jazz and brass honoring Louis Armstrong.

△ **Southern Decadence** *(late Aug, early Sep)*. A brash six-day celebration of LGBTQ+ culture culminates in the French Quarter on Labor Day.

Museum Month *(throughout Aug)*. Participating museums offer free entry to all visitors.

NOVEMBER

△ **NOLA Zydeco Music Festival** *(early Nov)*. Mandeville Shed in Crescent Park hosts a huge lineup of Cajun music and Zydeco.

Treme Creole Gumbo Fest *(mid-Nov)*. Louis Armstrong Park welcomes brass bands and gumbo variations from the city's restaurants.

Bayou Classic *(Thanksgiving weekend)*. Football fixture between Grambling and Southern University at the Superdome.

DECEMBER

△ **Celebration in the Oaks** *(Dec)*. City Park transforms with dozens of light installations, food stalls, and music tents.

Christmas *(Dec)*. The city holds festive events including concerts at St. Louis Cathedral and Christmas carols in Jackson Square.

New Year's Eve *(Dec 31)*. Fireworks on the Mississippi River, best viewed from the banks near the French Quarter, mark the start of the New Year.

A BRIEF
HISTORY

One of the U.S.'s oldest cities, New Orleans has been through wars, epidemics, and natural disasters. With a rich musical heritage and distinctive traditions, the city continues to forge its own unique identity from the cultures of the many peoples that have shaped it.

The City's Foundations

Prehistoric Indigenous communities, known collectively as the Poverty Point Culture, were the first people to inhabit the area of New Orleans – evidence suggests that the culture emerged around 3500 BCE. Over the centuries, these cultures evolved into a patchwork of distinct peoples, among them the Chitimacha, the Taensa, and the Choctaw, who thrived in settlements on the banks of the river and the shores of Lake Pontchartrain. Then, New Orleans was the site of a village known as Bulbancha (Choctaw for "place of many tongues"), an important Indigenous trading hub. When French traders arrived in Louisiana in the

1722

La Nouvelle-Orléans is declared the capital of French Louisiana.

Timeline of events

1682

French explorer La Salle reaches the Mississippi, claiming Louisiana for Louis XIV.

1718

Jean Baptiste Le Moyne, Sieur de Bienville, establishes a French settlement.

1720

The first ship of enslaved people is brought to New Orleans on July 7.

c.3500 BCE

Mound-building civilizations begin to flourish along the Mississippi.

1763

Treaty of Paris signed; Louisiana and New Orleans ceded to Spain.

1690s, they encroached on traditional hunting grounds and introduced diseases that decimated the Indigenous populations, and Bulbancha was gradually replaced by French trading posts.

In 1718, around 20 years after the French first arrived, Louisiana governor Jean-Baptiste Le Moyne officially established "Nouvelle-Orléans," the soon-to-be capital of French Louisiana. Yet the early colony did not prosper. Brutal treatment by the settlers incited unrest among local people – the Natchez rose up in 1729 and the Chickasaw Wars were fought from the 1720s until the 1760s.

Changing Hands

The following decades saw New Orleans passed between various powers. Following France's defeat in Europe's Seven Years' War, Louisiana became a Spanish colony in 1763. During this time, New Orleans saw a boom in sugar production and it soon became a major port, trading in cotton and enslaved people. The city also welcomed a host of French Creole refugees from the Haitian Revolution, who built Creole-style houses and expanded the practice of voodoo. In 1800, ownership changed once again, and Spain quietly ceded Louisiana back to France.

1 A map of New Orleans from the early 1900s.

2 French explorer La Salle received in the Mississippi delta by the Taensa peoples, before claiming the territory for France in 1682.

3 Bienville laying out plans for the city of Nouvelle-Orléans, 1718.

4 Enslaved Africans working on a sugar plantation in New Orleans, 1700s.

1783
End of Revolutionary War creates the new nation of USA east of Louisiana.

1765
First Acadians arrive from Nova Scotia, settling west of New Orleans.

1788
Fire on March 21 (Good Friday) destroys 856 buildings in the French Quarter.

1791
Toussaint L'Ouverture leads revolt in Saint Domingue (Haiti).

1795
The U.S. and Spain sign a treaty opening the Mississippi River to American trade.

The Louisiana Purchase and the Battle of New Orleans

It wasn't long before French military leader Napoleon Bonaparte sold the land to the U.S. for $15 million to help fund his wars in Europe. On December 20, 1803, under President Jefferson, the Louisiana Purchase was officially ratified. Along with territories stretching to the Rocky Mountains, Louisiana was signed away by the French, and the U.S. almost doubled in size. Louisiana became a U.S. state on April 30, 1812, six weeks before the U.S. declared war on Great Britain. In January 1815, despite the Treaty of Ghent, which had ended the war the month before, British forces launched a fresh attack on New Orleans. General Andrew Jackson led an army of pirates, frontiersmen, gentlemen, and free men of color to victory in the Battle of New Orleans, fought in modern-day Chalmette, 6 miles (10 km) southeast of the city, bringing an end to the hostilities.

Steamboats, Cotton, and Sugar

In the early 19th century, the cotton industry flourished in the South thanks to advances in technology such as the invention

[1] Cheering the 1803 Louisiana Purchase.

[2] Battle of New Orleans in 1815.

[3] Port of New Orleans.

[4] Nuns tend victims of a yellow fever epidemic.

$324m

in trade was cleared by New Orleans' steam-boats in 1860.

Timeline of events

1801
Louisiana sold to the U.S.

1803
Louisiana Purchase ratified on December 20.

1812
The first steamboat, the *New Orleans*, arrives in the city in January.

1812
Louisiana becomes a U.S. state on April 30.

1814
Treaty of Ghent, signed on December 24, ends the War of 1812.

of the cotton gin and development of the steamboat. With its favorable position on the Mississippi, New Orleans became a significant port from which cotton was shipped to the rest of the world. A domestic slave trade sustained labor on the city's plantations, where cash crops of cotton, tobacco, indigo, and sugarcane were cultivated by enslaved people, often under brutal conditions.

With increasing global exports of commodities, the city's economy boomed. By 1840, it was the third-largest city in the nation, and the largest in the South, with a population of 102,000. Immense wealth led to expansion; in 1852 the French Opera House was built and the city developed its reputation for courtly life, gambling, and easy living. Europeans continued to arrive, with many Germans settling upstream from New Orleans as farmers, and Irish people east of Louisiana Avenue. Between 1817 and 1860 the city was blighted by epidemics of cholera and yellow fever, with 23 epidemics killing more than 28,000. Meanwhile, bitter tensions over the issue of slavery grew between the South and the North, where laws had freed many of those in bondage by the end of the 18th century.

↑ Docker loading a cotton bale onto a steamboat

1815
Andrew Jackson leads the Battle of New Orleans, defeating the British on January 8.

1820–30
Development of the city's steamboats opens trade to the interior of the country.

1831–5
New Orleans becomes the world's largest cotton market.

1852
The city of Lafayette is annexed, becoming the Garden District.

1853
Yellow fever epidemic kills 8,000 between July and November.

Civil War and Reconstruction

The Civil War brought an end to the city's prosperity. In 1861 Louisiana seceded from the Union, and in 1862 New Orleans was captured by Union troops and occupied for the remainder of the conflict. After the war, the city struggled to recover – both the cotton industry and the slave trade, the source of its wealth, were destroyed. Enslaved people were liberated in 1865, and during the period of Reconstruction (1865–77), Black Freedmen founded schools and were elected to political office; however, African Americans still suffered violence from groups such as the Ku Klux Klan. After federal troops withdrew in 1877, the legal and social gains made by African Americans were eroded as former Confederates resumed power and public segregation was enforced.

A New New Orleans

In the early 20th century, the city emerged as the birthplace of jazz, with the new improvisational music flourishing in Storyville bars (p116). Though World War I briefly boosted business in the shipyards, New Orleans suffered during the Depression of the early 1930s. In World War II, business returned to the shipyards,

↑ Carpenter working on a World War II boat at a New Orleans shipyard

Timeline of events

1877
Reconstruction ends; Federal troops leave New Orleans.

1862
Union General Benjamin Butler occupies the city on May 1.

1896
Supreme Court decision Plessy v. Ferguson permits racial segregation.

1917
Storyville deemed too tempting for World War I sailors, and abolished on October 2.

1954
Supreme Court ruling Brown v. the Board of Education orders the desegregation of public schools.

the site of production for boats used in Allied landings. Under the mayoralty of deLesseps Story Morrison (1946–61), the city experienced a period of regeneration, with the construction of the Pontchartrain Expressway and Crescent City Connection. This era saw progress in civil rights too: desegregation of public education began in 1954, and the Voting Rights Act of 1965 changed the political landscape. In 1978 Ernest N. "Dutch" Morial was elected as the city's first African American mayor.

New Orleans Today

New Orleans is today a vibrant, forward-thinking city, known for its famous Mardi Gras festivities, its distinct music scene, and its resilience against natural disasters. The recovery improvements necessitated by Hurricane Katrina (p54) proved vital in August 2021, when Hurricane Ida made landfall in Louisiana with the strongest gusts to ever hit the state. The upgraded levee system withstood this major stress test, and flooding within the city was minimal. However, New Orleans remains at risk of sinking underwater due to rising sea levels and the continuous draining of surrounding swampland.

1 During the Civil War, Federal troops occupy the city in 1862, under Union General Benjamin Butler.

2 Attendees from around the globe arriving at the city's 1884 Cotton Centennial Exposition.

3 The huge cantilever bridge, the Crescent City Connection, linking the city's north and south across the Mississippi.

4 Musical performance honoring New Orleans' 2018 Tricentennial.

1975

The Louisiana Superdome constructed, at a cost of $163 million.

2005

Hurricane Katrina hits on August 29. Floodwaters inundate 80 per cent of the city.

2010

The BP oil spill seeps into the Gulf of Mexico and Lake Pontchartrain.

2018

Latoya Cantrell is sworn in as the first female mayor of New Orleans.

2021

Hurricane Ida hits New Orleans with sustained winds of 150 mph (240 km/h).

FLOODING IN NEW ORLEANS

Hitting New Orleans in August 2005, Hurricane Katrina has been called the most devastating disaster in U.S. history. More than 850,000 homes were damaged and the official death toll in Louisiana alone exceeded 1,800 people. Despite the flood defense systems that have been implemented since, New Orleans is still at risk of extreme flooding and the threat of submersion underwater as early as 2050 is very real.

HURRICANE KATRINA

Katrina was a disaster of unprecedented magnitude, combining a powerful hurricane, a huge storm surge of sea water, and levee failures that left much of the city inundated by floodwaters for weeks. In the wake of the disaster, the city descended into chaos, with citizens left pleading for help from their rooftops or sheltering in the Superdome in appalling conditions. The Federal Emergency Management Agency (FEMA) was criticized for its slow response, but eventually the military arrived to oversee a massive evacuation. In late 2005, residents slowly started returning to the city. The recovery effort proved a monumental undertaking, with billions of dollars committed to the project.

A SINKING CITY

Since Katrina, the Army Corps of Engineers has built a more advanced flood control system to protect the city. However, New Orleans' outdated pump system and the threat of climate change mean flooding is still a major concern. The city is sinking at around one to two inches per year - half of it is already below sea level - and rising oceans mean that New Orleans could be permanently submerged by 2050. While the city is unlikely to be abandoned (pundits have touted a Venice-like island city surrounded by giant dykes), much of the surrounding land will be flooded. The impact on the local economy is impossible to estimate.

CAUSES OF SINKING

In the late 19th century, the city began draining surrounding swampland for expansion; this caused underground air pockets to collapse and the soft alluvial soil that the city was built on to subside. Sediment and soil that would normally be deposited along the riverbanks has been reduced by dams and levees, and more groundwater has been pumped out by industry, causing further subsidence.

Timeline

2005
▲ Hurricane Katrina hits on August 29. Floodwaters inundate 80 per cent of the city.

2006
Following efforts by the US military, all NOLA neighborhoods are reopened.

2007
▶ The US Army Corps of Engineers set to build new flood controls.

2012
The city's new flood defense system, the Gulf Intracoastal Waterway West Closure Complex, operates for the first time in response to Hurricane Isaac and is a success.

↑ Flood waters inundating New Orleans on August 30, 2005

2013

The Greater New Orleans Urban Water Plan (UWP), a collaborative, multibillion dollar post-Katrina redevelopment plan for the New Orleans metropolitan area, is released.

2021

▼ The defense system is tested once again by Hurricane Ida and withstands it.

2014

▲ Former mayor, Ray Nagin, is found guilty of fraud, bribery, and related charges that took place before and after Katrina.

2022

All projects to repair and improve the flood prevention system are completed at an estimated final cost of $15.6 billion.

EXPERIENCE

UPPER FRENCH QUARTER

For many visitors, the French Quarter is synonymous with New Orleans. Founded in 1718 by Jean-Baptiste Le Moyne de Bienville, the original 20 blocks of Nouvelle-Orléans were laid out here on a grid pattern in 1721. Under Spanish rule, in the late 18th century, the district developed as a hub of trade, and the landmark Cathedral, Cabildo, and Presbytère formed the civic and religious heart of the colony.

The Louisiana Purchase of 1803 ushered in an era of economic and cultural growth, but following the Civil War, the quarter declined, and many wealthy merchants moved elsewhere. By the 20th century, the French Quarter's crumbling landmarks were in need of repair, but cheap rents attracted writers and artists, lending the area its alternative ambience.

The Upper French Quarter is the heart of the district. An example of quintessential New Orleans architecture, with pretty Creole cottages and Spanish-style lacy galleries, the neighborhood escaped Hurricane Katrina with little wind or flood damage. Through it all, the Vieux Carré (old square) has retained its beautiful street-scapes and romantic atmosphere.

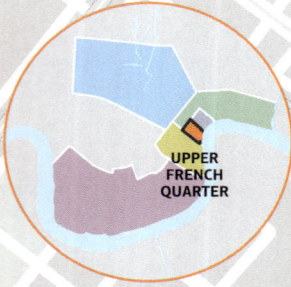

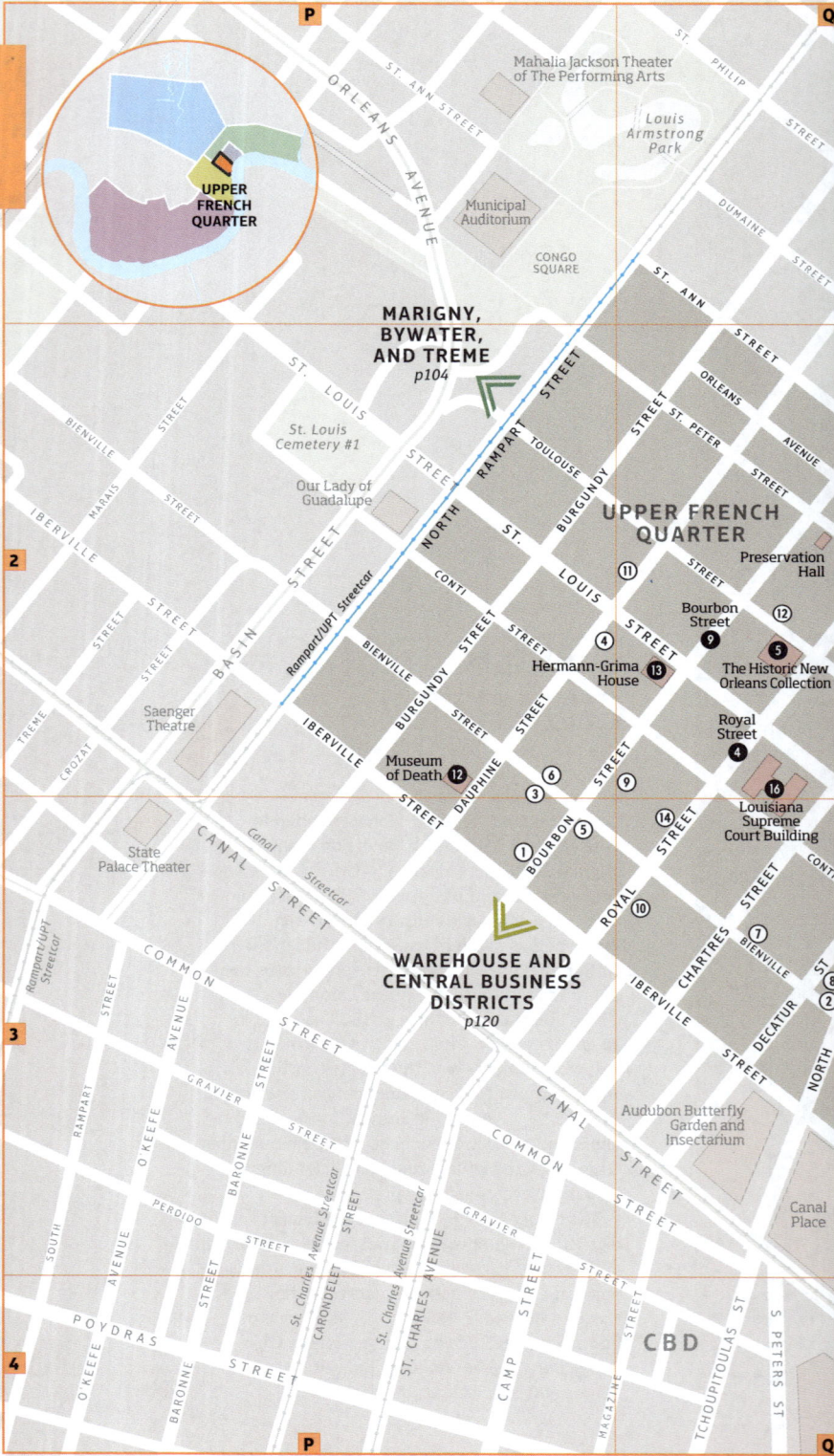

UPPER
FRENCH
QUARTER

Mahalia Jackson Theater
of The Performing Arts

ST. PHILIP
STREET

Louis
Armstrong
Park

ORLEANS AVENUE

ST. ANN STREET

DUMAINE STREET

Municipal
Auditorium

CONGO
SQUARE

ST. ANN STREET

MARIGNY,
BYWATER,
AND TREME
p104

STREET

ORLEANS
AVENUE

ST. PETER
STREET

RAMPART

TOULOUSE STREET

BURGUNDY STREET

UPPER FRENCH
QUARTER

STREET

St. Louis
Cemetery #1

NORTH

STREET

ST.

Preservation
Hall

2

BIENVILLE STREET

STREET

Our Lady of
Guadalupe

CONTI
STREET

STREET

STREET

LOUIS

Bourbon
Street

11

Hermann-Grima
House

4

9

13

12

5

The Historic New
Orleans Collection

IBERVILLE STREET

Saenger
Theatre

BASIN

STREET

Rampart/UPT Streetcar

MARAIS STREET

STREET

TREME

CROZAT

STREET

STREET

BURGUNDY

STREET

IBERVILLE
STREET

Museum
of Death

12

DAUPHINE STREET

STREET

6

STREET

Royal
Street

4

3

9

16

Louisiana
Supreme
Court Building

State
Palace Theater

CANAL STREET

Streetcar

BOURBON STREET

5

14

ROYAL STREET

CHARTRES STREET

3

WAREHOUSE AND
CENTRAL BUSINESS
DISTRICTS
p120

1

10

7

BIENVILLE STREET

1

8

2

Rampart/UPT
Streetcar

COMMON
AVENUE

GRAVIER STREET

STREET

STREET

IBERVILLE
STREET

DECATUR
STREET

NORTH

RAMPART STREET

O'KEEFE AVENUE

BARONNE STREET

PERDIDO STREET

St. Charles Avenue Streetcar

CARONDELET
STREET

ST. CHARLES AVENUE

St. Charles Avenue Streetcar

GRAVIER STREET

CANAL STREET

COMMON STREET

Audubon Butterfly
Garden and
Insectarium

STREET

Canal
Place

SOUTH

O'KEEFE
AVENUE

BARONNE
STREET

POYDRAS
STREET

STREET

CAMP STREET

ST. CHARLES AVENUE

MAGAZINE STREET

CBD

TCHOUPITOULAS ST.

S. PETERS ST.

4

Map labels:

BURGUNDY STREET
URSULINES STREET
DAUPHINE STREET
BOURBON STREET
AVENUE
ST. PHILIP STREET
BARRACKS STREET
ROYAL STREET

LOWER FRENCH QUARTER

Old Ursuline Convent

CHARTRES STREET
DECATUR ST

LOWER FRENCH QUARTER
p86

Père Antoine Alley and St. Anthony's Garden

Central Grocery

The Presbytère
Pirate's Alley
St. Louis Cathedral
Pontalba Buildings
The 1850 House
The Cabildo
Le Petit Theatre
Jackson Square

New Orleans Pharmacy Museum
Shops at JAX Brewery
Napoleon House
STREET
DECATUR

French Quarter Visitor Center

PETERS ST
STREET
NORTH FRONT STREET
Riverfront Streetcar

Steamboat *Natchez*

Woldenberg Riverfront Park

M i s s i s s i p p i

Audubon Aquarium

Caesars Hotel & Casino

0 meters 250
0 yards 250
N
4
R
R

UPPER FRENCH QUARTER

Must Sees
1. St. Louis Cathedral
2. The Presbytère
3. The Cabildo
4. Royal Street
5. The Historic New Orleans Collection
6. Steamboat *Natchez*

Experience More
7. Jackson Square
8. The 1850 House
9. Bourbon Street
10. Pontalba Buildings
11. Père Antoine Alley and St. Anthony's Garden
12. Museum of Death
13. Hermann-Grima House
14. Le Petit Theatre
15. Pirate's Alley
16. Louisiana Supreme Court Building
17. New Orleans Pharmacy Museum
18. Napoleon House
19. French Quarter Visitor Center

Eat
1. Galatoire's
2. Felipe's Mexican Taqueria
3. GW Fins
4. Bayona

Drink
5. Old Absinthe House
6. Arnaud's French 75 Bar
7. The Chart Room
8. Beachbum Berry's Latitude 29

Stay
9. Royal Sonesta
10. Hotel Monteleone
11. Audubon Cottages
12. The Celestine

Shop
13. M. S. Rau Antiques
14. Keil's Antiques

❶ Ⓜ️ 🛍️

ST. LOUIS CATHEDRAL

📍Q2 🏠Jackson Square 🚇St. Charles Ave, Canal, Riverfront
🚌5, 55 🕐9am–4pm daily 🌐saintlouiscathedral.org

Dedicated to King Louis IX of France, who died in 1270, St. Louis is the oldest continuously active Roman Catholic cathedral in the country. New Orleans' most recognizable landmark, the cathedral towers over Jackson Square, its mix of Spanish and French Neo-Gothic architecture a stately illustration of its history.

Two earlier churches once stood on this site: the first, a wooden church built in 1718, was destroyed by a hurricane in 1722; and the second, more robust construction was erected in 1727, but consumed by the great fire of 1788 that destroyed much of the French Quarter. The church was rebuilt by the Spanish from 1789, and made a cathedral in 1794. Restorations continued through the early 19th century, some to designs by renowned architect J. N. B. de Pouilly – as such, the cathedral as it stands today reveals little of its original Spanish structure. It is flanked by the most important buildings of the early colony, the Cabildo and the Presbytère, both former seats of Spanish government. The breathtaking interior is well maintained by the Archdiocese of New Orleans.

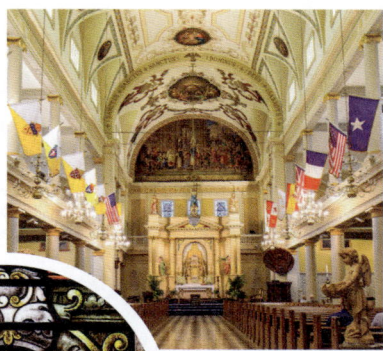

↑ The cathedral's grand interior, decorated with Baroque murals

← Elaborate stained-glass windows adorning the basilica

The carved-wood Baroque altars were constructed in Ghent, Belgium, and brought to the cathedral in pieces.

A great mural of St. Louis announcing the Seventh Crusade.

Stained-glass windows with figures of Catholic saints adorn the cathedral's interior.

The steeples, portico, and pilasters were added in 1851.

Ceiling murals by Alsatian artist Erasme Humbrecht (1872) portray biblical stories.

← An illustration of the Roman Catholic St. Louis Cathedral

St. Louis Cathedral flanked by the Presbytère and the Cabildo

2 🎨

THE PRESBYTÈRE

📍 Q2 🏠 751 Chartres St 🚋 St. Charles Ave, Canal, Riverfront
🚌 5, 55 🕐 9am-4pm Tue-Sun 🌐 louisianastatemuseum.org

Set proudly alongside St. Louis Cathedral, overlooking Jackson Square, the Presbytère was constructed in 1794 as a complement to the Cabildo. A National Historic Landmark since 1970, today the site forms part of the Louisiana State Museum.

This striking building, which was designed in 1791 by architect Gilbeto Guillemard (1747–1808), intended to serve as a rectory to the adjacent cathedral (p62). First known as the Casa Curial (Ecclesiastical House), the Presbytère was sited on the former residence or "presbytery" of Capuchin monks, from which it derives its French name. The building's construction was complicated by the sudden death of its financer, Don Andres Almonaster y Rojas, in 1798. In 1805, wardens of the cathedral took control of construction, and the building was completed in 1813.

The Louisiana Supreme Court was housed here until 1853, when the church sold the building to the city. The city's civil courts occupied the Presbytère until 1910. The property was transferred to the Louisiana State Museum in 1908, and the Presbytère opened to the public in 1911.

Today, the Presbytère holds two permanent exhibits, the first focusing on hurricanes Katrina and Rita, and their impact on Louisiana. The second collection celebrates the festival of Mardi Gras, exploring its origins in 18th-century Louisiana through to the jubilant festivities enjoyed in New Orleans today.

→
Seahorse costume on display in the Mardi Gras exhibit

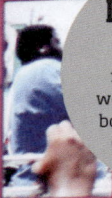

Did You Know?

Hurricane Rita
followed just four
weeks after Katrina –
both storms reached
Category 5 at sea.

MUSEUM GUIDE

Two large permanent
exhibitions are installed
on the first and second
floors, showing differ-
ent sides of New
Orleans' culture. On the
first floor, "Living with
Hurricanes: Katrina and
Beyond" explores the
impact of the 2005
hurricanes on the city
of New Orleans, with
moving eyewitness
accounts, interactive
displays, and movies.
On the second floor is
a vivid celebration of
carnival – "Mardi Gras:
It's Carnival Time in
Louisiana" – with cos-
tumes, ballgowns, and
pieces of brightly
colored floats among
the collections.

←

Louisiana residents
sharing their experiences
of Katrina and Rita

[1] The imposing exterior of the
Presbytère and St. Louis Cathedral,
illuminated at night.

[2] Cajun costumes and memorabilia
on display in the museum's Mardi
Gras collection.

[3] Interactive "Living with Hurricanes"
exhibit exploring the levee system
that protects the city.

MARDI GRAS

Each year, New Orleans' Carnival attracts over a million visitors. Since the 1700s, the period between Twelfth Night (January 6) and Ash Wednesday (the start of Lent) has been celebrated with lavish balls presented by private citizen groups known as "krewes." The first such group was the Mystic Krewe of Comus, founded in 1856 – it was soon joined by Rex (1872) and Proteus (1882). New krewes continue to emerge today, with membership open to members' relatives, or for a fee. In addition to private balls, krewes put on public parades with ornate costumes and floats, which take place for ten days before Mardi Gras.

PARADE FLOATS

Each krewe has 14 or more colorful floats, some still made of traditional papier-mâché, that are pulled through the city during the parades. Many floats are constructed at Blaine Kern's Mardi Gras World and can be seen there all year long (p147). The Presbytère (p64) presents a colorful display of Mardi Gras floats and history.

MARDI GRAS COLORS

The purple, green, and gold Carnival decorations derive from a costume worn by the king of Carnival, "Rex," during an 1872 parade. Today, these colors symbolize justice (purple), faith (green), and power (gold), and adorn throws (souvenir trinkets tossed from the floats), made from items like doubloons, beads, and dolls. The traditional food of Carnival, king cake, is decorated with Mardi Gras colors, and contains a small porcelain figure of a baby, representing the baby Jesus.

↑ Rich cinnamon king cake adorned with frosting and a plastic baby Jesus

MARDI GRAS INDIANS

The Mardi Gras Indians form a significant part of the Carnival celebrations. Their parades began in the late 19th century, when members from African American communities processed through the backstreets of Mardi Gras. With their exuberantly beaded costumes, feathered headdresses, and krewes named after imaginary "tribes," these groups blend West African, Caribbean, Indigenous, and European influences. Mardi Gras Indians can be spotted parading at Jazz Fest (p174) and on St. Joseph's Day, and their traditions are explored at the Backstreet Cultural Museum in Treme (p115).

→ The Parade of Rex processing along Canal Street, and (inset) Mardi Gras Indians celebrating in beaded costumes

PARADE KREWES

1 Krewe of Muses
Named for the ancient Greek daughters of Zeus, Muses is the most prominent all-female krewe. They delight crowds by throwing lavishly decorated shoes on their route.

2 Krewe of Bacchus
The Bacchus Parade on the Sunday before Mardi Gras features more than 25 floats, including some of the largest and longest, such as the heralded "Bacchagator."

3 Krewe of Zulu Parade
The Zulu Social Aid and Pleasure Club produces this festive parade, held on the morning of Mardi Gras, just before Rex. One of the most famous Krewe of Zulu carnival kings was Louis Armstrong, crowned in 1949.

4 Krewe of Rex Parade
The king of the city's most established krewes is, appropriately enough, Rex, which first appeared in 1872. Each year Rex crowns a prominent New Orleanian the "king" of Mardi Gras.

5 Krewe of Armeinius
Founded in 1968, Armeinius is the largest LGBTQ+ krewe in the city, best known for holding fabulous, uproariously funny balls.

3 ⟨⟩ ⟨⟩

THE CABILDO

📍 Q2 🏠 701 Chartres St 🚊 St. Charles Ave, Canal, Riverfront
🚌 5, 55 🕐 9am–4pm Tue–Sun 🌐 louisianastatemuseum.org

Set beside St. Louis Cathedral and the Presbytère, the Cabildo is the third in the trio of buildings framing the north of Jackson Square. Now a museum, this landmark houses exhibits that delve into the colorful and turbulent history of the city.

The original Cabildo building was destroyed by the great French Quarter fire of 1788. The structure seen today was rebuilt and financed by philanthropist Don Andrés Almonaster y Rojas in 1794. It served as a capitol for the legislative assembly of the Spanish colonial government, then as the City Hall.

Following the Louisiana Purchase of 1803 (p50), a December 20 ceremony was held in the Cabildo to mark France's transfer of the territory to the U.S. From 1853 to 1910, the Cabildo housed the state Supreme Court. Landmark court cases, such as the Plessy v. Ferguson case of 1896 (p52) were held here in the Sala Capitular (Meeting Room).

Today, the Cabildo forms part of the Louisiana State Museum (LSM). Collections include a permanent display on the Battle of New Orleans, and rotating exhibitions on the history and culture of Louisiana.

↑ Exploring an interactive exhibit about the Battle of New Orleans

The Cabildo, set beside St. Louis Cathedral on Jackson Square →

💬 INSIDER TIP
Friendly Crowd

Join Friends of the Cabildo, a volunteer-run group that supports the LSM, on their fascinating walking tours of the French Quarter, held daily at 10:30am and 1:30pm *(friends ofthecabildo.org).*

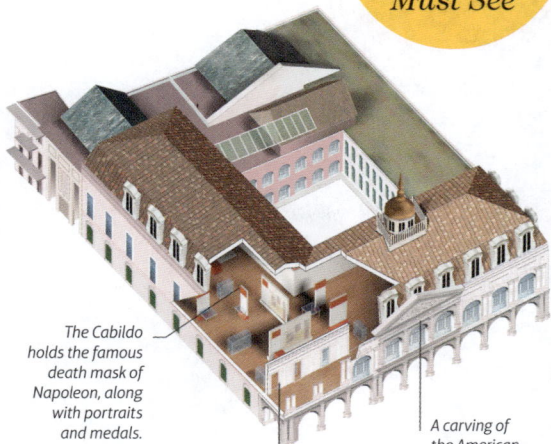

The Cabildo holds the famous death mask of Napoleon, along with portraits and medals.

A carving of the American eagle by Pietro Cardelli sits on the facade.

The Louisiana Purchase was signed in the Sala Capitular.

← The impressive 18th-century Cabildo overlooking busy Jackson Square

TOP 4 **COLLECTION PIECES**

Napoleon's Death Mask
This rare bronze cast of the French Emperor's face was made after his death in 1821.

The Battle of New Orleans (1839)
Awe-inspiring painting of the Battle of New Orleans by Eugene Louis Lami (1800–1890).

The Iberville Stone
A chunk of marble placed by the French-Canadian explorer Iberville to mark the location of the new French colony in Biloxi in 1699.

Carte de la Louisiane (1718)
Guillaume de L'Isle's map was printed in two editions; the second locates New Orleans.

Did You Know?

LaBranche House is said to be haunted by ghosts of both the owner's mistress and wife.

→ The LaBranche House (No. 700) with its pretty galleries and hanging ferns

↓ The houses lining a block of Royal Street, from Nos. 403 to 441

Benjamin Latrobe designed the Louisiana State Bank (No. 403) building, as well as the U.S. Capitol's south wing.

Built for a Spanish merchant in around 1802, the building housing Brennan's (No. 417) later became a bank. Brennan's restaurant moved here in 1954.

4

ROYAL STREET

Q2 **St. Charles Ave and Canal streetcars** **5, 55**

Running through the historic heart of the city, Royal Street is the pride of the French Quarter. Many of its beautiful buildings date back to the 18th century, when the thoroughfare was the city's financial center and most fashionable street. Today, this pretty parade is alive with shops, restaurants, and bars, along with galleries and museums.

Aside from the many fine antiques shops and restaurants that pepper Royal Street, many of the handsome landmarks here have been transformed into museums and galleries: at No. 533, the Historic New Orleans Collection occupies a complex of houses built in 1792 (p72) and at No. 541 you'll find the Galerie Rue Royale, showcasing contemporary European and American art. Meanwhile No. 700, LaBranche House, which was constructed in 1835 for sugar planter Jean Baptiste LaBranche, is among the city's most photographed buildings, famous for its fine oak-leaf ironwork and attractive hanging ferns.

↑ A quartet of street musicians providing open-air entertainment on Royal Street

SHOP

M. S. Rau Antiques
Established in 1912, M. S. Rau is internationally renowned for its range of antique furniture and objets d'art.

Q2
622 Royal St
rauantiques.com

Keil's Antiques
A family-run business dating from 1899, Keil's stocks superb antique jewelry, as well as chandeliers, furniture, and mirrors.

Q3
325 Royal St
keilsantiques.com

Moss Antiques (No. 411) offers a range of French antiques.

The Sazerac cocktail was born at Antoine Peychaud's Pharmacy (No. 437) when pharmacist Antoine Peychaud mixed brandy with his bitters and served the potion in a coquetier (egg cup).

5 Ⓜ ▢ ⏥

THE HISTORIC NEW ORLEANS COLLECTION

📍 Q2 🏛 Merieult House: 533 Royal St; Seignouret-Brulatour Building and Tricentennial Wing: 520 Royal St; Williams Research Center: 410 Chartres St 🚃 St. Charles Ave, Canal 🚌 55 🕐 9:30am–4:30pm Tue–Sat, 10:30am–4:30pm Sun 🚫 Public hols 🌐 hnoc.org

Founded in 1966, this vast collection of photographs, prints, paintings, and artifacts is a comprehensive record of New Orleans' history and culture going back more than 300 years. The works are on display at several historic French Quarter buildings.

What began as a personal collection of materials gathered by local couple General and Mrs. L. Kemper Williams has become the pre-eminent treasury of archives on the city. The works are housed in 18th- and 19th-century premises across three campuses in the French Quarter. The Williams Research Center holds the collection's archives, while the Seignouret-Brulatour Building houses a permanent gallery dedicated to the history of the French Quarter. Currently Merieult House is closed until 2028 for a major renovation. Note, entry to the collection is free but advance booking is required.

Did You Know?

The Historic New Orleans Collection encompasses over one million artifacts.

[1] The Reading Room at the Williams Research Center, an invaluable local resource.

[2] The facade of Merieult House at 533 Royal Street, which holds the Louisiana History Galleries and the Williams Gallery.

[3] *Portrait of Lydia Brown* (1922-28) by Josephine Marien Crawford, displayed in the French Quarter Gallery's Art and Literature Collection.

← The sumptuous interior of the Counting House, and *(inset)* the tranquil inner courtyard, Royal Street's Merieult House Campus

TOUR THE COLLECTIONS

A variety of guided tours of the historic collection are available throughout the French Quarter buildings. These include the New Orleans Mosaic, a 35-minute walking tour of the French Quarter History Galleries (11:30am Fri–Sun), featuring fascinating stories about immigrant communities, artists, and musicians, and the complex legacies of slavery and civil rights activism. There are also guided tours of temporary special exhibitions and live demonstrations of the restored Aeolian pipe organ by the residential player in the Seignouret-Brulatour Building (11–11:30am Wed–Sun).

6 ⟨⟩ 🍴 🛍️

STEAMBOAT NATCHEZ

📍R3 🏠Woldenberg Riverfront Park wharf 🚋Riverfront 🚌5, 55 🕐Harbor jazz cruises: 11:30am and 2:30pm daily; dinner jazz cruise: 7pm daily 🌐steamboatnatchez.com

For a reminder of the old days of river travel, take a two-hour trip on the Steamboat *Natchez* – pride of the riverfront in downtown New Orleans – and cruise along the Mississippi in style with a swinging soundtrack of jazz.

Ninth of its name, this incarnation of the *Natchez* has been sailing since 1975, but the original steam engines and steering system were built in 1925. In the 19th century, steamboats traveled the length of the Mississippi, taking between three and five days to get from Louisville, Kentucky, to New Orleans. The boatmen were notorious brawlers who went looking for women and liquor at the end of a trip and established New Orleans' reputation as the "City of Sin." In their heyday, from 1830 to 1860, some 30 steamboats lined up at the levee. The steamboat era ended by the close of the 19th century with the development of railroads and highways. Today, the *Natchez* can be seen gliding along the river on daily two-hour jazz cruises and, every so often, competing in a paddle steamer race.

> 🔺 GREAT VIEW
> **Steam Player**
>
> Breathtaking skyline views are possible a few minutes into the river tour on this steamboat. Head to the Hurricane Deck after setting off and you should be able to spy most of New Orleans' downtown.

The stylish *Natchez* paddle steamer, pride of the Mississippi River ↓

Bowthruster

Bridge

Gigantic ramps were used to board, load, and offload the steamboat.

The *Magnolia Suite* in the lower deck is used for private events.

The copper bell is inlaid with 250 silver dollars to produce a purer tone.

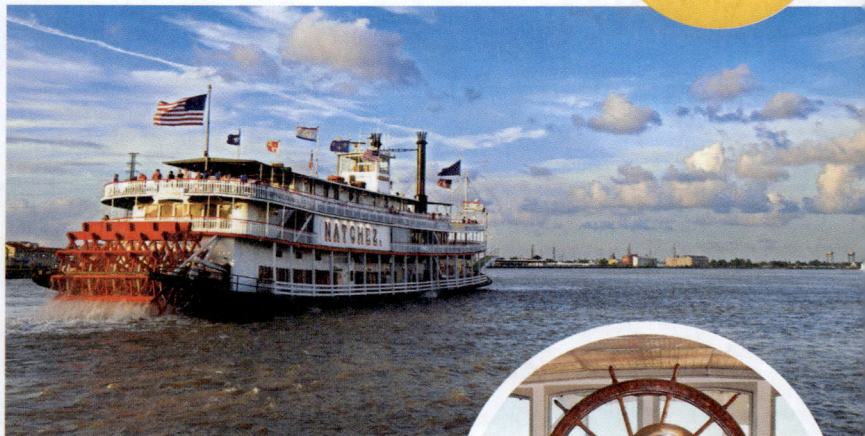

Majestic Steamboat *Natchez* cruising along the Mississippi, and *(inset)* the Dukes of Dixieland playing on board ↑

A telegraph is used for communication between the Pilot House and the Chief Engineer in the engine room.

Lifesavers are distributed around the ship.

Gift shop

The 32-note steam-powered calliope organ can be heard playing jaunty tunes from miles around.

The Hurricane Deck features live jazz music.

NATCHEZ.

A casual buffet dinner is served in the dining room on the second deck, accompanied by live jazz music from the Dukes of Dixieland.

These powerful steam engines were built for the U.S. Steel Corporation's sternwheeler Clairton in 1925.

Twenty-five tons of white oak propel the steamboat along the river.

EXPERIENCE MORE

7

Jackson Square

📍 Q2 🚋 Riverfront 🚌 5, 55

Today an attractive and lively meeting place, this square was named the Place d'Armes in the early French colony, when it was little more than a muddy field. Here, the troops were drilled, criminals were placed in the stocks, and executions were carried out. In 1850 it was renamed for the champion of the Battle of New Orleans (p50), after the Baroness Pontalba laid out the gardens and pathways of the square in a radial pattern, with walkways stemming out from the center. Under her auspices, the Pelanne brothers designed the handsome wrought-iron fence that encloses the square. At the center stands a statue of General Andrew Jackson astride a rearing horse. The inscription "The Union must and shall be preserved" on the plinth was added by General Benjamin Butler, when he occupied the city during the American Civil War (p52). Today, there are plenty of benches where visitors can sit and enjoy the charm of the historical houses that surround the square. Outside the park, artists rent space and hang their works on the enclosing fence, and on the flagstones around the square, tarot card readers, jazz players, and clowns entertain visitors throughout the week.

---

8 🎨 Ⓜ

The 1850 House

📍 R2 🏠 523 St. Ann St 🚌 5, 55 🕐 9am–4pm Tue–Sun 🌐 Public hols Ⓦ louisiana statemuseum.org/ museum/1850-house

Situated in the residence above the Lower Pontalba Building, the 1850 House is the Louisiana State Museum's faithful recreation of a mid-19th-century antebellum apartment. Accessed by a dramatic circular staircase, the bedrooms contain all the innovations of their day, including walk-in closets and private bathrooms. Also displayed are decorative arts and everyday artifacts of the period.

TOP 3 **FRENCH QUARTER HISTORICAL FIGURES**

Jean-Baptiste le Moyne de Bienville (1680–1767)
French-Canadian founder of "La Nouvelle Orleans" (1718) who oversaw the French Quarter's design.

Micaela Almonester, Baroness de Pontalba (1795–1874)
Creole aristocrat, entrepreneur, and property developer whose name graces the Pontalba Buildings.

Marie Laveau (1801–1881)
The "Voodoo Queen" of New Orleans was a free-born Creole woman who had a major impact on the city's religious and social life in the 19th century (p113).

← Artists displaying colorful works in busy Jackson Square

⑨ Bourbon Street

📍Q2 🚋Canal 🚌100

Its reputation as a party hub aside, this legendary street's name has nothing to do with the whiskey, despite the string of bars lining the thoroughfare; rather, it refers to the French royal family of Bourbon. While its infamy is not entirely unearned (during Mardi Gras, the lacy balconies above the sidewalks sag from the weight of drunken revelers), Bourbon Street is great for dining, architecture, and music. At No. 733, the intimate **Fritzel's Jazz Club** has attracted the best musicians since 1969, and just a few minutes' walk away, **Preservation Hall** has helped preserve New Orleans jazz since its inception in 1961, hosting top-quality jazz night after night.

Fritzel's Jazz Club

🏠733 Bourbon St
🌐fritzelsjazz.com

Preservation Hall

♿ 🏠726 St. Peters St
🌐preservationhall.com

⑩ 💻 🛍 Pontalba Buildings

📍Q2 🏠St. Peter & St. Ann sts 🚊Riverfront 🚌5, 55

In 1848 Baroness Pontalba (Micaela Almonester) supervised the building of these block-long apartments flanking the uptown and downtown sides of Jackson Square. They were built at a cost of just over $300,000, and at the time considered the best and largest apartments of their kind.

At the age of 15, Micaela had married the foppish aristocrat Celestin Pontalba, a distant cousin, and moved to Paris. There, her father-in-law tried to force her to sign over her entire estate. When she refused, he attempted to kill her, but only succeeded in shooting off two of her fingers.

She courageously separated from her husband in 1848 and returned to New Orleans. The baroness, like her father, the philanthropist Don Andrés Almonester y Rojas, was a developer. With plans brought back from Paris, she proceeded to build apartments like the ones she had seen in Paris. The design of the initials A and P (for Almonester and Pontalba) in the cast-iron railings of the buildings' galleries is attributed to one of the baroness's sons, an artist.

EAT

Galatoire's

This century-old institution serves up French Creole classics in its elegant dining room. Friday lunchtimes are one of the city's most decadent traditions, and dressing up is essential.

📍P3 🏠209 Bourbon St
🌐galatoires.com

$$

Felipe's Mexican Taqueria

Head to this family favorite to sample Mexican classics, or enjoy a freshly made margarita.

📍Q3 🏠301 N Peters St
🌐felipestaqueria.com

$⑤⑤

GW Fins

The menu changes almost daily at this seafood spot, giving fish a truly original head-to-tail treatment.

📍P2 🏠808 Bienville St
🌐gwfins.com

$$

Bayona

The charming, cozy Creole cottage setting gives a romantic ambience, while the menu spans the globe, with American classics and Asian and European favorites.

📍P2 🏠430 Dauphine St
🌐bayona.com

$$⑤

← The Parisian-style Pontalba apartment buildings overlooking Jackson Square

STAY

Royal Sonesta

Enjoy an oasis of Art Deco decor and contemporary art amid the Bourbon Street clamor. Visit its destination restaurant (R'evolution), 19th-century oyster bar, and atmospheric jazz venue.

🔲 Q2 🏠 300 Bourbon St
🆆 sonesta.com

$$$

Hotel Monteleone

This independent, fifth-generation-run hotel dates back to the 19th century. It is famed for its handsome facade, literary associations (Faulkner and Capote drank here), and rotating Carousel bar.

🔲 Q3 🏠 214 Royal St
🆆 hotelmonteleone.com

$$$

Audubon Cottages

With its private gardens and butler service, Audubon is one of the most discreet and luxurious properties in the city, once favored by Elizabeth Taylor.

🔲 Q2 🏠 509 Dauphine St
🆆 auduboncottages.com

$$$

The Celestine

A boutique property, revamped to recapture the romance of its glory days in the 1950s, Celestine is replete with antiques. The tranquil courtyard is a delight.

🔲 Q2 🏠 727 Toulouse St
🆆 thecelestinenola.com

$$$

↑ The tranquil St. Anthony's Garden, set out beneath St. Louis Cathedral

11

Père Antoine Alley and St. Anthony's Garden

🔲 Q2 🚇 Riverfront 🚌 5, 55

This alley is named for one of the city's most beloved clergymen, Father Antonio de Sedella (Père Antoine), who served as pastor of St. Louis Cathedral for 40 years. He was admired for his compassionate ministry to the poor, whom he assiduously fed and clothed.

The fenced garden, once a dueling ground, features a great sculpture of the Sacred Heart. In the early morning and evening, the scent of sweet olives lingers in the air.

12

Museum of Death

🔲 P2 🏠 227 Dauphine St
🚌 5 🕐 10am–6pm daily
🆆 museumofdeath.net

This museum is not for young children or the fainthearted. For those with a strong stomach and an interest in the many aspects of mortality, it offers a macabre collection, including skulls and coffins, apparatus used by morticians, crime and morgue scenes, and artworks and letters from infamous serial killers. A shrunken head, graphic car accident

photographs, and newspaper front pages recording momentous and tragic moments in American and world history also feature in the collection. There's an array of taxidermy, and a skeleton of an alligator chewing on a human leg bone.

The museum's exhibits are constantly expanding. New Orleans is a city with a special relationship to death, and while this museum isn't for everyone, its presence here is appropriate.

13

Hermann-Grima House

🔲 Q2 🏠 820 St. Louis St 🚌 5
🕐 10am–4pm Wed–Mon; tours: 10am, 11am, 1pm, 2pm & 3pm Wed–Mon
🚫 Public hols 🆆 hgghh.org

This gabled brick house stands out because it is one of the few examples of American Federal-style architecture in the French Quarter. William Brand built it in 1831 for Samuel Hermann, a German-Jewish merchant. He lost his fortune in 1837 and had to sell the house to Judge Felix Grima. The house features a central doorway with a fanlight and marble steps. Inside, the floors and doors are made of cypress, and the rooms have marble fireplaces. The three-story service

HEART OF THE DOMESTIC SLAVE TRADE

In 1808 the federal government ended the transatlantic slave trade, which meant that enslaved people were no longer brought into the U.S. from overseas. However, the 1803 Louisiana Purchase (when the U.S. bought Louisiana from France) had opened up land to slaveholders who demanded chattel labor. New Orleans became the nexus of the domestic slave trade and the largest slave market in the U.S. Much of this trade occurred within the French Quarter, then the heart of the city, including under the domed rotunda of the St. Louis Hotel, now the Omni Royal Orleans Hotel (p82), and Esplanade and Chartres Streets. It wasn't until 1865, when the federal government passed the 13th Amendment abolishing slavery in the U.S., that enslaved people were freed.

quarters, located in a separate building off the parterre behind the house, feature former quarters for enslaved workers. The house also offers a Urban Enslavement Tour, which focuses on the experiences of enslaved people in New Orleans.

---

14 ⟨⟩

Le Petit Theatre

📍Q2 🏠616 St. Peter St
🚌5, 55 🕐Hours vary,
check website 🌐lepetit
theatre.com

This tiny theater was the brainchild of the Drawing Room Players, a group of

actors who came together in 1916 under the management of Mrs. Oscar Nixon. Their first theater was located in the Lower Pontalba Building, but the current site was bought in 1922 and was used for the first American productions of Eugene O'Neill's *Beyond the Horizon* and Oscar Wilde's *Lady Windermere's Fan*. A courtyard with a fountain sits in the center of the building. Legend has it that the fountain is haunted by the spirit of a jilted bride.

In 2011, part of the building was converted into a restaurant. Tableau is part of the famous Dickie Brennan & Co. group of restaurants, and guests can choose between dining in the

courtyard or on the balcony overlooking Jackson Square.

The theater hosts a season of performances from September to June, and acts as a headquarters during the Tennessee Williams & New Orleans Literary Festival and Writers' Conference in March.

15

Pirate's Alley

📍Q2 🚌5, 55

Although there is no concrete evidence, a popular theory holds that this narrow cobbled row, extending alongside St. Louis Cathedral, was once the favorite haunt of the infamous pirate brothers Jean and Pierre Lafitte.

Today, the alley attracts visitors with its artistic atmosphere and open-air cafés and shops. At No. 624 is Faulkner House Books, in the building where William Faulkner wrote his first novel, *Soldier's Pay*, in 1925. Today, the store's shelves are lined with Faulkner first editions as well as works by other major Southern authors. Next door is Pirate's Alley Café, which stands on the site of a former Spanish colonial prison, built in 1769.

↑ Faulkner House Books at 624 Pirate Alley, once the residence of William Faulkner

Did You Know?

Many of Louisiana's current state laws are descended from the civil code first devised by Napoleon.

16

Louisiana Supreme Court Building

🅠 Q2 🏠 400 Royal St
🚋 Riverfront 🚌 55
🕐 Museum: 9am–5pm Mon–Fri 🌐 sclahs.org

When this massive granite and marble structure was built in 1908–10, the French Quarter was on the downslide. Erecting the splendid Beaux Arts court building was an early exercise in urban renewal. Despite a few protests, an entire block of historic 18th- and early 19th-century buildings was razed to make way for it. The Louisiana Supreme Court occupied it from 1910 to 1958. Thereafter, it began to decline and massive trees were planted on site to conceal the building's exterior. It was then home to a string of state agencies, none of which kept up the maintenance on this architecturally intricate structure. In the 1990s, the state finally launched a reno-vation program, and since 2004, the building has once again served as the home of the Louisiana Supreme Court, the Louisiana Law Library, and other state legal offices. A small museum on the first floor includes exhibits on the development of Louisiana law.

Browsing the collections of the Pharmacy Museum, and *(inset)* the museum's historic storefront ↑

17

New Orleans Pharmacy Museum

🅠 Q2 🏠 514 Chartres St
🚌 55 🕐 11am–4pm Tue–Sat; tours: 10–11am Wed–Sun (reservations required) 🔒 Public hols 🌐 pharmacy museum.org

This museum is located on the site of the first licensed pharmacy in the United States, operated by Louis Joseph Dufilho from 1823 to 1855. The original display cases and mahogany cabinets contain some gruesome-looking early surgical tools – saws, knives, and bloodletting instruments – as well as herbal remedies, many of which were forerun-ners of today's drugs. These include a bottle of salicin, an early form of aspirin produced by Bayer & Co. from black willow bark. The Pharmacy Museum also features a splendid 1855 marble soda

↑ The imposing facade of the Louisiana Supreme Court Building

sandwich (p27). It occupies two buildings, one of which is a two-story structure, built in 1798, facing St. Louis Street; the second, built in 1814, is a three-story building with a mezzanine. Together, they were the home of Mayor Nicholas Girod, who planned to free Napoleon from imprisonment on St. Helena Island. With the help of Dominique You and a pirate band, Girod intended to bring him to this refuge, but Napoleon died before the mission could be undertaken. Today, the walls of the house are adorned with all kinds of Napoleonic decor and memorabilia. Both buildings are attributed to leading New Orleans architect and artist Jean-Hyacinthe Laclotte, and the balcony railings were crafted by prolific blacksmith William Malus. The cupola on the roof is a New Orleans landmark.

19 🅜

French Quarter Visitor Center

📍 Q3 🏠 419 Decatur St
🚌 5, 55 🕘 9:30am–4:30pm
Tue-Sat 🕒 Public hols
🌐 nps.gov

This visitor center serves as the primary introduction to the Jean Lafitte National Historical Park & Preserve (p194) and the New Orleans Jazz National Historical Park. It has displays on the history, geography, and culture of the Mississippi River Delta region, including dioramas and interactive exhibits – the jazz park promotes the origins of jazz and its development through performances, ranger talks, and other programs. Rangers from both parks give talks at 10am Tuesday–Saturday and the Arrowhead Jazz Band perform a live concert at 2pm on Tuesdays.

fountain at which appealing sodas were first concocted to help the medicine go down. The second floor features a 19th-century sick room, a fine collection of eye glasses, homeopathic remedies, and an impressive collection of 19th-century dental instruments. The walled courtyard garden is filled with medicinal herbs.

18 🍴 🍺

Napoleon House

📍 Q2 🏠 500 Chartres St
🚌 55 🕘 11am–10pm daily
🌐 napoleonhouse.com

One of New Orleans' most atmospheric bars, Napoleon House is famous for its Pimm's Cup and for a warm version of the muffuletta, a traditional New Orleans deli

DRINK

Old Absinthe House

This bar dates back to 1807, when pirates and ne'er-do-wells drank within its storied walls. Today it's a lively Bourbon Street spot, and one of the few places in the city with a full absinthe service.

📍 P3 🏠 240 Bourbon St
🌐 ruebourbon.com/old-absinthe-house

Arnaud's French 75 Bar

This bijoux annex to Arnaud's Restaurant oozes old-world charm and serves up mouth-watering versions of the eponymous French 75 cocktail, a refreshing champagne and gin mix.

📍 P2 🏠 240 Bourbon St
🌐 arnauds restaurant.com

The Chart Room

A true French Quarter dive bar, open 24 hours and specializing in cheap drinks and loud music, the Chart Room gives visitors a good story to take home.

📍 Q3 🏠 300 Chartres St
📞 (504) 522-1708

Beachbum Berry's Latitude 29

Jeff "Beachbum" Berry is among the world's foremost mixologists and a figurehead of the popular tiki cocktail bar revival. Come here for phenomenal fruity, boozy concoctions in striking glassware.

📍 Q3 🏠 321 N Peters St
🌐 latitude29nola.com

A SHORT WALK
JACKSON SQUARE

Distance 0.5 miles (0.8 km) **Time** 10 minutes
Nearest Streetcar Riverfront

In the historic heart of the French Quarter, Jackson Square is surrounded by a striking and harmonious collection of buildings. This block initially served as a military parade ground, or *place d'armes*, where troops were trained and drilled, executions carried out, and public meetings held. The Cathedral, Cabildo, and Presbytère face the square. The plaza was redesigned in 1848, when Baroness Pontalba built the two elegant apartment buildings on the upriver and downriver sides of the square.

Today, the square makes a pleasant place to wander, amid performing musicians, hotdog stands, and the stalls of local artists displaying their works.

Tennessee Williams wrote A Streetcar Named Desire in an apartment at **632 St. Peter Street**.

Le Petit Theatre du Vieux Carré, *established in 1916, moved to its current location in 1919 (p79). The building is a replica of the original.*

The Omni Royal Orleans Hotel *is constructed on the site of the 1836 St. Louis Hotel.*

TOULOUSE ST

CHARTRES STREET

WILKINSON

START

The French Quarter's beloved **Napoleon House** *bar is devoted to the emperor's memory, with portraits and other memorabilia adorning the walls.*

DECATUR STREET

FINISH

0 meters 50
0 yards 50
N

Entrance to Le Petit Theatre du Vieux Carré, designed by architect Richard Koch

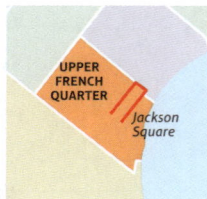

UPPER
FRENCH
QUARTER

*Jackson
Square*

← A Lucky Dogs hot dog stand
sitting outside the Cabildo
and St. Louis Cathedral

St. Louis Cathedral (p62), **the
Presbytère** (p64), *and* **the Cabildo**
(p68) *were the most important religious
and administrative buildings in the
French and Spanish periods.*

ST. ANN STREET

The handsome
**Pontalba
Buildings**, *built
in 1848 for $302,000,
are located on the
upriver and down-
river sides of the
square (p77).*

ST. PETER ST.

The 1850 House
*displays opulent
furniture and
decorations that
convey the middle-
class lifestyles of the
antebellum era (p76).*

*A statue of General
Jackson sits in the
center of* **Jackson
Square** *(p76), where
artists hang their
works on the fence.*

Did You Know?

Designed by Louis H.
Pilié, the square was
modeled on the
Place des Vosges in
Paris, France.

A SHORT WALK
AROUND THE MISSISSIPPI RIVERFRONT

Distance 1 mile (1.6 km) **Time** 25 minutes (plus the 10-minute ferry ride) **Nearest Streetcar** Riverfront

New Orleans owes its very existence to the Mississippi River, one of the world's great waterways and an iconic feature on the cultural, historic, and economic landscape of America. This walk provides superb vistas from both sides of the river, explores a portion of the levee system, and, thanks to a ride on the Algiers Ferry, gives you a chance to experience its swirling waters up close. The ferry ride is brief but offers excellent views of the New Orleans skyline and various craft that ply the river.

*Begin at **Washington Artillery Park** (p99), a raised platform with excellent views of Jackson Square (p76) and the river.*

*Descend the stairs on the river side of the platform to reach the **Moon Walk** (p99), a paved walkway named for former New Orleans mayor Maurice "Moon" Landrieu.*

*Pass the berth for the **Steamboat Natchez** (p74), a paddle wheeler that offers river trips, and listen out for the music from its steam calliope organ.*

*Meander through sculpture-studded **Woldenberg Riverfront Park** (p129), where green open spaces are popular with picnickers and joggers.*

*The area around the **Audubon Aquarium** (p135) is filled with marine sculptures, shaded park benches, and vendors serving refreshments.*

*If the ferry is not in dock at the terminal, take some time to explore the adjacent **Spanish Plaza** (p131) with its fountain ringed by tile mosaics.*

*The Canal-Algiers ferry departs **Canal Street Ferry Terminal** every 30 minutes at quarter to and a quarter past the hour (p128), transporting visitors across the river to Algiers Point (p205).*

JACKSON SQUARE

START

Moon Walk Riverfront Park

DECATUR STREET

N PETERS ST

Steamboat Natchez

Woldenberg Riverfront Park

PETERS STREET

N FRONT ST

IBERVILLE ST

NORTH

Canal Place

CANAL STREET

Audubon Aquarium of the Americas

SOUTH PETERS ST

Harrah's Casino

SPANISH PLAZA

World Trade Center

Mississippi

Did You Know?

The Spanish Plaza was gifted to New Orleans by Spain in a gesture of friendship.

| 0 meters | | 300 |
| 0 yards | | 300 |

N

Crossing the Mississippi on the 10-minute ferry trip from Canal Street to Algiers

Locator Map
For more detail see p60 and p122

UPPER FRENCH QUARTER

Around the Mississippi Riverfront

The ferry docks in **Old Algiers Point**, *a village established in 1719 (p128). Turn left and follow the trail of crushed shells that top the grassy levee.*

The **Algiers Courthouse** *is a grand Romanesque Revival structure built in 1896 after a devastating fire wiped out much of the neighborhood.*

Descend the set of colorfully painted concrete steps down to **Patterson Road** *and then on to Olivier Street and Pelican Avenue, each lined with colorful Creole townhouses and shotgun-style houses.*

At the end of Pelican, turn right at **Bouny Street** *and continue up to the ferry terminal for the return trip.*

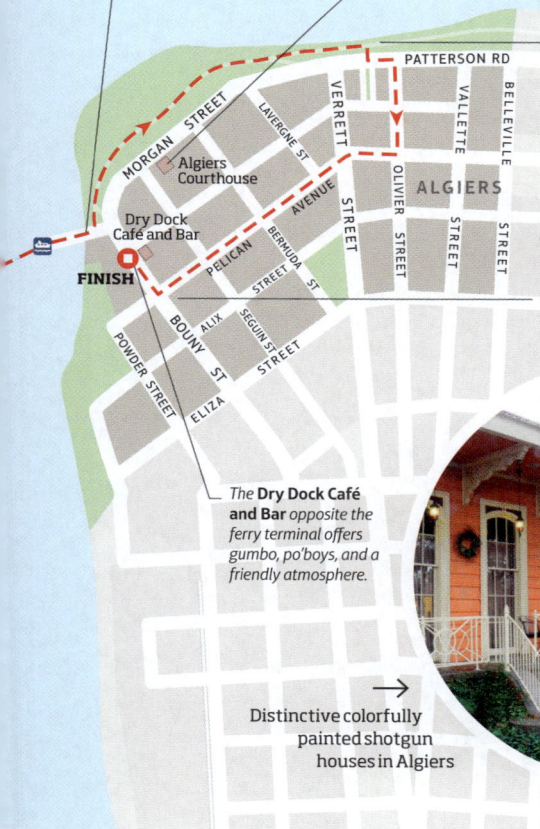

PATTERSON RD

MORGAN STREET
LAVERGNE ST
VERRETT STREET
VALLETTE STREET
BELLEVILLE STREET
OLIVIER STREET
STREET
STREET

Algiers Courthouse

ALGIERS

Dry Dock Café and Bar

PELICAN AVENUE
BERMUDA STREET

FINISH

BOUNY ST
ALIX ST
SEGUIN STREET

POWDER STREET
ELIZA

The **Dry Dock Café and Bar** *opposite the ferry terminal offers gumbo, po'boys, and a friendly atmosphere.*

Distinctive colorfully painted shotgun houses in Algiers

LOWER FRENCH QUARTER

Featuring handsome Creole-style houses and ornate ironwork galleries, this is the more residential part of the French Quarter. It extends from beyond St. Ann Street to Esplanade Avenue, which, in the 19th century, housed the aristocratic French Creole community. This area is home to some of the city's oldest buildings, such as the Old Ursuline Convent, dating from 1752, the only remaining French colonial structure in New Orleans.

In the south of this quarter, the area that surrounds the French Market has long been a place for meeting and mixing; in the city's early days, it was an Indigenous trading post on the banks of the Mississippi. Under French then Spanish colonial rule, it was a busy center for international trade. Imported goods flowed in from overseas, and African, German, Italian, and Irish traders set up market stalls to sell their wares. In the 19th century, nearby Gallatin Street (now French Market Place) became the quarter's most notorious thoroughfare, its dimly lit brothels and disreputable saloons tempting visiting sailors.

The French Market still throngs with activity, but today makes a pleasant spot to browse for local souvenirs, fresh produce, and sizzling street food. There are plenty of bars here too, including Lafitte's Blacksmith Shop, one of the city's oldest. The surrounding streets, lined with historic houses, afford some respite from the crowds.

LOWER FRENCH QUARTER

Must See

❶ French Market

Experience More

❷ Old Ursuline Convent
❸ New Orleans Historic Voodoo Museum
❹ New Orleans Jazz Museum
❺ Historic BK House & Gardens
❻ Soniat House
❼ Gallier House
❽ St. Mark's United Methodist Church
❾ Lalaurie House
❿ Café du Monde
⓫ Gauche House
⓬ Central Grocery
⓭ Esplanade Avenue
⓮ Lafitte's Blacksmith Shop
⓯ Cornstalk Fence
⓰ Madame John's Legacy
⓱ Washington Artillery Park and Moon Walk

Eat

① Clover Grill
② Verti Marte
③ Coop's Place

Drink

④ Bar Tonique
⑤ Cane and Table
⑥ Molly's at the Market
⑦ Port of Call

Stay

⑧ Lamothe House
⑨ Lanaux Mansion
⑩ Lafitte Hotel & Bar

Shop

⑪ Fifi Mahoney's

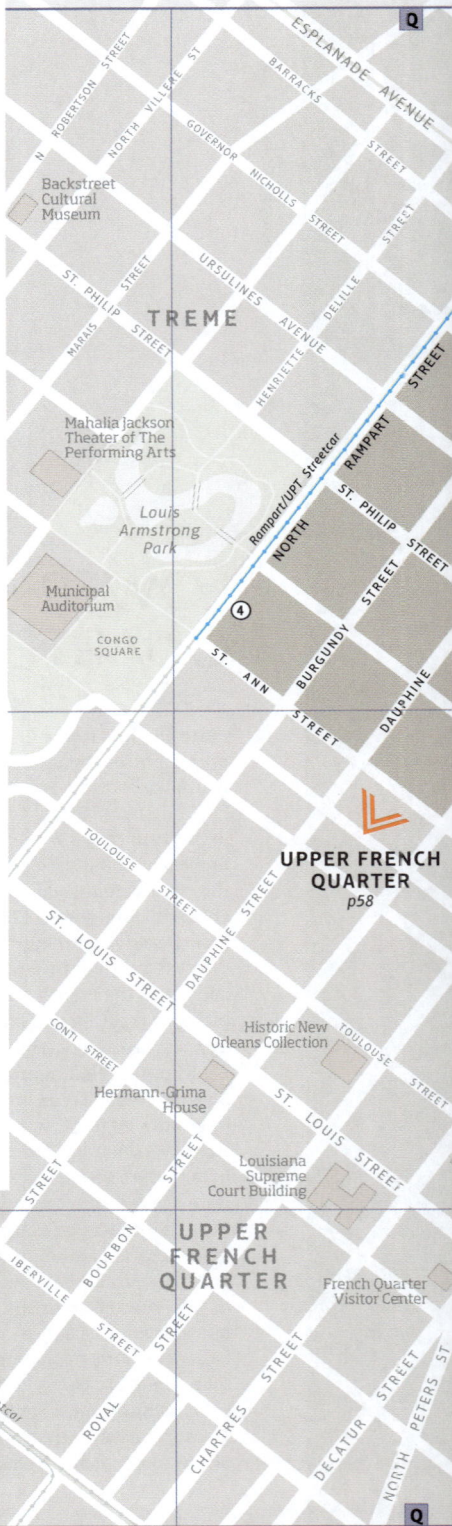

ESPLANADE AVENUE

BARRACKS STREET

ROBERTSON STREET

NORTH VILLERE ST

GOVERNOR NICHOLLS STREET

N. ROBERTSON STREET

Backstreet Cultural Museum

URSULINES AVENUE

ST. PHILIP STREET

MARAIS STREET

HENRIETTE DELILLE STREET

TREME

Mahalia Jackson Theater of The Performing Arts

Louis Armstrong Park

Municipal Auditorium

CONGO SQUARE

Rampart/UPT Streetcar

NORTH RAMPART STREET

ST. PHILIP STREET

BURGUNDY STREET

DAUPHINE STREET

❹

ST. ANN STREET

UPPER FRENCH QUARTER
p58

TOULOUSE STREET

DAUPHINE STREET

ST. LOUIS STREET

CONTI STREET

Historic New Orleans Collection

TOULOUSE STREET

Hermann-Grima House

ST. LOUIS STREET

Louisiana Supreme Court Building

UPPER FRENCH QUARTER

State Palace Theater

CANAL STREET

Canal Streetcar

DAUPHINE STREET

IBERVILLE STREET

BOURBON STREET

ROYAL STREET

French Quarter Visitor Center

COMMON STREET

GRAVIER STREET

CHARTRES STREET

DECATUR STREET

NORTH PETERS ST

Q

P

Q

1

2

3

1 🍴 💬 🛍️

THE FRENCH MARKET

📍R2 🚌N Peters St to Barracks St 🚋Riverfront Stops 1, 2, 3 🚌55
🕐10am–6pm daily 🌐frenchmarket.org

The historic French Market runs alongside the Mississippi River, set between Jackson Square and the Old U.S. Mint. A people-watcher's paradise, it's one of the city's most colorful places to shop, stroll, and sample delicious local treats.

More than 200 years ago, Indigenous peoples first came to this riverside location to trade baskets, beads, and *filé* (ground sassafras leaves used in gumbo). As the port grew in the 1800s, the market flourished, with African American women selling coffee and *calas* (hot rice cakes), German farmers offering their produce, and Italian butchers selling meat. At the far end, the flea market (open until 5pm) stands on the site of the notorious neighborhood once called the "port of the missing men," due to the deaths and disappearances of many men who visited the local bars and brothels here. The present French Market buildings date from the 1930s and officially cover the six blocks of shops and cafés between St. Ann and Barracks streets. Inside the market is Dutch Alley, a triangular plaza with a performance tent and an artists' co-op. At the open-air Farmers' Market, which begins at Ursulines Street, you can shop for Cajun spices and pralines, buy local artworks, or choose from a variety of mouthwatering snacks at the food stands.

1813

Built this year, the Meat Market Building is the oldest standing structure in the market.

1 Established in 1862, Café du Monde is located on the south side of the market.

2 A garden shop in the French Market selling fresh, locally grown produce.

3 A distinctive yellow archway marks the entrance to the market, which also hosts farmers' and artisan markets on Wednesdays and Saturdays.

↑ The vibrant French Market, a great place to pick up handmade souvenirs

CREOLE TOMATO FESTIVAL

During the second weekend in June, the French Market celebrates the arrival of a local favorite: the Creole tomato. Grown in the rich alluvial soil of the river parishes, these fat, sweet fruits are the star of special dishes from crêpes to crawfish pies. This quirky festival features tomato-eating contests, a Bloody Mary Market, cooking demonstrations, live music, and more.

EXPERIENCE MORE

2 🔲 🎨 🏛

Old Ursuline Convent

📍 R2 🏠 1100 Chartres St
🚊 Riverfront 🚌 55 🕐 10am–2pm Tue–Sat 🌐 oldrs
ulineconventmuseum.com

Dating from 1752, this convent is the oldest building in the Mississippi Valley. In the 1820s, it became the first official residence for the bishops and archbishops of New Orleans, and the home of the archdiocesan archives.

Inside the current chapel, consecrated in 1845, visitors can admire the splendid pine and cypress ceiling, Bavarian stained-glass windows, and a window depicting the Battle of New Orleans (p50). A formal French garden containing a handsome iron gazebo lies in front of the building.

Near the convent is St. Mary's Catholic Church, dating back to 1845, which has beautifully preserved statues and stained-glass windows, plus a functional Pilcher organ built in 1890.

3 🔲 🎨 🏛

New Orleans Historic Voodoo Museum

📍 Q2 🏠 724 Dumaine St
🚊 Riverfront 🚌 5, 55
🕐 10am–6pm daily
🌐 voodoomuseum.com

This fascinating museum is the best place to learn more about this religious practice, a blend of African, Catholic, and Haitian spiritual beliefs. Interesting exhibits on voodoo's history and art are displayed here.

4 🔲 🎨 🏛

New Orleans Jazz Museum

📍 R1 🏠 400 Esplanade Ave
🚊 Riverfront 🕐 9am–4pm
Tue–Sun 🌐 nolajazz
museum.org

Housed in the Old U.S. Mint (part of the Louisiana State Museum portfolio) the New Orleans Jazz Museum's comprehensive collections include rare and significant recordings, tapes, and pressings,

URSULINE NUNS

Sent by King Louis XV to set up a base to care for the poor and sick, as well as to provide education for young girls, the first Ursuline nuns journeyed to New Orleans from Rouen, France, arriving in 1727. Fourteen nuns made the arduous seven-month voyage across the Atlantic and up the Mississippi. Despite the challenging conditions on arrival, they established a school and set up a hospital, treating the enslaved population and wounded soldiers.

← The entrance to the Old Ursuline Convent, and *(inset)* inside the convent's chapel

including a 1917 disc of the first jazz recording. The instruments belonging to famous musicians, including a cornet owned by legendary Louis Armstrong, are also on display, along with photographs, paintings and prints showing the early days of jazz.

There is a live performance venue where concerts, lectures, and theatrical shows are held.

5 ⊗ ⓜ

Historic BK House & Gardens

📍R1 🏠1113 Chartres St
🚊Riverfront 🚌5, 55
🕐By tour only: 10am–3pm Mon-Tue & Thu-Sat hourly 🌐bkhouse.org

Twin staircases lead up to this Federal-style townhouse, designed by architect François Correjolles in 1826. It is

→ Central courtyard and fountain of the Historic BK House & Gardens

associated with several famous New Orleans residents, including master chess player Paul Morphy, who was born here in 1837, when it belonged to his grandfather, Joseph Le Carpentier. The house derives its name in part from Civil War confederate General P. G. T. Beauregard, who lived here briefly in 1866–7.

Frances Parkinson Keyes wrote many of her 51 novels here, and restored the property to its Victorian style. Today, many of the novelist's personal possessions are on display, along with those of the Beauregard family. The rooms are arranged around a courtyard, which contains a fountain that Keyes brought from Vermont, her home state.

EAT

Clover Grill
This 1950s style, 24-hour diner is a favorite when it comes to satisfying late-night cravings. Enjoy mouth-watering burgers grilled on a hubcap and served in a retro setting.
📍Q2 🏠900 Bourbon St
🌐clovergrill.com

⑤⑤⑤

Verti Marte
A French Quarter institution, this deli at the back of a convenience store is as casual as it gets, but the tasty, hearty po'boy sandwiches are a local favorite.
📍R1 🏠1201 Royal St
🌐vertimartenola.com

⑤⑤⑤

Coop's Place
The dining room may be no-frills, but the food is some of the best homestyle Cajun and Creole fare you'll taste, especially the signature jambalaya.
📍R2 🏠1109 Decatur St
🌐coopsplace.net

⑤⑤⑤

DRINK

Bar Tonique

Half craft cocktail joint, half casual neighborhood tavern, this is a perfect spot to relax after a long walk around the Vieux Carré. Sip a Dark and Stormy or an Old Fashioned in calm surrounds.

⚲Q1 ⌂820 Rampart St
🅦bartonique.com

Cane and Table

Drinks are billed as "proto-tiki" – expect tasty precursors to daiquiris and the fancy cocktails you know and love. A Cuban ambiance permeates the menu.

⚲R1 ⌂1113 Decatur St
🅦caneandtable
nola.com

Molly's at the Market

Open late into the night, this lively Irish bar is always buzzing. Mix with locals and curious tourists as the genial bartenders pull pints of Guinness and concoct their famous frozen Irish coffees.

⚲R2 ⌂1107 Decatur St
🅦mollysatthe
market.net

Port of Call

It might be famous for its burgers, but this nautical-themed restaurant also has a bar serving sweet, tropical punch-style tipples with names such as the Red Turtle and Windjammer.

⚲R1 ⌂838 Esplanade
Ave 🅦portofcall
nola.com

↑ Sunlight streaming into the exquisitely furnished interior of Soniat House

6

Soniat House

⚲R1 ⌂1133 Chartres
St 🚋Riverfront 🚌5,
55 🕐To the public
🅦soniathouse.com

This historic residence was built in 1829 as a townhouse for wealthy sugar planter Joseph Soniat Dufossat and his family. Joseph was the second son of Chevalier Guy Saunhac du Fossat, who had been sent to Louisiana by Louis XV of France in 1751 to work as a military engineer.

The house combines classic Creole style – the flagstone carriageway, a courtyard, an external spiral staircase, and lacy iron galleries – with Greek Revival detail in the mantels and moldings. In the 1940s, the Nathaniel Felton family restored it completely. Today it is a small hotel, exquisitely furnished with antiques and decoration.

7 ♿ Ⓜ

Gallier House

⚲R1 ⌂1132 Royal St 🚌5,
55 🕐9:30am–3:30pm Wed–
Mon 🕐Some public hols
🅦hgghh.org

In 1857 James Gallier, Jr. designed this attractive residence, using elements of Creole architecture, such as the carriageway and gallery

configurations, and American styles, such as the internal halls (p101). The interior incorporated many innovations, including a hot-water and ventilation system. The kitchen was also placed inside, thanks to advances in cooking technology. Designer James Gallier, Jr. was the son of the city's renowned architect James Gallier, Sr., who designed the portico of the Louisiana State Bank building (p70), and Gallier Hall (p132).

Today the house is part of the Hermann-Grima + Gallier Historic Houses Museum (p78). Among the rooms to visit here

→

The graceful exterior of Lalaurie House, belying its grim history is the "sick room," a sparsely furnished room for the unwell. Many households had such a room, which was not surprising in a city that had 23 yellow fever epidemics between 1718 and 1860.

8

St. Mark's United Methodist Church

Q1 **1130 N Rampart St** **Rampart: UPT** **frenchquarterumc.org**

Also known as the Methodist Church of the Vieux Carré, this pretty chapel on Rampart, at the corner of Governor Nicholls, was completed in 1924 in Spanish Mission style and shares space with a community center. The beautiful interior is all wood and white paint, with a timber ceiling and an original 1922 Moller pipe organ. Founded when the French Quarter was going through hard times, struggling with poverty and crime, the church has a long history of community activism, supporting the women's suffrage movement of the 1910s and the civil rights movement of the 1950s and 1960s. Today it's best known for its homeless outreach program and LGBTQ+ advocacy.

9

Lalaurie House

R1 **1140 Royal St** **5, 55** **To the public**

Residents of the French Quarter still tend to hurry past this otherwise delightful building because of its grim associations and reputation for ghosts. It was built in 1832 for a distinguished couple, Dr. Leonard Louis Nicolas Lalaurie and his wife, Delphine, two socialites who were well known for their lavish and fashionable parties.

However, guests at these social events could not help but notice the condition of the servants, who were painfully thin and seemed to be terrified of Madame Lalaurie. Suspicions of maltreatment were eventually confirmed on April 10, 1834, when a fire broke out at the residence. When neighbors rushed in to extinguish the fire, they found seven enslaved workers, half-starved and manacled. A story in the local press further fueled the outrage, and a mob arrived intent on destroying the place. During the melee, Madame Lalaurie and her husband escaped unharmed. After her death in Paris in 1842, it is believed that her body was returned to New Orleans and secretly buried in St. Louis Cemetery #1 (p112) or #2 (p114). During the Civil War, the house served as a Union headquarters; later it was used as a school, music conservatory, and gaming house.

Some locals still swear that the house, now a private residence, is haunted, and that the clanking of chains can be heard in the night.

↑ Guests at the historic Café du Monde, and *(inset)* a sample of the café's fare

10 Café du Monde

📍 R2 🏠 800 Decatur St
🚉 Riverfront 🚌 5, 55
🕐 7:15am–11pm daily (to midnight Fri–Sat) 🚫 Dec 25
🌐 shop.cafedumonde.com

Everyone who visits the city should stop here for the famous sugar-dusted *beignets* (square donuts), along with *café au lait* (or the chicory-flavored version), iced coffee, or a glass of milk. This coffee-house, established in 1862, is perfect for relaxing at a table under the arcade and listening to the street musicians.

In the mid-19th century, as many as 500 coffeehouses operated in the French Quarter. Coffee was one of the city's most important commodities, and the coffee trade helped the economy to recover after the Civil War, when New Orleans vied with New York City to control coffee imports. During the Civil War, locals drank coffee flavored with peanuts and pecan shells to make the supply last.

11 Gauche House

📍 R1 🏠 704 Esplanade Ave at Royal St 🚉 Riverfront
🚌 5 🚫 To the public

The beautiful cast ironwork of Gauche House is uniquely integral to its overall design, which accounts for the building's harmonious appearance. Little of the ironwork in New Orleans was constructed at the same time as the building – it was usually added later. Numerous patterns are used on the fence, the gate, the balconies, and the parapet, casting spellbinding shadows on the stucco exterior on sunny days. A bacchant surrounded by grapevines adorns the balcony, cast in Saarbrücken, Germany. Rows of anthema and other Greek floral motifs decorate the roof's edge and the fence posts. Architect James Freret designed the house for crockery merchant John Gauche in 1856.

12 Central Grocery

📍 R2 🏠 923 Decatur St
🚉 Riverfront 🚌 5, 55
🕐 9am–5pm daily
🌐 centralgrocery.com

This historic store, one of the few Italian delis left

INSIDER TIP
Sandwich Savvy

Visit Central Grocery before the lunchtime rush, as the line can sometimes stretch all the way out of the door. If you're going to try a muffuletta, a half portion is usually plenty for one person.

The fashionable elite once paraded in their carriages past the many elegant residences on Esplanade Avenue, some of which have survived to this day.

in the French Quarter, sells all kinds of Italian food, including pasta, provolone, mozzarella, sausages, olive oil, and parmesan. In the 1890s, many Italians began to move to the French Quarter and became major stallholders at the nearby French Market (p90). Today, customers gather at the counters at the back of the store to order another specialty, the muffuletta, a sizable sandwich filled with deli meats and cheeses. The most vital ingredient, however, is the olive salad – a blend of olives, celery, carrots, cauliflower, and capers.

→

Charming, old buildings lining the Esplanade Avenue

13

Esplanade Avenue

🚉 R1 🚌 46, 48

Today Esplanade Avenue is the dividing line between the French Quarter and Faubourg Marigny, and it extends from the Mississippi to Bayou St. John. As early as the 1830s, this broad, tree-lined street cut through what was the most aristocratic Creole neighborhood of impressive villas and townhouses. The fashionable elite once paraded in their carriages past the many elegant residences on Esplanade Avenue, some of which have survived to this day. A stroll along this stretch reveals over 190 homes built before 1900. Many of these were designed by the city's foremost architects, whose styles range from Greek Revival to Italianate and Queen Anne. Most are still private residences, but some have been converted into bed-and-breakfasts. One of these is the Lanaux Mansion on the corner of Chartres Street. Built in 1879, the house featured in the movie *The Curious Case of Benjamin Button*. This area was once a notorious slave market – a plaque commemorates Solomon Northup, who was sold at an auction here in 1841 after being kidnapped (recounted in the film *12 Years A Slave*).

STAY

Lamothe House
Step back in time in this atmospheric, 19th-century townhouse.

🚉 R1 🏠 621 Esplanade Ave 🌐 frenchquarter guesthouses.com

$$$

Lanaux Mansion
Set in an ideal location, this delightful hotel exudes historic charm and has a friendly staff.

🚉 R1 🏠 547 Esplanade Ave 🌐 thelanaux mansion.com

$$$

Lafitte Hotel & Bar
The guest rooms at this Creole mansion exude period charm.

🚉 Q1 🏠 1003 Bourbon St 🌐 lafittehotel andbar.com

$$$

14

Lafitte's Blacksmith Shop

📍 Q1 🏠 941 Bourbon St
🚌 55, 89 🕐 10am–3am daily
🌐 lafittesblacksmith
shop.com

This is reportedly the oldest bar in New Orleans. It is an example of the French brick-between-posts (p100) style of building, and was constructed before 1772, although the precise date is unknown. Inside, several small fireplaces warm the place on cool evenings, and there is also a compact patio containing a sculpture of Adam and Eve embracing on a bed of ivy. The sculpture was created by an artist in lieu of payment for his bar tab.

Despite its name, there is no proof that the notorious pirate brothers Jean and Pierre Lafitte operated a smithy here as a front for their smuggling activities. Very little documentation of their lives exists, so many myths have been woven around these two figures. They operated as smugglers and were prominent slave traffickers, selling all manner of contraband, including seized slave ships, when the importation of enslaved people into the United States was forbidden in 1808. They earned local gratitude by warning the Americans of the planned British attack on New Orleans, and with their band they fought bravely in the ensuing battle. Regardless of whether this shop was indeed occupied by the Lafitte brothers, the building certainly existed to witness Jean Lafitte brazenly walking the streets when posters calling for his capture were plastered all over town.

Further along Bourbon Street stands another bar, called Lafitte's (originally Café Lafitte in Exile). It is so called because, until the early 1950s, Lafitte's Blacksmith was frequented by an LGBTQ+ crowd; when the bar changed hands, its new owner refused to renew the lease, and in 1953 its regular patrons were driven into exile. They established their new quarters just up the street, making Lafitte's one of the oldest gay bars in the U.S. It is open 24 hours a day and has outdoor seating both upstairs and downstairs.

15

Cornstalk Fence

📍 Q2 🏠 915 Royal St
🚌 5, 55

This handsome cast-iron landmark is one of three remaining in the city (p150). It was erected around 1850, when cast iron began to replace wrought iron (p152). Cornstalks are entwined with morning glories, and each element is painted in its natural color – yellow for the ears of corn, green for the stalks, and blue for the morning glories. A butterfly decorates the central portion of the gate, and a spray of holly adorns the bottom. It was cast by the prestigious Wood & Perot in Philadelphia.

16 🖼️ 🖼️

Madame John's Legacy

📍 Q2 🏠 632 Dumaine
St 🚊 Riverfront 🚌 5, 55
🕐 For refurbishments 🌐 lou
isianastatemuseum.org

Dating from 1789, this is one of the oldest surviving residences in the Mississippi

↑ Enjoying a drink outside Lafitte's Blacksmith Shop, the oldest bar in New Orleans

↑ A section of the intricate cast-iron Cornstalk Fence

Valley. It is a typical Creole plantation-style house, supported on brick piers that rise some 9 ft (3 m) off the ground. A veranda, accessible via French windows from all rooms, extends around the first floor.

The house's name refers to George Washington Cable's famous story *Tite Poulette* (1873), in which the hero leaves a residence as a legacy to his mistress, who sells the building, deposits the cash in a bank, and loses it all when the bank fails. Cable modeled the home in his story on this residence. In the late 19th century, the house was converted into rental apartments.

Today, exhibits in the first-floor galleries relate the history of the house and its several owner-residents. Among them were Jean Pascal, a Provençal sea captain who built the original house on this site before being killed during the Natchez revolt in 1729; and pirate-admiral René Beluche,

who was born here and later served in the Venezuelan Revolutionary Navy. The galleries on the second floor are used for contemporary art exhibitions.

In 2022 Madame John's Legacy closed for refurbishments – check the website before visiting.

17

Washington Artillery Park and Moon Walk

📍 R2 🏠 Decatur St (between St. Ann St and St. Peter St) 🚋 Riverfront 🚌 5, 55

Washington Artillery Park faces Jackson Square from across Decatur Street. Inside the park is an austere concrete amphitheater with a central staircase leading to the Moon Walk. This community boardwalk was named after Mayor Maurice "Moon" Landrieu, who approved the construction of a boardwalk that made the riverfront area accessible to the public in the 1970s.

Today, Moon Walk is favored by street performers. Crowds gather to witness impromptu performances by solo artists, including guitarists, clarinetists, saxophonists, trombonists, and steel drummers, who play with an open music case at their feet to collect donations. Standing on the Moon Walk, you can enjoy a welcome break from the city's humidity, as the constant breeze along the waterfront makes the temperature feel

much cooler than in the rest of the city. It also provides an excellent vantage point from which to view the river, Jackson Square, and the surrounding area.

Stone steps lead right down from the boardwalk to the edge of the Mississippi River, where you can sit and dangle your feet in the whiskey-colored water or watch the steamboats, ocean-going barges, and other river traffic float past. Do not attempt to stand in the river, however, as the current is deceptively rapid and powerful.

If you do want to get closer to the water, there are plenty of river cruises – from quick sightseeing trips across the river on the Algiers ferry *(p128)*, to romantic nighttime dinner cruises aboard the Steamboat *Natchez* accompanied by live jazz music *(p74)*.

SHOP

Fifi Mahoney's

New Orleans loves to dress up, and this wig store and hairdressers is the perfect place to bring your fancy-dress vision to life. It also has a wide range of jewelry and accessories.

📍 Q2 🏠 934 Royal St 📞 (504) 525-4343

→ A memorial Civil War cannon in Washington Artillery Park

THE ARCHITECTURE OF NEW ORLEANS

New Orleans is one of the few American cities to retain much of its historic architecture. Some French Quarter buildings date back 150 years or more, while those lining Esplanade Avenue tend to be the 19th-century former residences of the French Creole elite. The Garden District's splendid mansions are designed in a variety of period styles. It is not always easy to categorize the city's architecture, as buildings here combine multiple elements, in typical New Orleanian fashion.

FRENCH COLONIAL

Only a few buildings remain from this period, such as the Old Ursuline Convent *(p92)* and Lafitte's Blacksmith Shop *(p98)*. Most were destroyed by a series of fires: in 1788, 856 wooden buildings were destroyed; and in 1794, a further 212. However, the city's many Creole cottages reflect the style of this era. Single-storied, and featuring a pitched roof, these brightly colored residential cottages are a mix of French and Caribbean in style, popularized across the Gulf coast in the early 19th century.

↑ Laffitte's Blacksmith Shop, one of the city's few French colonial-style buildings

SPANISH COLONIAL

After the 1788 and 1794 fires, the Spanish decreed that any building of more than one story must be constructed of brick. The houses that were subsequently built can still be seen in the French Quarter. They often combine residence and store, and feature arcaded walls, heavy doors and windows, and a flagstone alleyway leading to a loggia and fountain-graced courtyard. Napoleon House, in the French Quarter, is a typical three-storied Spanish house *(p81)*.

↑ Spanish colonial-era Napoleon House, with its flat roof and heavy stone walls

← A Queen Anne-style raised center-hall cottage on Esplanade Avenue, and *(inset)* shotgun cottages in the French Quarter

AMERICAN TOWNHOUSE

Americans from the Atlantic states brought their own architecture with them, erecting Federal-style homes that stand out from the French or Spanish cottages. Historic BK House & Gardens is a fine example of this kind of building, with its cast-iron detailing and Palladian portico *(p93)*.

RAISED CENTER-HALL COTTAGE

Most of these raised cottages feature timber eaves and an alleyway leading to a rear courtyard. The interior usually contains four symmetrical rooms separated by a center hall. This style emerged in the South in the early 19th century and was popular with the upper middle classes. Esplanade Avenue is lined with several kinds of these raised cottages *(p97)*.

SHOTGUN HOUSE

These were so called because a bullet fired from a shotgun through the front door would go straight through the house and out the back as all the doors were aligned. They became popular in the 1810s–1830s to accommodate an influx of immigrant workers. There are many traditional examples in Marigny *(p104)*.

THE CREOLE PLANTATION HOUSE

Refugees from Saint Domingue (Haiti) brought this style of dwelling to New Orleans. This one-story residence is raised on brick pillars (to catch the breezes and avoid flooding) and incorporates a wraparound veranda. Typical examples are Pitot House *(p175)*, and Laura *(p185)*.

↑ Historic BK House & Gardens, with its galleries and architraves supported by Greek Revival columns

↑ Laura, a Creole Plantation House, with wide verandas and a flagstone piazza

A SHORT WALK
LOWER FRENCH QUARTER

Distance 0.6 miles (0.9 km) **Time** 15 minutes
Nearest Streetcar Riverfront

The area surrounding the French Market is loaded with atmosphere, and has long been a place for meeting and mixing. First an Indigenous trading post, the market developed as part of the French and then Spanish colonies. In the 19th century, it became a thriving hub of trade, thronging with international merchants and traders selling their wares, and customers meeting to drink coffee. Today the French Market still bustles with activity, with fresh produce, street food, and local souvenirs loading the many stalls. The surrounding area has plenty of bars and restaurants, and some of the oldest and most important buildings in the French Quarter.

Soniat House *has been restored to its original splendor, and serves as a lovely small hotel (p94).*

Historic BK House & Gardens, *former home of Frances Parkinson Keyes, is now a museum (p93).*

Set in a former residence, **Gallier House** *is an informative showcase of 19th-century life (p94).*

0 meters 50
0 yards 50

N

START

CHARTRES STREET

GOV. NICHOLLS ST

DECATUR STREET

Commissioned in 1745 and completed in 1752, the **Old Ursuline Convent** *(p92) is the oldest building in the Mississippi Valley.*

↑ Soniat House, with its delicate ironwork balconies

↑ A restaurant counter within the busy French Market

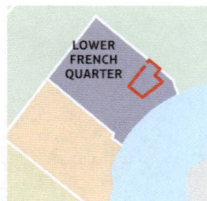

Locator Map
For more detail see p88

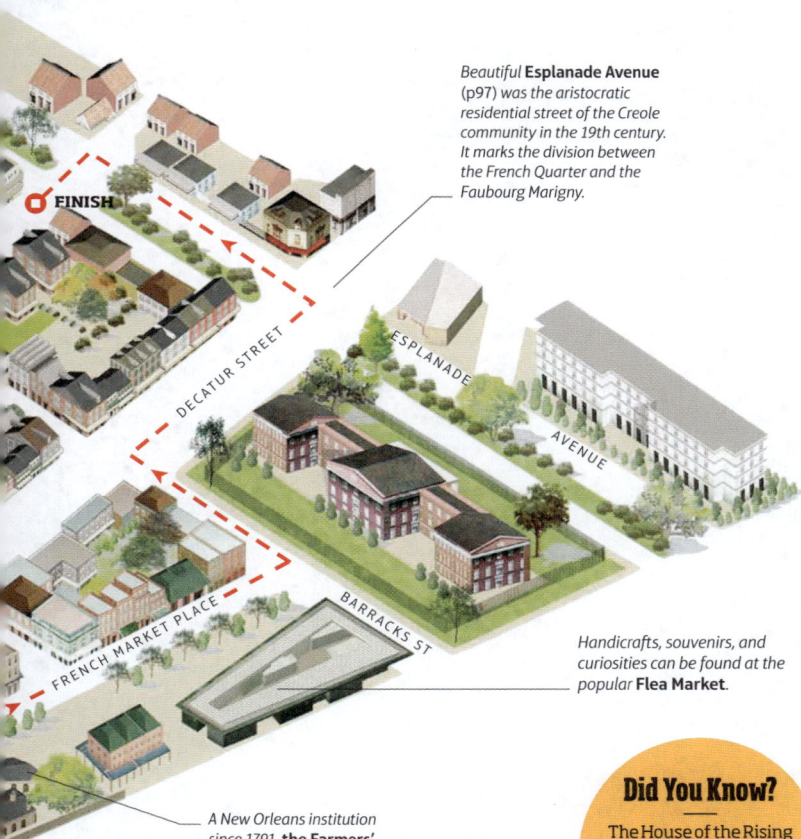

FINISH

Beautiful **Esplanade Avenue** (p97) *was the aristocratic residential street of the Creole community in the 19th century. It marks the division between the French Quarter and the Faubourg Marigny.*

DECATUR STREET

ESPLANADE AVENUE

FRENCH MARKET PLACE

BARRACKS ST

Handicrafts, souvenirs, and curiosities can be found at the popular **Flea Market**.

A New Orleans institution since 1791, **the Farmers' Market** at the French Market is the place to visit to stock up on fresh produce (p90).

Did You Know?

The House of the Rising Sun (from the famous song) is thought to have been located at No. 1614 Esplanade Avenue.

MARIGNY, BYWATER, AND TREME

Faubourg Marigny emerged as New Orleans' first suburb in 1805, when Bernard de Marigny subdivided his family's old plantation. The small plots quickly blossomed into a vibrant working-class district, settled by French Creoles, free people of color, and German immigrants. It was once home to Jelly Roll Morton, Sidney Bechet, and other leading jazz musicians of New Orleans. The brightly painted Creole cottages and shotgun houses are now part of the Marigny historic district, and Frenchmen Street has one of the city's liveliest music scenes. An arty ambience continues into adjoining Bywater.

The area just west of the French Quarter is the Faubourg Treme, the nation's oldest African American neighborhood. Congo Square, where enslaved people gathered to make music in the 18th and 19th centuries, is hailed as the birthplace of jazz. Other landmarks include historic churches and the elaborate above-ground mausoleums in St. Louis Cemeteries #1 and #2.

G   H   J   K

3

ST. BERNARD AVENUE

BROAD STREET

N DORGENOIS

N DABADIE STREET
ONZAGA STREET

LAHARPE STREET

BAYOU ROAD

Degas
House

N GALVEZ STREET
N KERLEREC STREET

ESPLANADE   AVENUE

URSULINES   AVENUE

LONDON AVENUE

ST. ANTHONY STREET

TOURO STREET

FRENCHMEN STREET

ELYSIAN

FIELDS

NORTH   TONTI   STREET

NORTH   GALVEZ   STREET

NORTH   ROCH   STREET

N CLAIBORNE

ROBERTSON ST

SPAIN STREET

DERBIGNY   STREET

N   CLAIBORNE   AVENUE

ROBERTSON   AVENUE

ELYSIAN

MARIGNY AVENUE

4

DOMAINE   STREET

ORLEANS   AVENUE

Lafitte   Greenway

MID-CITY
p162

N CLAIBORNE AVENUE

NORTH ROBERTSON STREET

N VILLERE ST

MARAIS STREET

KERLEREC ST

COLUMBUS STREET

ST. BERNARD   AVENUE

ANNETTE STREET

ST. ANTHONY STREET

NORTH VILLERE

URQUHART

PAUGER

TOURO

FRENCHMEN

McSHANE PLACE

RAMPART   STREET

JAMNOLA   ❹

FIELDS

ST. CLAUDE

MARAIS STREET

BURGUNDY   STREET

DAUPHINE   STREET

ROYAL   STREET

SPAIN   STREET

Washington
Square   ❽

❺   New Orleans African
American Museum

TREME

Mahalia Jackson
Theater of the
Performing Arts

❻   Backstreet
Cultural
Museum

ENRIGHT   DELILE ST

N RAMPART STREET

ESPLANADE   AVE

MARIGNY

❻
❽   ❹

DECATUR   STREET

5

Lafitte   Greenway

❼   Lafitte
Greenway

Louis
Armstrong
Park   ❶

TREME ST

ST. LOUIS ST

N PETERS   STREET

❿   Frenchmen
Street

St. Louis
Cemetery # 2

❸

ROBERTSON ST

Municipal
Auditorium

CONGO
SQUARE

Rampart/St Streetcar

DAUPHINE ST

Esplanade
Avenue Wharf

St. Louis
Cemetery #1   ❷

BASIN ST

LOWER
FRENCH QUARTER
p86

St. Louis
Cathedral

French
Market

TREME ST

IBERVILLE   STREET

Our Lady of
Guadalupe   ❾

UPPER
FRENCH QUARTER
p58

BOURBON STREET

ROYAL ST

CHARTRES STREET

JACKSON
SQUARE

Steamboat
Natchez

6

WAREHOUSE AND
CENTRAL BUSINESS
DISTRICTS
p120

CANAL   STREET

COMMON   STREET

The Historic New
Orleans Collection

N PETERS   STREET

MORGAN ST

City
Hall

LOYOLA   AVENUE

O'KEEFE   AVENUE

ST. CHARLES AVENUE

CARONDELET STREET

Canal
Place

Audubon
Aquarium

BOURBON ST

7

Civil
Courts

CBD

Caesars Hotel &
Casino

POYDRAS   STREET

N PETERS   STREET

PL. DE FRANCE

G   H   J   K

MARIGNY, BYWATER, AND TREME

Must Sees
1. Louis Armstrong Park
2. St. Louis Cemetery # 1

Experience More
3. St. Louis Cemetery # 2
4. JAMNOLA
5. New Orleans African American Museum
6. Backstreet Cultural Museum
7. Lafitte Greenway
8. Washington Square
9. Our Lady of Guadalupe
10. Frenchmen Street
11. Marigny Opera House
12. Studio BE
13. Crescent Park

Eat
1. The Joint
2. Bar Redux
3. Bacchanal
4. Adolfo's
5. Pizza Delicious

Shop
6. Frenchmen Art Bazaar
7. Euclid Records
8. Frenchmen Art and Books

FRANKLIN AVE

NORTH ROBERTSON STREET

PORT STREET

N. FERDINAND STREET

PRESS STREET

N. VILLERE STREET

LOUISA STREET

St. Vincent de Paul Cemetery

GALLIER STREET

INDEPENDENCE STREET

N CLAIBORNE AVENUE

N ROBERTSON STREET

AVENUE

URQUHART STREET

MARAIS STREET

FELICIANA STREET

N. VILLERE STREET

URQUHART STREET

MARAIS STREET

ST. ROCH STREET

FRANKLIN AVENUE

PORT STREET

N. FERDINAND STREET

RAMPART STREET

BURGUNDY STREET

MONTEGUT STREET

CLOUET STREET

LOUISA STREET

ST. CLAUDE AVENUE

PAULINE STREET

N RAMPART STREET

POLAND AVENUE

DAUPHINE STREET

Marigny Opera House 11

Royal

Studio BE 12

New Orleans Centre for Creative Arts

PIETY STREET

GALLIER STREET

CONGRESS STREET

INDEPENDENCE STREET

PAULINE STREET

N STREET

BURGUNDY STREET

DAUPHINE STREET

5

7

BYWATER

ALVAR STREET

MAZANT STREET

ROYAL STREET

1

3

2

Industrial Canal

Crescent Park 13

CHARTRES STREET

5

Mississippi

PATTERSON ROAD

VERRETT STREET

AVENUE

AVENUE

WHITNEY AVENUE

6

ALGIERS

VALLETTE STREET

ELIZA STREET

ELMIRA STREET

ATLANTIC STREET

7

OPELOUSAS

DRIVE

SLIDELL STREET

0 meters 600

0 yards 600

N

MARIGNY, BYWATER, AND TREME

L

M

N

2

3

4

5

6

7

Sculpture by Steve Kline set beside the water in Louis Armstrong Park →

1 🖼

LOUIS ARMSTRONG PARK

📍H5 🏠Louis Armstrong Park: Rampart St between St. Peter St and St. Ann St; Mahalia Jackson Theater for the Performing Arts: 1419 Basin St; Congo Square: N Rampart St between St. Peter St and St. Philip St 🚌5, 48, 88, 89 🌐Mahalia Jackson Theater for the Performing Arts: mahaliajacksontheater.com

Named for the legendary trumpeter Louis "Satchmo" Armstrong, this spacious park stands on hallowed jazz ground. Within the park, Congo Square and the Mahalia Jackson Theater play host to music festivals and concerts, while shaded paths around the artificial lake make for pleasant wandering, year round.

Congo Square

Under the Code Noir (a 1724 French edict concerning the treatment of enslaved workers), slaveholders were forbidden to work enslaved people on Sunday in order to encourage them to attend church. Such minimal amounts of freedom allowed the enslaved of New Orleans to retain their African heritage, more so than those in other parts of America. On Sunday afternoons, during the 18th and early 19th century, enslaved and free people of color would gather in Congo Square, now part of Armstrong Park, to meet with friends and family. They would sing, dance, and play music, performing the *calinda*, an African line dance, and the *bamboula*. These dances sowed the seeds of jazz music in New

Mahalia Jackson Theater for the Performing Arts

Louis Armstrong Park

CONGO SQUARE

Municipal Auditorium

NORTH RAMPART ST

Locator Map
For more detail see p106

LOUIS ARMSTRONG IN NEW ORLEANS

Born on August 4, 1901, Armstrong spent much of his childhood singing on the streets in a quartet until he was sent to a juvenile detention home after firing a pistol in public. It was there that he learned to play the trumpet, and soon he was challenging such leading players as Joe "King" Oliver and Freddie Keppard. He left New Orleans in 1922 to join King Oliver in Chicago, and went on to build an international career, entertaining audiences until his death in 1971. Today, Elizabeth Catlett's 1976 sculpture of the legendary musician is set in Armstrong Park.

Orleans, and Congo Square is remembered as one of the birthplaces of jazz. Today, the park hosts music festivals like Essence (p47) and Jazz Fest (p174). During Mardi Gras, Krewe du Kanaval, who celebrate New Orleans' Haitian heritage, perform parades and dances here.

← Krewe du Kanaval celebrating Mardi Gras with dancing and parades in Congo Square

Mahalia Jackson Theater for the Performing Arts

This world-class theater is named for the celebrated New Orleanian gospel singer Mahalia Jackson (1911–72), who began her career singing in the local church, where her father was a pastor. Despite her strict upbringing, she fell in love with the syncopated rhythms of blues but never sang the more bawdy songs in its repertoire. Jackson was discovered in the 1930s and made her first recording in 1934. Her career took her to Carnegie Hall, the Newport Jazz Festival, and other major music venues. Jackson was active in the civil rights movement and a supporter of Martin Luther King, Jr.

The theater suffered flood damage after Hurricane Katrina but has since been restored, and today showcases broadway musicals and works of theater, along with shows by famous musicians and comedians, and dance performances.

↑ The Mahalia Jackson Theater for the Performing Arts perched on the lake

109

HISTORY OF NEW ORLEANS JAZZ

A modern American art form, jazz music appeared from the late 19th to early 20th century. Incorporating meandering improvisation, call and response patterns, and intricate rhythmic percussion, its roots lie in the melange of genres played in 19th-century New Orleans. Blending elements of blues, ragtime, classical music, and European brass, jazz emerged in the clubs of Storyville, and evolved in the city's parades, dances, and funerals.

CONGO SQUARE

Known as the birthplace of jazz, Congo Square is where enslaved people gathered to celebrate their one day off, playing music and dancing (p108).

STORYVILLE JAZZ

Many early jazz artists were classically trained musicians, who entertained in the bordellos of Storyville (p116) – Buddy Bolden, King Oliver, Jelly Roll Morton, Sidney Bechet, and Freddie Keppard among them.

RIVERBOAT JAZZ BANDS

After Storyville was closed in 1917, many of New Orleans' best musicians moved to perform on the city's riverboats like Steamboat Natchez (p74).

STREETS OF JAZZ

Many jazz greats, Armstrong included (p109), started out playing on the streets. This tradition continues, with bands playing on every corner, and second lines marching the neighborhoods (p114).

↑ New Orleans-born jazz legend Louis Armstrong performing in 1968

→ Sidney Bechet (left) performs with Jelly Roll Morton's New Orleans Jazzmen in 1939

Local Legends

Sidney Bechet (1897–1959)

▽ Solo clarinetist and saxophonist, and composer, Bechet toured the world. He moved to Paris in 1950.

Danny Barker (1909–94)

▽ Played guitar and banjo with the big bands in 1930s and 1940s New York City before returning to New Orleans.

Jelly Roll Morton (1890–1941)

△ A pianist and one of the first great jazz composers, Jelly Roll Morton began his career in Storyville.

Lil Hardin (1898–1971)

△ Pianist, composer, and singer who collaborated with (and married) Louis Armstrong.

Blanche Thomas (1922–77)

A favorite in the bars along Bourbon Street, Thomas sang the blues with artists like Al Hirt.

Terence Blanchard (1962–)

▽ A trumpeter and composer, famous for scoring and playing the music for the films of director Spike Lee.

Louise "Blue Lu" Barker (1913–98)

▲ A jazz and blues singer, said to have influenced famous stars like Billie Holiday and Eartha Kitt.

Boswell Sisters (performed 1925–36)

A trio of singers whose up-tempo tunes propelled them to national radio in the 1930s.

Trombone Shorty (1986–)

▲ A multi-genre maverick who has been playing his signature horn since he was four, hence the nickname.

ST. LOUIS CEMETERY #1

⚲H5 🏠501 Basin St 🚌80, 91 ⏰For tours only
ⓦcemeterytourneworleans.com

Spanning one square block, St. Louis Cemetery #1 is the final resting place for many thousands. Its narrow alleyways lined with elaborately carved mausoleums make for a fascinating wander.

This cemetery opened in 1789 and is the oldest in the city. By 1829, St. Louis #1 was already filled, mostly with victims of yellow fever. Although Catholic, the cemetery did accept Protestants (though these graves were later moved). The narrow alleyways are full of mausoleums, many in advanced stages of decay. In New Orleans, people are usually buried above ground rather than below, because the city sits below sea level, and therefore deep digging is not allowed in many areas.

Numerous legendary local figures are buried here in impressive crypts. The largest tomb belongs to the Société Française de Bienfaisance, which contains 70 vaults. The tallest monument, sculpted by Pietro Gualdi in 1857 for $40,000, belongs to the Italian Society. Under rules set by the Archdiocese of New Orleans, all visitors to St. Louis Cemetery #1 must be accompanied by a licensed tour guide.

> 💬 INSIDER TIP
> **Beat the Heat**
>
> There's barely any shade in the cemetery, and the big vaults here tend to block the breeze, meaning that this spot can get very hot. If you're visiting in a warmer month (essentially anytime outside of winter) make sure to bring a lot of water and wear a wide-brimmed hat.

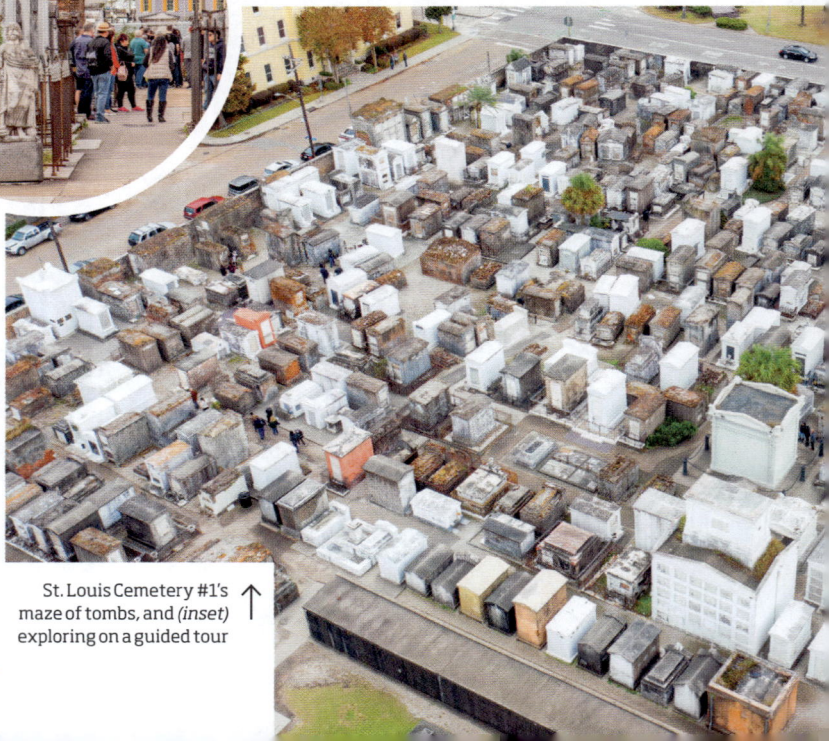

St. Louis Cemetery #1's maze of tombs, and *(inset)* exploring on a guided tour ↑

↑ Nicholas Cage's mausoleum, where the actor plans to be interred

↑ Paying respects at the tomb of Marie Laveau

Henry Latrobe

A plaque memorializes Benjamin Henry Latrobe (1764-1820), an architect who came to New Orleans to build a waterworks. He died in 1820 of yellow fever. No one knows where his remains are. In 1823 many bodies were moved from St. Louis Cemetery #1 to Lafayette Cemetery No. 1 and then to Metairie Cemetery in the 1950s. Latrobe's body got lost in the shuffle.

Barthélemy Lafon

This famed Creole architect (1769-1820) was a Classics-loving city planner who named the streets in the Lower Garden District after the Greek muses. He was known to work closely with local smugglers and pirates to expand his fortune.

Bernard de Marigny

▶ A French-Creole aristocrat, Marigny (1788-1871) is known for having introduced craps (dice) to the United States. At age 15, he inherited the sum of $7 million, but gambled the money away.

Marie Laveau

◀ The most famous mausoleum belongs to "Voodoo Queen" Marie Laveau (1801-81). People visit her tomb (though some believe it is not the correct one) to leave offerings. Some have also left "X" markings, which symbolize a request that she grant a wish; however, this is considered vandalism by the Glapion family, descendants of Laveau who own the tomb.

Homer Adolph Plessy

A free person of color, Plessy (1862-1925) challenged the Separate Car Act segregation law, and was tried in the Plessy v. Ferguson U.S. Supreme Court case in the 1890s.

Ernest Nathan Morial

▶ A leading civil rights advocate, Ernest "Dutch" Morial (1929-89) was the first African American mayor of New Orleans. Morial served from 1978 to 1986, contributing to the city's urban development. His son, Marc Morial, would also serve as mayor.

EXPERIENCE MORE

3 Ⓜ

St. Louis Cemetery #2

⚐ H5 ⌂ Iberville to St. Louis St, between N Claiborne Ave and N Robertson St ☎ (504) 482-5065 🚌 48, 46, 52, 57 🕐 To the public

By the end of the colonial period, and mostly because of a devastating series of cholera and yellow fever epidemics (p51), this cemetery was established as the natural extension of St. Louis Cemetery #1 (p112) around 1823. The final resting place for much of New Orleans' 19th-century Creole aristocracy, it contains remarkably ornate mausoleums. Among the notables buried here are General Jean Baptiste Plauché, who fought with Andrew Jackson at the Battle of New Orleans (p50), jazz musician Danny Barker, and pirate Dominique You. A common legend says that Napoleon Bonaparte's followers were waiting for his arrival in New Orleans from his exile in St. Helena, but since he died beforehand on December 20, 1821, a funeral service for him was held in the cemetery. Due to concerns regarding vandalism, all tours have been suspended.

---

4 🏛 🛍

JAMNOLA

⚐ K4 ⌂ 940 Frenchmen St Ⓢ St. Claude Ave & Elysian Fields Ave 🚌 55, 91 🕐 10am–6pm Mon, Thu & Sun, 10am–8pm Fri & Sat Ⓦ jamnola.com

This immersive museum ("Joy Art Music – New

💬 INSIDER TIP
Second Look

Second line parades trace back to the jazz funeral, when mourners and a brass band would be followed by a "second line" of revelers. Today, these parades, organized by the city's Social Aid and Pleasure Clubs, enliven the Treme neighborhood many Sundays from September to May. Watch (or even join in) as the celebrations unfold.

↑ A wide avenue in St. Louis Cemetery #2, and (inset) the elaborate Joseph Barelli tomb

→ Mardi Gras celebrations outside the Backstreet Cultural Museum

> **The tombs are like impressive residences, often enclosed within beautiful wrought-iron gates, featuring elaborate motifs.**

Orleans") opened in permanent digs in 2025. Inside are 29 highly vibrant exhibits showcasing the city's culture through multi-colored art and music. The work has been created via collaborations with over 100 local artists and it takes around 45 minutes to walk the whole thing. Expect a cascade of eye-catching installations, from giant crawfish and blinged out alligators, to feather chandeliers and a giant bust of Lil Wayne.

VODOU WORSHIP

Vodou (or voodoo as it is commonly known today) arrived in New Orleans from Africa, via the Caribbean, where it originated as a form of ancestor worship among the West African peoples who were enslaved and brought to North America. With the revolution in Saint Domingue (Haiti) in 1793, enslaved workers and free people of color arrived as refugees and increased the practice in the city. The most famous of all 19th-century vodou leaders was Marie Laveau (c. 1801–81). Mythologized as the "Voodoo Queen," it is thought that she used Catholic elements like prayer, incense, and saints in her rituals, which she opened to the public for an admission fee. Laveau is reputed to have held celebrations along the Bayou St. John on St. John's Eve, a festival observed by the Catholic calendar. She is buried at St. Louis Cemetery #1 (p113).

5

New Orleans African American Museum

📍 H4 🏠 1417–1418 Governor Nicholls St 🚋 N. Rampart St at Ursulines Ave 🕐 11am–4pm Thu–Sun 🌐 noaam.org

To learn more about the history and culture of Treme, stop by the African American Museum, where displays highlight Black artists, Creole language and culinary traditions, and rare black and white photographs and documents. The site has

the Meilleur-Goldthwaire House, built in 1828 and an excellent example of Creole architecture. Try the *calas* (rice beignets) at the on-site Calas Café. The main museum is currently operating in the smaller admin building while its main property is undergoing a multi-year renovation.

6

Backstreet Cultural Museum

📍 J5 🏠 1531 St. Philip St 🚋 St. Claude at Pauger 🚌 Ursulines Ave 🕐 10am–4pm Tue–Sat 🌐 backstreetmuseum.org

What looks like a residential home offers a rare glimpse into one of the city's more secretive cultural groups: the Mardi Gras Indians (p66). African and Indigenous American influences are at play in the costumes and traditions of these colorful Mardi Gras groups, who parade in feathered and sequined masks and costumes each year. Seeing the outfits up close on display, you can appreciate the detail that goes into every rhinestone on these handmade wonders. It also has information and artifacts relating to the city's unique traditions of jazz funerals, second lines, and Social Aid and Pleasure Clubs.

7
Lafitte Greenway

H5 **W** lafittegreen
way.org

Stretching from Armstrong Park to Bayou St. John in Mid-City, this 2.6-mile (4.2-km) park is a pleasant green lung amid urban New Orleans. A former railroad, the Lafitte Greenway has a hybrid bicycle-walking path running through it, which is peppered with exercise stations. The route is also lined with both permanent and temporary public art installations, including colorful murals and modern sculptures. Exercise caution where the path crosses major streets; despite the presence of flashing cross-walk signs, drivers may not always notice bicycle infrastructure or right of way.

Various events are hosted at the Lafitte Greenway throughout the year, including movie screenings, a Halloween Spooktacular, and the Greenway Supernova, a vibrant arts and music festival.

8
Washington Square

K5 **A** Frenchmen St between Royal St and Dauphine St **5, 55**
9am–6pm daily

Washington Square, one of the earliest parks to be laid out in New Orleans, was created in 1808, and named after the Washington 141st Field Artillery Regiment in 1838. It lies at the center of the Faubourg Marigny on Elysian Fields, and is a good place to throw a frisbee or have a ball game, or just to relax on the green areas it offers. There are open-air concerts and plays here in summer and caroling in December.

9
Our Lady of Guadalupe

H6 **A** 411 N Rampart St
48, 46, 52, 57 **6:30am–5pm Mon–Sat, 6am–7pm Sun** **W** judeshrine.com

Originally consecrated as the Mortuary Chapel of St. Anthony, this church was built on the outskirts of the French Quarter in 1826, when funerals were no longer being held in St. Louis Cathedral for fear of spreading yellow fever (p51). In 1918, it was renamed and put under the administration of the Missionary Oblates of Mary Immaculate.

The church is distinguished by several brilliantly colored stained-glass windows, each representing a different saint honored by devoted New Orleanians. The most visited altar is dedicated to St. Jude, known as the "patron saint of hopeless causes," but a more light-hearted one stands to the left of the exit; this is dedicated to New Orleans' very own St. Expedite, whose name is not in

---

STORYVILLE

From 1897 to 1917, the 38 blocks bounded by Iberville, Basin, Robertson, and St. Louis were set aside as a legal red-light district by alderman Sidney Story. Saloons and brothels lined Basin Street, and bawdy houses clustered along Dauphine, St. Louis, Conti, and Bienville. At No. 317 Basin Street, Countess Willie Piazza held court, and regularly employed pianist Jelly Roll Morton. The district was officially closed in 1917 by the Navy Department. In the 1930s, the Federal government leveled Storyville to make way for low-income housing. Consequently, little remains of Storyville today, but it has inspired many works of fiction, including the 1978 movie *Pretty Baby* (below).

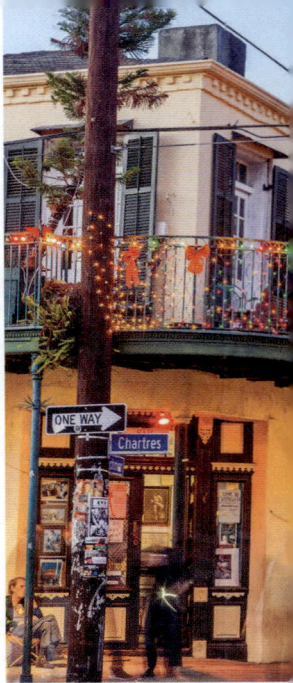

Did You Know?

In the early 1900s, sex workers were listed in the "Blue Book," available at bars all over Storyville.

Colorful lights and palm trees brightening up Frenchmen Street

any official dictionary of saints. According to legend, a crate marked with the word *spedito!* ("rush!") arrived in the chapel one day. The statue inside it was removed and mounted on the wall, and its name was confused with the word on the box. To this day, locals visit the altar to pray for help when they need something in a hurry. St. Expedite is also associated with voodoo, which is why the church is sometimes referred to as the "Voodoo Church." Our Lady of Guadalupe is the official place of worship for the police and fire departments, whose altar stands to the right of the main altar. Today, the church is best known for its weekly "Jazz Mass" (9:30am Sunday), where hymns and prayers are blended with live jazz music.

10

Frenchmen Street

K5 **Elysian Fields**

Named after a group of French rebels executed under Spanish rule, the Marigny section of this street has traditionally been a local's secret. More visitors are now coming here, drawn by the mix of music, lively bars, and restaurants, and the nightly art market. Every evening, live jazz bands strike up in various venues, including famous clubs such as the swinging **Spotted Cat** (one of the city's oldest jazz clubs), intimate **Blue Nile**, and jazz bistro **Snug Harbor**. There is often a one-drink minimum, but you'll be rewarded with impeccable live traditional jazz and, if you're lucky, some swing dancing by talented locals.

Brass bands entertain on the corner of Frenchmen and Chartres, and street poets and artists line the pavements. Most music venues on Frenchmen have gigs around 6pm, 9pm, and 11pm or midnight. On weekends, Frenchmen becomes more or less an open-air pedestrian festival. Several late-night dining options are available, most notably **Three Muses**, where you can enjoy tapas with live music and cocktails.

SHOP

Frenchmen Art Bazaar
The city's most innovative artists sell their work at this atmospheric nightly market. Vibrant visual arts, handicrafts, and clothing are all on sale.

K5 **619 Frenchmen St** **frenchmenartbazaar.com**

Euclid Records
One of the city's oldest indie music stores, this record store is a treasure trove of all genres, and the staff are well informed and helpful.

L5 **3301 Chartres St** **euclidrecordsneworleans.com**

Frenchmen Art and Books
One of the few remaining indie bookstores in the city is this Frenchmen Street institution. New and used editions abound, and there is a wonderful selection of art prints.

K5 **600 Frenchmen St** **frenchmenartandbooks.com**

Spotted Cat
😊 **623 Frenchmen St** **spottedcatmusicclub.com**

Blue Nile
🍷😊 **532 Frenchmen St** **bluenilelive.com**

Snug Harbor
🍷😊 **626 Frenchmen St** **snugjazz.com**

Three Muses
🍷😊 **536 Frenchmen St** **3musesnola.com**

EAT

The Joint

Fans of this BBQ joint's home-smoked ribs, brisket, and pulled pork pack the place out daily.

📍M5 🏠701 Mazant St
🌐alwayssmokin.com

$$$

Bar Redux

On the outskirts of the Bywater, this charming dive has a good kitchen and a varied program of music and comedy.

📍M5 🏠801 Poland Ave
🌐barredux.tumblr.com

$$$

Bacchanal

Pick up a bottle and a cheese plate and enjoy the live jazz at this expanded venue with an inviting backyard.

📍M5 🏠600 Poland Ave
🌐bacchanalwine.com

$$$

Adolfo's

Climb the rickety stairs to this cozy Italian restaurant for an evocative ambience and delicious home-made dishes.

📍K5 🏠611 Frenchmen St 🌐adolfosnew orleans.com

$$$

Pizza Delicious

With its unusual daily specials and a range of vegetarian and vegan offerings, this kitchen is known for serving some of the best pizza in town.

📍L5 🏠617 Piety St
🌐pizzadelicious.com

$$$

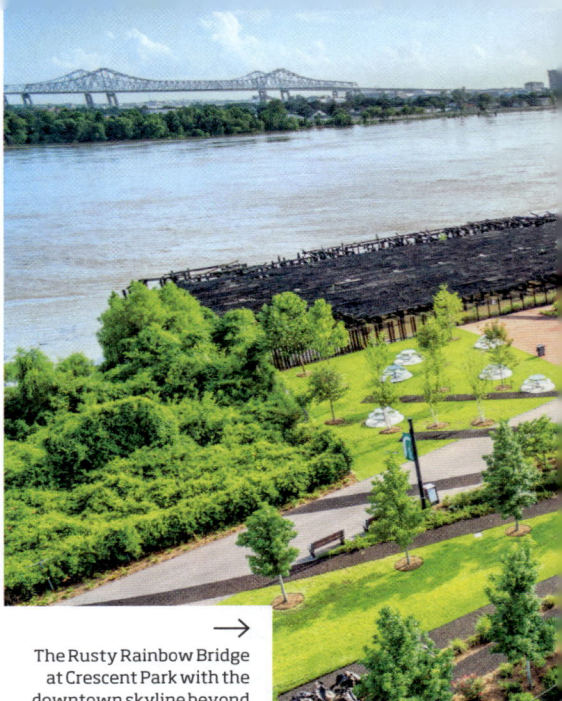

→

The Rusty Rainbow Bridge at Crescent Park with the downtown skyline beyond

11

Marigny Opera House

📍L5 🏠725 St. Ferdinand St ⏰For performances
🌐marignyoperahouse.org

Many New Orleans venues are former churches, but none is quite as impressive as this self-proclaimed "church of the arts." The building itself, dating back to 1853, was originally the Holy Trinity Catholic Church, serving the German Catholic community of the Marigny. Architect Theodore Giraud designed the church using elements of the Romanesque and Baroque styles, and the building is dominated by its elegant twin bell towers with onion-shaped domes. In 2011 this historic landmark was transformed into a venue for classical music, dance, and theater. The opera house now has an impressive program of operatic productions and contemporary dance, and is home to the award-winning Marigny Opera Ballet company, which produces original pieces to live musical accompaniment. The venue has also become a popular venue for weddings, including those of famous musicians such as singer Solange Knowles and Patrick Carney of the Black Keys.

12

Studio BE

📍L5 🏠2941 Royal St
🚇Elysian Fields ⏰2–8pm Wed–Sat 🌐studiobe nola.com

This huge studio warehouse is dedicated to showcasing the work of New Orleans-based visual artist Brandan Odums (also known as BMike), who specializes in striking, colorful, large-scale murals and paintings illustrating scenes from African American culture in the city and Black cultural leaders and icons. After a stint as a music video director for hip-hop luminaries such as Curren$y, Juvenile, and Yasiin Bey (Mos Def), Odums began to experiment with the

medium of graffiti, founding guerilla art hubs in dilapidated housing developments. He is now one of the most in-demand street artists in the world.

The varied exhibits on show at Studio BE show off the whole range of Odums' talent, with mixed-media pieces including sculpture and video. For most people, though, the real stars of the show, and the works for which he is most famous, are the incredible floor-to-ceiling portraits. The gallery is an inspiring example of successful community art and a welcome contrast to the more conventional tastes of the Uptown art galleries.

> **Bike paths, dog runs, and picnic areas with great views of the city skyline were built, and the area was given a brand new lease of life as Crescent Park.**

New Orleans' art scene will reward visitors willing to explore beyond the popular paintings of jazz musicians and colorful landscapes of the French Quarter, and this warehouse gallery is well worth anyone's time.

13

Crescent Park

📍 L5 🏠 Crescent Park Trail, Mississippi Riverside 🚆 Elysian Fields 🕐 6am–7:30pm daily 🌐 crescentparknola.org

A few years ago, the banks of the Mississippi River along the Marigny and Bywater neighborhoods were an unsightly, disused stretch of industrial wasteland, and the nearby residents had no access to the riverside. In 2015, as part of the post–Hurricane Katrina revitalization project, this all changed, and the riverside was redeveloped into a mile and a half of linear green spaces for public use. Bike paths, dog runs, and picnic areas with great views of the downtown city skyline were built, and the area was given a brand new lease of life as Crescent Park. Some of the industrial spaces have been preserved and repurposed as event facilities for concerts, weddings, and parties.

The most famous element of the park is the Rusty Rainbow Bridge, a striking, curved iron walkway that reaches across the train tracks. Stroll the length of the park for a scenic route from the Bywater into the Marigny and the French Quarter.

📷 PICTURE PERFECT
Pretty Crescent City

Crescent Park follows the gentle bend of the Mississippi - make your way down to the park's riverside at the Marigny end to snap an extraordinary panorama of the city's skyline.

WAREHOUSE AND CENTRAL BUSINESS DISTRICTS

When the Americans arrived in New Orleans following the Louisiana Purchase of 1803, they developed a community on the upriver side of Canal Street, in Faubourg Ste. Marie. Separated from the Creole French Quarter by a median of "neutral ground" along the center of Canal Street, this neighborhood was known as the American Sector. As global trade from the port of New Orleans flourished, a commercial and residential district grew behind the waterfront. The Central Business District, or CBD, is still the city's commercial hub, its narrow streets lined with Victorian warehouses, banks, and offices. The 1970s saw a wave of demolitions along the riverfront as historic buildings began to crumble, and modern skyscrapers rose along Poydras Street, along with the enormous Superdome.

Southwest from Poydras Street is the Warehouse District, where 19th-century brick buildings once housed goods at the busy port in the days before containerized shipping. Following a steady period of decline in the 20th century, the 1984 World's Fair transformed this semi-dilapidated neighborhood. Today, the Ogden Museum of Southern Art, and vibrant clusters of galleries and theaters, lend this quarter its nickname: the Arts District.

Municipal
Auditorium

CONTI STREET

IBERVILLE ST

CANAL STREET

TULANE AVENUE

PERDIDO STREET

SOUTH GALVEZ STREET

S ROMAN STREET

ST LOUIS ST

NORTH CLAIBORNE AVENUE

Canal Streetcar

IBERVILLE STREET

Rampart/LPT Streetcar

MID-CITY
p162

**MARIGNY, BYWATER,
AND TREME**
p104

BASIN STREET

TREME ST

CROZAT ST

BIENVILLE STREET

IBERVILLE STREET

13 Saenger
Theatre

6

GRAVIER STREET

Public
Library

COMMON STREET

11 **3**

CANAL STREET

12

SOUTH CLAIBORNE AVENUE

LAFAYETTE STREET

CLARA ST

PERDIDO STREET

MAGNOLIA STREET

FRERET STREET

LASALLE STREET

S ROBERTSON STREET

S VILLERE STREET

LIBERTY STREET

Duncan
Plaza

GRAVIER STREET

O KEEFE STREET

PERDIDO STREET

ST CHARLES AVENUE

POYDRAS STREET

SUGAR BOWL DRIVE

W STADIUM DRIVE

Caesars
Superdome
12

DAVE DIXON DRIVE

LASALLE STREET

S LIBERTY STREET

LOYOLA AVENUE

RAMPART STREET

POYDRAS

8

CAMP STREET

Smoothie
King Center

GIROD STREET

S STREET

GIROD ST

LAFAYETTE STREET

BARONNE STREET

Gallier Hall

11

Lafayette
Square

JULIA ST

Post Office and
Federal Building

JULIA STREET

SOUTH STREET

O KEEFE STREET

CARONDELET STREET

ST CHARLES STREET

GIROD ST

CLIO STREET

Union
Station

Greyhound
Bus Station

5

HOWARD AVENUE

JULIA STREET

St. Patrick's
Church
6

MARTIN LUTHER KING JR BOULEVARD

THALIA STREET

CALLIOPE ST

**WAREHOUSE
DISTRICT**

St Charles Ave Streetcar

Contemporary
Arts Center,
New Orleans

ST ANDREW STREET

RAMPART STREET

Museum
of the Southern
Jewish Experience **7**

Ogden Museum of
Southern Art

Confederate
Memorial Hall

1

14

15

2

The National
WWII Museum

JACKSON AVENUE

PONTCHARTRAIN EXPRESSWAY

**GARDEN DISTRICT
AND UPTOWN**
p138

POEYFARRE STREET

J. CHURCHILL

FELICITY STREET

EUTERPE STREET

POLYMNIA STREET

CAMP STREET

ST CHARLES AVENUE

St Charles Avenue Streetcar

MELPOMENE STREET

TERPSICHORE STREET

MAGAZINE STREET

CONSTANCE STREET

EUTERPE STREET

**WAREHOUSE
AND CENTRAL
BUSINESS DISTRICTS**

ST CHARLES AVENUE

i

Map labels:

Louis Armstrong Park

FRENCH QUARTER

St. Louis Cathedral

JACKSON SQUARE

Riverfront Streetcar

UPPER FRENCH QUARTER
p58

Steamboat Natchez

Woldenberg Riverfront Park

Canal Place

CBD

Caesars Hotel & Casino

Four Seasons Hotel

Audubon Aquarium

Ferry to Algiers

Spanish Plaza

Creole Queen

Riverwalk Outlets

Julia St Cruise Ship Terminal

Ernest N. Morial Convention Center

Mississippi

Mardi Gras World

MARDI GRAS BLVD

MAGELLAN STREET

Street names: N BAMPART STREET, DAUPHINE STREET, BOURBON STREET, CHARTRES STREET, ST LOUIS STREET, URSULINES STREET, GOVERNOR NICHOLLS STREET, ESPLANADE AVE, MAGAZINE STREET, CAMP STREET, TCHOUPITOULAS, COMMERCE STREET, PETERS STREET, FULTON STREET, CONVENTION CENTER BOULEVARD, LAFAYETTE ST, JULIA STREET, SOUTH PETERS STREET, JOSEPH STREET, ANDREW HIGGINS BLVD, CHASE STREET, GAIENNIE STREET, ERATO ST, HENDERSON STREET

0 meters 500
0 yards 500

N

WAREHOUSE AND CENTRAL BUSINESS DISTRICTS

Must Sees
1. Ogden Museum of Southern Art
2. The National WWII Museum

Experience More
3. Ferry to Algiers
4. Woldenberg Riverfront Park
5. Riverwalk Outlets
6. St. Patrick's Church
7. Museum of the Southern Jewish Experience
8. Canal Place
9. Casears Hotel & Casino
10. Spanish Plaza
11. Gallier Hall
12. Caesars Superdome
13. Saenger Theatre
14. Confederate Memorial Hall
15. Contemporary Arts Center, New Orleans
16. Audubon Aquarium

Eat
1. Cochon Restaurant
2. Compère Lapin
3. Domenica
4. Emeril's

Drink
5. Brewery Saint X
6. The Sazerac Bar
7. W.I.N.O

Stay
8. Le Pavillon
9. The Old 77 Hotel and Chandlery
10. The Eliza Jane
11. The Roosevelt

Shop
12. Meyer the Hatter

Did You Know?

The collection of Southern art here comes from 15 states, including Texas and Virginia.

❶ 🛠 🎨 🛍

OGDEN MUSEUM OF SOUTHERN ART

📍H8 🏠925 Camp St 🚌11 🚋St. Charles 🕐10am–5pm daily
🌐ogdenmuseum.org

This captivating museum showcases an array of artworks from the American South. Containing everything from Impressionist paintings to contemporary sculptures, it's one of the most comprehensive collections of Southern art in the world.

Opened in 2003, this museum is named for Roger H. Ogden, a philanthropist who donated the core collection of some 4,000 works by more than 400 Southern artists. The museum consists of a two-building complex connected by a corridor gallery. The Romanesque-style Patrick F. Taylor Library was designed by Henry Hobson Richardson in 1888. This architectural master-piece, with its splendid wood-panel rotunda, is incorporated into the more contemporary Goldring Hall. These two structures wrap around the Confederate Memorial Hall, so that the complex fronts Camp Street. The collection includes works by William Henry Buck, Clarence Millet, John McCrady, George Dureau, Robert Gordy, and Ida Kohlmeyer.

TOP 3 MUSEUM EXHIBITS

Folk Art
The permanent collection at the Ogden includes eye-popping, bold works of art by amateur painters and sculptors, like the self-taught artist Clementine Hunter.

Classical South
The work of classical Southern artists like Ellsworth Woodward captures the vibrancy of the local street scene from over a century ago.

Center for Southern Craft & Design
This studio and workshop for Southern artisans hosts a monthly pop-up market where you can find the perfect souvenir.

Shawne Major's 2008 work *Eating Cake* at the Ogden, and *(inset)* the museum's exterior

INSIDER TIP
Ogden After Hours

On select Thursdays, the festive Ogden After Hours held at the museum features live music, refreshments, book signings, specially curated exhibits, and hands-on art activities. Check the website for upcoming dates.

The museum consists of a two-building complex connected by a corridor gallery. The Romanesque-style Patrick F. Taylor Library was designed by Henry Hobson Richardson in 1888.

2 ⌖ ⌖ ⌖ ⌖

THE NATIONAL WWII MUSEUM

📍H8 🏛945 Magazine St and Howard Ave 🚌10, 11 🕐9am–5pm daily 🚫Thanksgiving, Dec 24 & 25, Mardi Gras 🌐national ww2museum.org

Originally founded in 2000 as the National D-Day Museum, this hugely impressive archive is a magnificent memorial to the U.S. servicemen and women who helped secure the Allied victory in World War II.

This museum honors the veterans of World War II and the role played by the U.S. military in the conflict. There's also a local connection in the form of New Orleans shipbuilder Andrew Higgins, whose company built many of the U.S. landing craft used in the war. The Home Front, the European and Pacific Theaters, and the D-Day Invasion are the museum's principal exhibits, combining everything from news reports to interactive personal stories to the era's vehicles and weapons. Displays include the immersive, hands-on submarine exhibit – Final Mission: USS Tang Submarine Experience – and a poignant 4D movie presentation, Beyond All Boundaries; this multimedia epic is presented in the state-of-the-art Solomon Victory Theater and narrated by Tom Hanks. An ambitious multi-year expansion added the Higgins Hotel and the Hall of Democracy in 2019, and the Liberation Pavilion in 2023, dedicated to the end of World War II, the Holocaust, and the immediate postwar years.

← The Campaigns of Courage pavilion, covering the European and Pacific theaters of war

→ A World War II German motorcycle from the museum's collection

THE HIGGINS BOAT

Louisiana was the home of Higgins Industries, which manufactured a revolutionary amphibious landing craft – The Higgins Boat. Trialed in the state's renowned swamps and marshes, the craft was perfectly suited for testing wartime conditions. Around 20,000 were deployed during World War II.

Did You Know?

The museum has its own female vocal trio, the Victory Belles, who sing wartime-era songs.

←

Iconic aircraft, tanks, and trucks in the U.S. Freedom Pavilion: the Boeing Center

EXPERIENCE MORE

3

Ferry to Algiers

◎ J7 🏠 Pier is at the end of Canal St 🚉 Riverfront 🚌 55 🌐 friendsofthe ferry.org

From the foot of Canal Street, a ferry will take you over the Mississippi to the historic neighborhood of Algiers on the West Bank (p205). Algiers was established in 1719 and is the second oldest part of the city. For over a century, it was used as a holding area for enslaved people, who were held here before being sold on.

The area was not connected directly to the rest of the city until a bridge was built in the late 1950s, so it has a distinct, small-town feel. It is packed with beautiful late-Victorian churches, homes, parks, and busi-nesses, and at its heart is the Romanesque Revival-style Algiers Courthouse, dating from 1896, which is visible from the French Quarter across the river. It continues to serve as a courthouse for the residents of the entire city, and is home to various municipal offices.

At the beginning of the 20th century, Algiers was home to many of the early jazz artists, such as Red Allen, Jimmy Palao, and Kid Thomas Valentine. Today, the Algiers courthouse is the setting for much of the **Make It In Old Algiers Festival**, a weekend-long event celebrating the role of the area in the development of jazz. Visitors can enjoy great live music and various arts and crafts, and sample typical New Orleans cuisine. The festival takes place in late March or April each year.

Make It In Old Algiers Festival
🌐 oldalgiersmain street.org

GREAT VIEW
Mississippi Magic

The Algiers ferry can be caught from just behind Caesars Casino. A few minutes after the ferry leaves the pier, you'll be rewarded with an absolutely breathtaking view of the city skyline.

↑ The city skyline seen from the Canal Street ferry at dusk

4 Woldenberg Riverfront Park

📍 J6 🏠 2 Canal St
🚊 Riverfront 🚌 10, 11, 55
🕐 Dawn-dusk daily

The 16-acre (6.5-hectare) Woldenberg Park extends along the riverfront from St. Peter Street up to the Riverwalk Outlets, providing an outstanding garden setting studded with contemporary sculptures. The park is named for Malcolm Woldenberg, a local businessman and philanthropist, who helped to build it. From Jackson Square, visitors can access the riverfront park via Washington Artillery Park and Moon Walk. Here, many of the city's street performers can be found. Moon walk is named after local politician Moon Landrieu, widely regarded as having paved the way for the first Black mayor, "Dutch" Morial, to be elected in 1978 (p53).

←

A bronze Malcolm Woldenberg with a young companion at Woldenberg Riverfront Park

5 Riverwalk Outlets

📍 J7 🏠 1 Poydras St
🚊 Riverfront 🚌 3, 55, 57, 65
🕐 10am-7pm Mon-Sat, 10am-6pm Sun 🌐 river walkneworleans.com

This riverside shopping mall, designed by the same company that developed Boston's Faneuil Hall, contains more than 75 stores, including brand-name favorites like Coach, Levi's, Ralph Lauren, and Gap. The entire top floor houses a food court, while on the ground floor is a branch of the iconic Café du Monde, known for its delicious beignets and chicory coffee.

The mall also has an outdoor walkway that runs along the Mississippi, giving visitors one of the best views of the river and its traffic in the city. International and other cruise ships dock alongside the marketplace, the most notable being the Paddlewheeler *Creole Queen* (p131). A number of information plaques along the walkway describe everything from the types of boats plying their trade on the river to the seagulls that drift up from the Gulf of Mexico.

EAT

Cochon Restaurant
This rustic-looking dining room is a celebration of all things porcine, with meats prepared on the premises to the exacting standards of the in-house recipes.

📍 J8
🏠 930 Tchoupitoulas St
🌐 cochonrestaurant.com

$ $ $

Compère Lapin
This cool, sophisticated restaurant serves Caribbean food, bringing innovative twists to St. Lucian and Creole classics.

📍 H7
🏠 535 Tchoupitoulas St
🌐 comperelapin.com

$ $ $

Domenica
One of the best Italian restaurants, Domenica serves popular dishes, including roasted cauliflower with whipped feta, thin-crust pizzas, and *cacio e pepe* pastas.

📍 H6 🏠 123 Baronne St
🌐 domenica restaurant.com

$ $ $

Emeril's
The flagship joint of the city's most famous chef, Emeril Lagasse, is where classic New Orleans dishes live up to his reputation.

📍 J8
🏠 800 Tchoupitoulas St
🌐 emerils restaurants.com

$ $ $

6 Ⓜ

St. Patrick's Church

📍H7 🏠724 Camp St
🚋St. Charles 🚌10, 11
🕐9am-4pm Mon-Fri
🌐oldstpatricks.org

This church was completed in 1841 to minister to the Irish Catholic population at the urging of Father James Ignatius Mullon. The brothers Charles and James Dakin were the original architects, but James Gallier Sr., the mastermind behind Gallier Hall (p132), replaced them. St. Patrick's is an impressive architectural feat, with a 185-ft- (60-m-) high tower, and splendid stained-glass vaulting in the sanctuary.

Behind the altar are three paintings by the French artist Leon Pomarede. At the center is a copy of Raphael's *The Transfiguration*, flanked by *St. Patrick Baptizing the Irish Princesses* and *Christ Walking on Water*. Each of these works dates to 1841. Although the Irish community has largely moved away from the area, the congregation still draws loyal followers from other districts. Today, Father Mullon is remembered as an ardent Confederate. He prayed publicly for a Confederate victory, and when General Benjamin Butler (p52) accused him of refusing to bury a Union soldier, he volunteered that he would be "very happy to bury them all." At noon on St. Patrick's Day, a mass is attended by most Catholics as an important part of the festivities held all over the city.

7 ✏️ 🛍️

Museum of the Southern Jewish Experience

📍H8 🏠818 Howard Ave
🕐10am-5pm Wed-Mon
🚫Public and Jewish hols
🌐msje.org

The Jewish experience in the American South – a narrative of discrimination, assimilation, and activism, through World War II, the Holocaust, and the Civil Rights Movement – is explored in detail at this well-presented and carefully curated museum. A mix of interactive displays and several rooms full of artifacts, ranging from diaries to Judaica (Jewish literary or historical materials), collected through the ages, make up the exhibits. Stop by the gift shop for a variety of interesting items, including books and apparel, as well as novelty *mezuzah* and Mardi Gras *kippahs*.

8 🍴 🍽️ 🛍️

Canal Place

📍J7 🏠333 Canal St and N Peters St 🚋Canal, Riverfront 🚌5, 10, 55
🕐11am-7pm Mon-Sat, noon-6pm Sun 🌐canal placestyle.com

Downtown's most upscale shopping mall is anchored by Saks Fifth Avenue, and contains stores such as Brooks Brothers, J. Crew, Banana Republic, Anthropologie, and Tiffany & Co. The third floor features the food court, plus the only downtown cinema that shows global and art-

---

SHOP

Meyer the Hatter

Hats are de rigueur at almost every occasion in New Orleans, so why not treat yourself to a well-made classic from this independent hat-maker – the largest in the South – that has been here since 1894.

📍H6 🏠120 St. Charles Ave
🚫Sun 🌐meyer thehatter.com

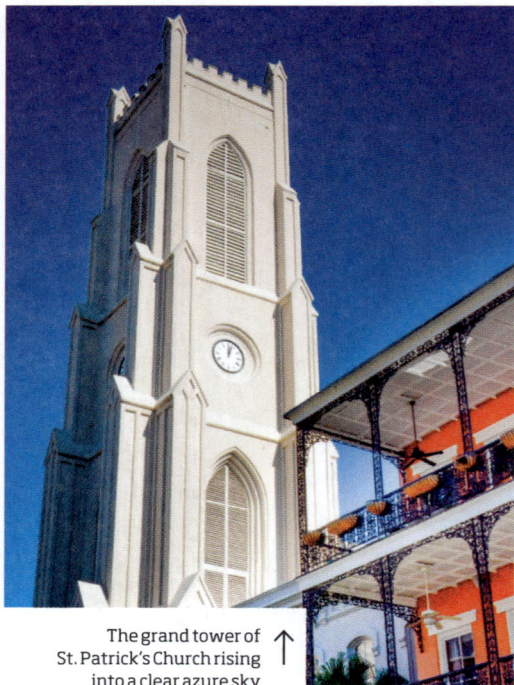

The grand tower of St. Patrick's Church rising into a clear azure sky ↑

The fountain at the Spanish Plaza, and *(inset)* tiles with the coat of arms of Las Palmas province

house films, the Prytania Theatres at Canal Place. This nine-screen theater showcases both Hollywood blockbusters and more independent cinematic fare; there's an attached bar if you need to top up before showtime.

---

9 🍴 🏪

Casears Hotel & Casino

📍 J7 🏠 8 Canal St 🚊 Riverfront 🚌 5, 10, 55 🕐 24 hrs daily 🌐 caesars.com/caesars-new-orleans

This casino is close to the riverfront, just a block away from the Mississippi. It is the only land-based casino offering table games in the whole city. Caesars also has a vast ballroom for functions, in addition to a wide range of games. Its live venue The Fillmore New Orleans (*thefillmorenola.com*) forms part of the complex. The hotel also features several restaurants and bars like the lavish Octavia, plus bowling at Fulton Alley.

---

10 🍴 🖥 🏪

Spanish Plaza

📍 J7 🏠 2 Canal St 🚊 Riverfront 🚌 10, 11

This small plaza, situated at the entrance to the Riverwalk Outlets, is a good place to take a rest and enjoy an uninterrupted view of the river. A fountain stands at its center, surrounded by a circular mosaic bench on which the coats of arms of Spain are depicted.

The *Creole Queen (p207)* paddlewheeler departs from the plaza and takes passengers downriver to the Chalmette Battlefield Park, the site of Andrew Jackson's victory at the Battle of New Orleans during the Civil War. Rangers provide a 40-minute tour of the site. Adjacent to the battlefield is Chalmette National Cemetery, where thousands of Union soldiers are buried. An antebellum house, the Malus-Beauregard home, stands on park property. This residence was built in 1833 and purchased in 1880 by the son of confederate General P. G. T. Beauregard. Note, the house is currently closed for renovation.

> The *Creole Queen* paddlewheeler takes passengers downriver to the Chalmette Battlefield Park, the site of Andrew Jackson's victory at the Battle of New Orleans.

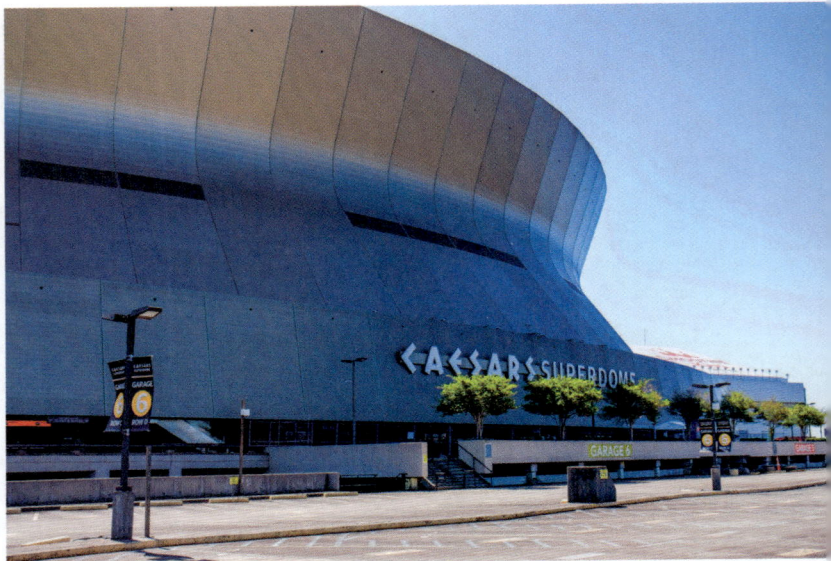

⑪

Gallier Hall

📍 H7 🏛 545 St. Charles Ave 🚋 St. Charles 🕐 To the public 🌐 gallierhall.com

James Gallier, Sr.'s Greek Revival masterpiece was built between 1845 and 1853, at a staggering cost of $342,000, and has long been at the center of the city's urban history. Constructed of bricks plastered and scored to look like stone, the building extends deeper than its narrow facade suggests. Six fluted Ionic columns support the tympanum on the facade, which is decorated with bas-reliefs of Justice and Commerce by prolific Russian-American sculptor Robert A. Launitz. Gallier Hall

← A bronze statue of Benjamin Franklin outside Gallier Hall

was built to serve as the headquarters of the Second Municipality when the city was briefly controlled by three separate governments. In 1852 it became City Hall, when the three were reunited. Many historical figures have lain in state here, including Jefferson Davis, president of the Confederacy, and General Beauregard. Perhaps most notably, Gallier Hall was the venue for the city's official surrender to Union forces in the Civil War.

The building faces Lafayette Square, which was laid out in 1788 as Place Gravier, and renamed in 1824. The square contains statues of statesman Benjamin Franklin by Hiram Powers, and famed Senator Henry Clay by Joel T. Hart. John McDonogh, the great benefactor of the New Orleans public schools, is remembered with a statue by Atallio Piccirilli.

Today, the building is a popular vantage point during Mardi Gras (*p66*). VIP viewing galleries are erected for the carnival parades, which pause here to allow the marching bands to perform for the gathering crowds.

⑫

Caesars Superdome

📍 G7 🏛 Sugar Bowl Dr 🚌 16 🚋 St. Charles 🕐 For sporting events only 🌐 caesarssuperdome.com

This vast landmark is home to local football teams the Saints and Tulane University's Green Wave. It is also the venue for the Sugar Bowl, the annual college football championships, and other sports and entertainment events. Built between 1971 and 1975, it occupies 52 acres (21 hectares), and stands 27 stories high.

The Superdome has become somewhat synonymous with the suffering of those affected by Hurricane Katrina. It was here that many thousands sought refuge from the flood waters. The building was severely damaged by wind as well as flooding.

The Superdome underwent a $560 million restoration to open just in time for the Super Bowl LIX in February 2025, which attracted over 65,000 fans and saw rapper Kendrick Lamar perform an elaborate

The flying saucer-shaped football stadium Caesars Superdome

halftime show. Adjacent is the **Smoothie King Center**, the "abydome," which opened in 1999. In 2002, the Charlotte Hornets professional basketball team moved here and became the city's home team. They have since been renamed the New Orleans Pelicans. The arena is also home to the Tulane University basketball team.

Smoothie King Center
♿ 🅿 1501 Girod St
Ⓦ smoothiekingcenter.com

⓭
Saenger Theatre
📍H6 🅿1111 Canal St
🚋St. Charles 🚌39, 46, 57
Ⓦsaengernola.com

Originally a cinema, this beautiful Italian Renaissance theater first opened in 1927. Once the flagship of brothers Julian and Abe Saenger's vast empire, today it is one of only a handful of theaters that continue to operate under the Saenger name.

Designed by local architect Emile Weil, it features a mezzanine and towering arcade, while the main theater space is made to look like the courtyard of an Italian villa, with archways and statuary decorating the walls. The ceiling is accented by some 150 tiny lights, which resemble stars in the night sky.

Heavily damaged by the flood of 2005, the Saenger sat empty for years. New owners have returned this landmark building to its former glory, with additional state-of-the-art technology, and the theater reopened in 2013 to host touring Broadway shows, big-name comedians, and famous musicians.

Did You Know?
Julian and Abe Saenger once owned 320 theaters, popularizing motion picture theaters in the South.

STAY

Le Pavillon
One of the city's oldest hotels, the Pavillion is renowned for the huge limestone pillars that grace its driveway. Impressive period artworks line the walls, hinting at its prestigious past.

📍H7 🅿833 Poydras St
Ⓦlepavillon.com

💲💲💲

The Old 77 Hotel and Chandlery
This converted 19th-century warehouse is now a trendy, art-focused hotel with the service levels to back up its looks, plus an enticing bar and restaurant.

📍H7 🅿535 Tchoupitoulas St
Ⓦold77hotel.com

💲💲💲

The Eliza Jane
Another conversion (this time a print shop), this hotel has a classical European ambience to it, a curated vintage feel to the rooms, and a fine French restaurant.

📍H7 🅿315 Magazine St
Ⓦhyatt.com

💲💲💲

The Roosevelt
This grand old institution has an impressively decadent lobby. The Sazerac Bar is a piece of local history with stories aplenty.

📍H6 🅿130 Roosevelt Way Ⓦhilton.com

💲💲💲

↑ A crowd going wild for Troy "Trombone Shorty" Andrews at the Saenger Theatre

14 Ⓐ Ⓜ

Confederate Memorial Hall

📍H8 🏠929 Camp St at Howard Ave 🚋St. Charles 🚌11 🕐10am–4pm Tue–Sat 🚫Public hols 🌐confederate museum.com

One of the oldest museums in the city, Confederate Memorial Hall focuses on narrating the personal stories of many individual Civil War combatants. Some were teenagers, like Landon Creek, who had fought in seven battles and was wounded three times by the age of 15. Several display cases contain objects relating to the occupation of the city by forces led by General

CONFEDERATE STATUES

As a Southern city, New Orleans has its fair share of statues erected to commemorate Confederate generals and the like. Many memorials were put up in the early 20th century to reinforce Jim Crow laws, and some became rallying points in opposition to the African American civil rights movement in the 1950s and 1960s. In 2017 Mayor Mitch Landrieu began removing some of the more prominent statues, most famously that of General Robert E. Lee in Lee Circle. The decision was met with significant resistance, with objectors using everything from lawsuits to firebombs to protect them. Landrieu saw it through, however, arguing that the monuments had promoted a "fictional, sanitized Confederacy."

Benjamin Butler, including a document that came to be known as "The Woman Order," announcing that all women who insulted Union officers, sang Southern songs, or wore Confederate colors, were to be locked up and treated as if they were "common harlots." The museum also holds a collection of items associated with Confederate president Jefferson Davis, from his cradle to his military boots. Several interesting exhibits are devoted to the Black regiments that served during the war – some 180,000 African American soldiers enlisted to fight for the Union, roughly 10 per cent of the entire army.

The original Memorial Hall – a small, stately chamber featuring heavy trusses, gleaming cypress paneling, and detailed Romanesque architecture – was built in

1891 as a meeting place for Confederate veterans to reflect on their Civil War experiences and to house and protect their valuable relics, including bullets, guns, flags, paintings, uniforms, letters, and photographs.

15 Ⓐ Ⓜ 🖥

Contemporary Arts Center, New Orleans

📍H8 🏠900 Camp St 🚋St. Charles 🚌11 🕐11am–5pm Wed–Mon 🚫Public hols 🌐cacno.org

This warehouse-style center is the city's premier multidisciplinary space for contemporary arts, including dance, painting, video, performance art, theater, and music. First established in 1976, the Contemporary Arts Center (CAC) began

This warehouse-style center is the city's premier multidisciplinary space for contemporary arts, including dance, painting, video, performance art, theater, and music.

The Great Maya Reef exhibit at the Audubon, and (inset) the building's exterior

Brewery Saint X

One of the city's best craft brewers operates this sleek bar and restaurant, with a wide range on tap, from German and Czech-inspired lagers to British cask-style beers, along with excellent cocktails.

📍H7 🏠734 Loyola Ave
🌐brewerysaintx.com

The Sazerac Bar

Secret deals, prohibition drama, and women's liberation all play a part in the colorful history of this hotel bar. Sip a sazerac beneath the huge murals.

📍H6 🏠The Roosevelt, 130 Roosevelt Way
🌐hilton.com

W.I.N.O

If you're a wine buff, you'll love this high-tech bar that lets you buy credit and then spend it via a chipped card on wines by the glass from its storage tanks.

📍J7 🏠610 Tchoupitoulas St
🌐winoschool.org

---

its life as a community-led organization driven by a dedicated group of artists in New Orleans' burgeoning arts district.

The complex combines the original structure with modern designs to its full advantage, presenting a unique, modern space, mostly illuminated with natural light, that houses four galleries and two theaters. The rotating shows in the galleries usually remain for one or two months. The center offers year-round lectures, camps, and workshops for adults and children. These include programs focused on creative expression in young artists and discussions on the connection between art and a just society, as part of an effort to better connect artists with the communities they're a part of. Guided tours are offered for individuals and groups.

16 🐟 🎭 🖼 🛍

Audubon Aquarium

📍J7 🏠1 Canal St at Mississippi River 🚌10, 11, 55 🕐10am–5pm daily 🕐Dec 24 and 25, Thanksgiving, Mardi Gras 🌐audubonnatureinstitute. org/aquarium org

The Audubon Aquarium is a multi-sensory immersion in undersea fauna. Dive into a kaleidoscope of fascinating underwater worlds, and observe a myriad of endangered sea creatures in mesmerizing natural habitats.

The collection spans the underwater world, from the Caribbean and the Amazon rainforest, to the waters that give New Orleans its lifeblood – the Mississippi – and the Gulf of Mexico. Highlights include the Great Maya Reef, where visitors

walk through a clear tunnel and feel as if immersed in a submerged Mayan city. In the Amazon Rainforest, piranhas lurk in the waters that flow under a forest canopy alive with tropical birds, wild orchids, and an anaconda. Around 500 different species make up the collection – many of which live in the Gulf of Mexico exhibit, the aquarium's largest tank.

A SHORT WALK
CENTRAL BUSINESS DISTRICT

Distance 1.2 miles (1.9 km) **Time** 25 minutes
Nearest Streetcar St. Charles Ave

The hustle and bustle that surrounds daily activity in the downtown area extends throughout the Warehouse and Central Business Districts (CBD). As well as the historic 19th-century buildings that exist between a profusion of newer structures, there are residential streets, and old warehouses converted into stylish spaces housing jazz bars, restaurants, hotels, galleries, and museums. New Orleans' downtown is a hub of commerce, entertainment, dining, and shopping, and its lively wide streets make for pleasant, varied wandering.

At 741 Baronne Street is **Leni's Cafe**, *a mom-and-pop diner that's been serving Southern classics since the 1940s.*

*Begin this walk by the St. Charles streetcar station on **Julia Street**. This popular thoroughfare is known as "Gallery Row" for the many small art galleries lining it.*

GRAVIER

O'KEEFE STREET

PERDIDO STREET

ST

POYDRAS

O'KEEFE STREET

BARONNE STREET

CARONDELET

ST CHARLES

Leni's Cafe

START
JULIA STRE

ST. JOSEPH ST

HOWARD AVENUE

CALLIOPE ST

Contemporary Arts Center

Ogden Museum of Southern Art

*Housed in a futuristic, brightly colored building, the **Ogden Museum of Southern Art** holds collections ranging from folk art to contemporary pieces (p124).*

*The **Contemporary Arts Center** was established in 1976 as one of the district's earliest spaces dedicated to the arts (p134). Today the complex promotes cutting-edge and experimental works.*

STEVE MARTIN FINE ART

← Julia Street, the heart of New Orleans' contemporary art scene

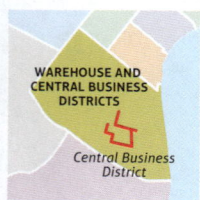

Locator Map
For more detail see p122

WAREHOUSE AND
CENTRAL BUSINESS
DISTRICTS

Central Business
District

↑ Relaxing in Lafayette Square during
the Crescent Blues and BBQ Festival

End this walk in grassy **Lafayette
Square**. *Presided over by grand Gallier
Hall (p132), this is the city's second-oldest
square after Jackson Square. Today it
plays host to the Crescent Blues and
BBQ Festival each autumn.*

On Camp Street, peek inside
the impressive **St. Patrick's Church** *to
admire its Gothic-inspired interior (p130).*

At No. 332, **LeMieux Galleries** *is one of
dozens of art spaces lining Julia Street,
exhibiting fine contemporary works by
Louisiana artists.*

FINISH

St. Patrick's
Church

National
WWII Museum

Cochon
Restaurant

0 meters   300
0 yards   300

N
↑

The **National
World War II
Museum** *honors
the American con-
tribution to the war
effort, with huge
displays of planes,
ships, and military
memorabilia (p126).*

Drop into **Cochon
Restaurant** *on
Tchoupitoulas Street for
an elegant lunch. The
pork-heavy menu riffs
on traditional Cajun
flavors (p129).*

→ Enjoying Cajun-
inspired small plates
at Cochon Restaurant

GARDEN DISTRICT AND UPTOWN

In 1832, a residential quarter was established on the former Livaudais Plantation. The land was subdivided and developed to create the city of Lafayette, which was incorporated into New Orleans in 1852. Here, between Jackson and Louisiana avenues, and St. Charles Avenue and Magazine Street, wealthy merchants, planters, and bankers built mansions in a variety of styles, ranging from Greek Revival to Italianate to Queen Anne. The area became known as the Garden District because of the lush gardens that were laid out around the mansions.

The neighborhood of Uptown was also established on a former plantation during the 1830s. This area, originally known as Faubourg Bouligny, prospered following the opening of the St. Charles Avenue streetcar in 1835. In 1850, the neighborhood was incorporated into the larger Jefferson City before becoming part of New Orleans in 1852. The 19th century also saw the establishment of the prestigious Tulane and Loyola universities, as well as the creation of Audubon Park out of the former Boré sugar plantation.

In 1874, both the Garden District and Uptown, alongside nearby neighborhoods such as Carrollton, became part of a new area of New Orleans known as uptown. The city's working-class and its gentry have long lived side by side in this area, but since Hurricane Katrina, gentrification has gathered pace and significantly raised home prices, driving out some of the local residents.

**GARDEN DISTRICT
AND UPTOWN**

A **B** **C** **D** **E**

6

CARROLLTON

Palmer Park

7

Carrollton Cemetery

22 Riverbend

19 Newcomb Art Museum

BROADMOOR

8

Levee Park

17 Tulane University

SOUTH CLAIBORNE

18 Amistad Research Center

16 Loyola University

5

9

UNIVERSITY DISTRICT

Evans Playground

St. Vincent Cemetery

Samuel Playground

Danneel Playground

20 Audubon Park

1 St. Charles Avenue Streetcar

10

21 Audubon Zoo

Touro Synagogue

3 **10**

Children's Hospital

12 *Laurence Square*

11

Riverview Park

TCHOUPITOULAS

12

Nashville Avenue Wharves

Port of New Orleans

Napoleon Ave Wharves

Milan Street Wharf

A **B** **C** **D** **E**

GARDEN DISTRICT AND UPTOWN

Must See

❶ St. Charles Avenue Streetcar

Experience More

❷ Claiborne Cottage
❸ Lafayette Cemetery No. 1
❹ Robinson House
❺ Briggs-Staub House
❻ Southern Food and Beverage Museum
❼ Toby's Corner
❽ Carroll-Crawford House
❾ Louise S. McGehee School
❿ Mardi Gras World
⓫ Musson-Bell House
⓬ Colonel Short's Villa
⓭ Brevard-Wisdom-Rice House
⓮ Opera Guild Home
⓯ Payne-Strachan House
⓰ Loyola University
⓱ Tulane University
⓲ Amistad Research Center
⓳ Newcomb Art Museum

⓴ Audubon Park
㉑ Audubon Zoo
㉒ Riverbend

Eat

① Commander's Place
② Stein's Deli
③ Saba

Drink

④ Avenue Pub
⑤ Cure
⑥ Courtyard Brewery

Stay

⑦ The Pontchartrain Hotel
⑧ Henry Howard Hotel
⑨ Columns

Shop

⑩ Hazelnut
⑪ Trashy Diva
⑫ Uptown Costume and Dancewear

WAREHOUSE AND CENTRAL BUSINESS DISTRICTS
p120

Southern Food and Beverage Museum

Mardi Gras World

Opera Guild Home

Claiborne Cottage
Louise S. McGehee School
Briggs-Staub House
Toby's Corner
Robinson House
Carroll-Crawford House
Colonel Short's Villa
Brevard-Wisdom-Rice House
Musson-Bell House
Payne-Strachan House
Lafayette Cemetery No. 1

GARDEN DISTRICT

IRISH CHANNEL

Mississippi

0 meters 800
0 yards 800

N

❶ 🚋

ST. CHARLES AVENUE STREETCAR

📍 D10 🚏 St. Charles Ave 🌐 norta.com

Board the beloved, olive-green St. Charles Avenue Streetcar for one of the city's most romantic rides. As you rumble uptown along Route 12, swaying in the handsome wooden seats, you'll pass city landmarks and centuries of history.

Boarding the streetcar is like stepping back in time. A National Historic Landmark, this kind of car was immortalized by Tennessee Williams in his drama *A Streetcar Named Desire*. For a leisurely city tour, ride 6 miles (10 km) from Canal Street through the CBD, along tree-shaded St. Charles Avenue to Carrollton Avenue. You'll pass many notable sights, including Lafayette Square, the Touro

Synagogue, and Claiborne Cottage, a classic raised cottage built in 1857 for the daughter of the first American Louisiana governor. Due to electrical damage sustained during Hurricane Katrina, the St. Charles Avenue Streetcar was out of commission for two years. The return of its familiar green cars was greeted with delight by New Orleanians during the holiday season of 2007.

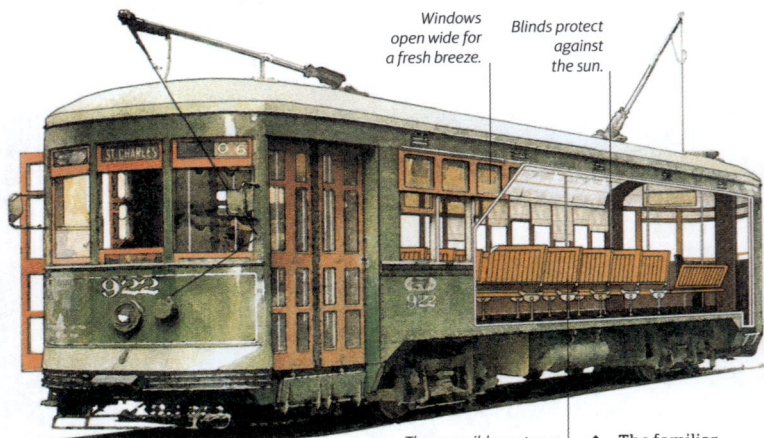

Windows open wide for a fresh breeze.

Blinds protect against the sun.

The reversible seats are made of slatted polished wood with brass handles.

↑ The familiar green St. Charles Avenue Streetcar

Timeline

1835
△ The first steam-powered streetcars begin running; a dedicated right of way is later established.

1867
Horse and mule power replaces the dirt and noise of the steam locomotives.

1893
△ Electric streetcars are installed and the line is extended along Carrollton Avenue.

1973
The St. Charles line is listed on the National Register of Historic Places.

2005
Due to damage from Hurricane Katrina, service is suspended.

2014
▽ National Park Service lists the line as a National Historic Landmark.

Did You Know?

Opened in 1835, St. Charles Avenue is the world's oldest continuously operating streetcar line.

Boarding the trolley at Canal at Carondelet, on the way to Carrollton Avenue ↑

EXPERIENCE MORE

2
Claiborne Cottage

G9 **2524 St. Charles Ave** **St. Charles** **11**
To the public

The history of this Greek Revival-style cottage is somewhat disputed, but the plaque in front states that it was built in 1857 for Sophronie Claiborne Marigny, the daughter of the first governor of Louisiana. She was married to Mandeville Marigny, the youngest son of Bernard de Marigny (p113), who introduced dice to the United States. The cottage variously served as a school, a convent, and a rectory throughout the first half of the 20th century. Later, it passed into the hands of the family of Anne Rice, who would go on to become one of New Orleans' most successful authors with her gothic horror *Interview with the Vampire*. Rice also used it as the setting of her 1997 novel *Violin*. In 2004 Rice sold Claiborne Cottage to entrepreneur and horse-breeder Evelyn B. Benoit, who restored it to its former glory.

> **In 2004 Rice sold Claiborne Cottage to entrepreneur and horse-breeder Evelyn B. Benoit, who restored it to its former glory.**

3
Lafayette Cemetery No. 1

F10 **1400 Washington Ave** **St. Charles** **11**
For renovation

This walled cemetery was laid out in 1833 by Benjamin Buisson to accommodate the residents of the adjacent Garden District. The second Protestant cemetery to open in New Orleans, it is the resting place of many German and British Protestants, as well as Americans who had migrated here from the east coast. By 1840 it was full, mostly with yellow fever victims, and a new cemetery was needed.

Among the notables buried here are Confederate General Harry T. Hays and Samuel Jarvis Peters (1801–85), an influential city politician and land developer. A Canadian, Peters arrived in New Orleans and quickly ascended to a powerful position by the time he was 30. He was one of the movers and shakers who developed the area above Canal Street, fashioning it into a Second Municipality comparable to the downtown Creole community below Canal Street. One of the most striking

> **INSIDER TIP**
> **Through the Keyhole**
>
> Although most of the mansions in the Garden District are private homes, you can tour some of them on one weekend a year. In December, the Holiday Home Tour, run by the Preservation Resource Center of New Orleans, sells tickets to fund their work (prcno.org).

Tombs lining the walkways of Lafayette Cemetery No. 1 amid lush greenery

memorials in this cemetery is the communal tomb built in 1852 to commemorate the Jefferson Fire Company #22. It is embellished with a typical pumper wagon.

The wall vaults or "ovens," a wall of inexpensive internment chambers, were added to the cemetery in 1858 to temporarily house the dead.

In Anne Rice's famous Gothic horror novel *Interview with the Vampire*, characters frequently wander around Lafayette Cemetery No. 1. This was also used prominently

as a location in the film adaptation of the book. The author staged her own mock burial here in 1995 to promote her book *Memnoch the Devil*.

④ Robinson House

📍 G10 🏠 1415 3rd St
🚋 St. Charles 🚌 11
🚫 To the public

One of the Garden District's grandest residences, this house was built for Virginia tobacco merchant Walter Robinson. Designed by Henry Howard, it was built between 1859 and 1865. The galleries of the Italian-style villa are supported with Doric columns on the first floor and Corinthian on the second. An unusual feature of this mansion is its curved portico, and it was one of the first buildings in the city to have indoor plumbing.

⑤ Briggs-Staub House

📍 G9 🏠 2605 Prytania St
🚋 St. Charles 🚌 11
🚫 To the public

This mansion was built for gambler Cuthbert Bullitt by

James Gallier Sr. in 1849. The house's Gothic Revival style is uncommon in this part of the city, because many Protestant Americans claimed it reminded them of Roman Catholic France. After Gallier had designed the building, Bullitt refused to pay for it, perhaps because of a gambling loss, and the house subsequently became the property of Charles Briggs, an English insurance executive.

EAT

Commander's Palace
Visit one of the city's most famous restaurants for modern takes on local favorites. The lunch service features the ever-popular 25-cent Martinis.

📍 G10 🏠 1403 Washington Ave
🌐 commanders palace.com

💲💲💲

Stein's Deli
Get here early on the weekends for delicious New York-style deli sandwiches and bagels. There's a fine craft beer selection and excellent coffee pop-ups.

📍 G10 🏠 2207 Magazine St 🌐 steinsdeli.com

💲💲💲

Saba
This bright, airy restaurant showcases contemporary Israeli cuisine with dishes that reflect the gastronomic diversity of the Jewish diaspora. It's upscale, but with a relaxed vibe.

📍 C11 🏠 5757 Magazine St
🌐 eatwithsaba.com

💲💲💲

↑ The imposing Briggs-Staub House, the Garden District's only Gothic Revival mansion

STAY

Pontchartrain Hotel

Exuding 1950s glamor, this hotel has one of the best rooftop bars in the city.

📍 G9 🏠 2031 St. Charles Ave 🌐 thepontchartrainhotel.com

$ $ $

Henry Howard Hotel

This debonair, mid-19th-century townhouse has a period feel.

📍 G9 🏠 2041 Prytania St 🌐 henryhowardhotel.com

$ $ $

Columns

The Italianate Columns hotel has an atmospheric veranda.

📍 E10 🏠 3811 St. Charles Ave 🌐 thecolumns.com

$ $ $

---

6 🛡️ 🍖 🍴 🍺 🛍️

Southern Food and Beverage Museum

📍 G8 🏠 1504 Oretha Castle Haley Blvd 🚋 St. Charles ⏰ 11am–5pm Thu–Mon 🌐 southernfood.org

A treasure trove for foodies, this delightful museum celebrates the food and drink of the American South and its starring role in the culture of the region. The former Dryades Market building provides an open, airy space for colorful displays that offer a fascinating insight into the iconic foods of New Orleans and beyond. The Gallery of the South features curated exhibits that highlight the food and foodways of 16 southern states. The Louisiana Gallery, for example, looks at sugar making, coffee drinking, crawfish harvesting and a range of dishes from beignets to jambalaya. On weekends, there are cooking demonstrations and other events.

The Museum of the American Cocktail is located here too, showcasing popular drinks and their social history. Don't forget to stop at La Galerie de l'Absinthe for a look at the anise-flavored spirit. In the restaurant, you can have a cocktail from the city's oldest bar, which was salvaged from the ruins of Hurricane Katrina.

7

Toby's Corner

📍 G9 🏠 2340 Prytania St 🚋 St. Charles 🚌 11, 27 🔒 To the public

Built around 1838 and thought to be the Garden District's oldest residence, this house was built for Thomas Toby, a successful wheelwright who lost his fortune financing the cause for Texan independence from Mexico. It was, in fact, his wife who paid for the construction of the house. Toby subsequently worked as a plantation manager until he died.

After the Civil War, the house was auctioned off for $5,000. Now it is privately owned and closed to the public, but its facade is a superb example of the Greek Revival style.

↓ The Southern Food and Beverage Museum's expansive foyer

8
Carroll-Crawford House

📍G9 🏠1315 First St
🚋St. Charles 🚌11
🚫To the public

This broadly proportioned house was built in 1869 for Joseph Carroll, a cotton merchant from Virginia. The surrounding gardens include venerable live oaks and other lush plantings. A two-story home with octagonal wings, the house is Italianate in design with fine cast-iron galleries.

The original carriage house can still be seen around the corner on Chestnut Street. The house's designer Samuel Jamison also constructed an identical building at 1331 First Street for rope dealer Joseph C. Morris.

9
Louise S. McGehee School

📍G9 🏠2343 Prytania St
🚋St. Charles 🚌11
🚫To the public

James Freret designed this elaborate French Second Empire home in 1872 for sugar planter Bradish Johnson for $100,000. Freret had recently returned from Paris and was enamored of the École des Beaux-Arts, which is evident in this mansion's Renaissance Revival style. When it was built, the house incorporated all of the fashionable interior design elements and conveniences of the day: a conservatory, a marble pantry, a passenger elevator, and a magnificent circular staircase. It is one of the few houses in the city to have a basement.

Since 1929, it has served as a private school for girls. The cafeteria was once a stable, and the gym is a refurbished carriage house. Note the steep mansard roof with its wrought-iron parapet and the unique bull's-eye window on the facade. The gardens contain some magnificent magnolias and ginger trees.

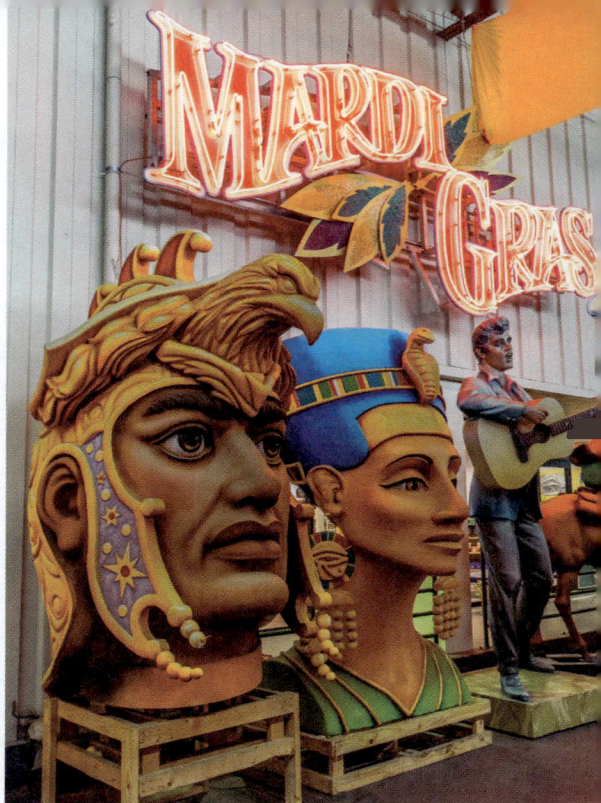
↑ Anthony, Cleopatra, and Elvis welcoming visitors to Blaine Kern's Mardi Gras World

10
Mardi Gras World

📍J9 🏠1380 Port of New Orleans Place 🚋Riverfront
🕘9am–5:30pm daily
🚫Public hols 🌐mardigras world.com

Blaine Kern is often called "Mr. Mardi Gras" because so many of the massive floats that roll through the streets during Carnival (p66) are constructed here in the 20 warehouse-dens of his company.

A tour of Mardi Gras World begins with a short film showing the floats in the parades and the stages of their production, from the original drawings to the manufacture of the final pieces. You can then don some costumes that krewe members have worn in past parades. Many of these are heavy and ornate. Visitors can also wander one of the warehouses to view gigantic fiberglass and Styrofoam figures overlaid with papier-mâché. The cost of the floats is borne by the krewes them-selves, with contributions from their members.

Did You Know?

Horse-drawn floats were introduced to Mardi Gras in 1840 by early carnival society, the Cowbellions.

Wrought-iron detailing at Colonel Short's Villa in the Garden District

The elegant iron-work of the Italianate Musson-Bell House ↑

11 Musson-Bell House

📍 G10 🏠 1331 3rd St
🚋 St. Charles 🚌 11, 27
🚫 To the public

This handsome Italianate villa was built in 1853 for Michel Musson (1812–85), a successful and prominent Creole cotton merchant and the New Orleans postmaster. Musson had close ties with his extended family, including his sister Celestine Musson Degas, who lived in France. Celestine's son, Edgar Degas, was to become one of the world's great artists and a founder of the Impressionist movement.

After the Civil War, Edgar Degas came to visit Louisiana, but it is unlikely he ever saw this house. The war had dealt Musson's fortunes a severe blow and he sold the house in 1869, moving his family to rented accommodation on Esplanade Avenue (p176).

The house has eight bedrooms, seven bathrooms, a stable and carriage house, as well as a cistern for water storage on the roof. The facade is girdled by magnificent cast-iron galleries.

12 Colonel Short's Villa

📍 G10 🏠 1448 Fourth St
🚋 St. Charles 🚌 11, 27
🚫 To the public

Henry Howard designed this large Italian-style residence in 1859 for Kentuckian Colonel Robert Short. The veranda, with fine iron railings, extends around three sides of the house. An exquisite ironwork fence, incorporating a motif of morning glory and cornstalks, encloses the gardens (p152). The story goes that the Colonel had it installed to please his wife, who missed the cornfields of her native Iowa. Unlike a similar fence at Gauche House in the French Quarter (p96), famous for its detailed ironwork, this one has not been painted and shows its original colors. In September 1863, Union troops seized the residence, but it was returned to the family after the Civil War. Although closed to the public, the famous cornstalk fence is much photographed.

13 Brevard-Wisdom-Rice House

📍 G10 🏠 1239 First St
🚋 St. Charles 🚌 11, 27
🚫 To the public

Fans of the Gothic author Anne Rice often stop to gawk at this stylish Greek Revival home, where she lived from 1989 to 2003. The house was designed for merchant Albert Hamilton Brevard in 1857 by James Calrow (who designed several other important houses in the Garden District) and cost some $13,000, at the time a formidable sum. Brevard-Wisdom-Rice House is adorned with ornate ironwork, including a fence incorporating a rose motif, earning the house its nickname, "Rosegate." Ionic and Corinthian columns support the galleries. The second owners of the property, the Clapp family, added the hexagonal wing in 1869. The gardens feature stunning camellias.

Anne Rice, who was born in New Orleans and grew up in the Irish Channel neighborhood, has portrayed the city in many of her *Vampire Chronicles* novels. She and her husband, poet-scholar Stan Rice, returned to New Orleans from San Francisco in 1988. Rice used this house as the setting for her occult horror novel *The*

> **Brevard-Wisdom-Rice House is adorned with ornate ironwork, including a fence incorporating a charming rose motif, earning the house its nickname, "Rosegate."**

Witching Hour (1990) and her *Mayfair Witches* series. She spent her teenage years living in Claiborne Cottage *(p144)* at 2524 St. Charles Avenue, which inspired much of her novel *Violin*. The author restored several historic buildings, but after her husband died in 2003, Anne moved to California where she died in 2021.

---

14 ⊘ Ⓜ

Opera Guild Home

📍 G9 🏠 2504 Prytania St 🚋 St. Charles 🚌 11 🕐 For events only 🌐 operaguild home.org

William Freret designed the original Greek Revival section of this house, known as the

Davis-Seebold Residence, in 1859 for a wealthy merchant. In 1965 it was bequeathed to the Women's Guild of the New Orleans Opera Association, a non-profit organization that preserves the rich opera traditions of New Orleans. It now serves as the administration office for New Orleans Opera and is used for meetings and receptions. It was also used as a filming location for Tarantino's *Django Unchained*. In the 19th century, New Orleans was a major opera center, although its original French Opera house, designed by James Gallier, Jr., burned down in 1919.

The octagonal tower of the Opera Guild Home, and *(inset)* a memorial plaque outside ↓

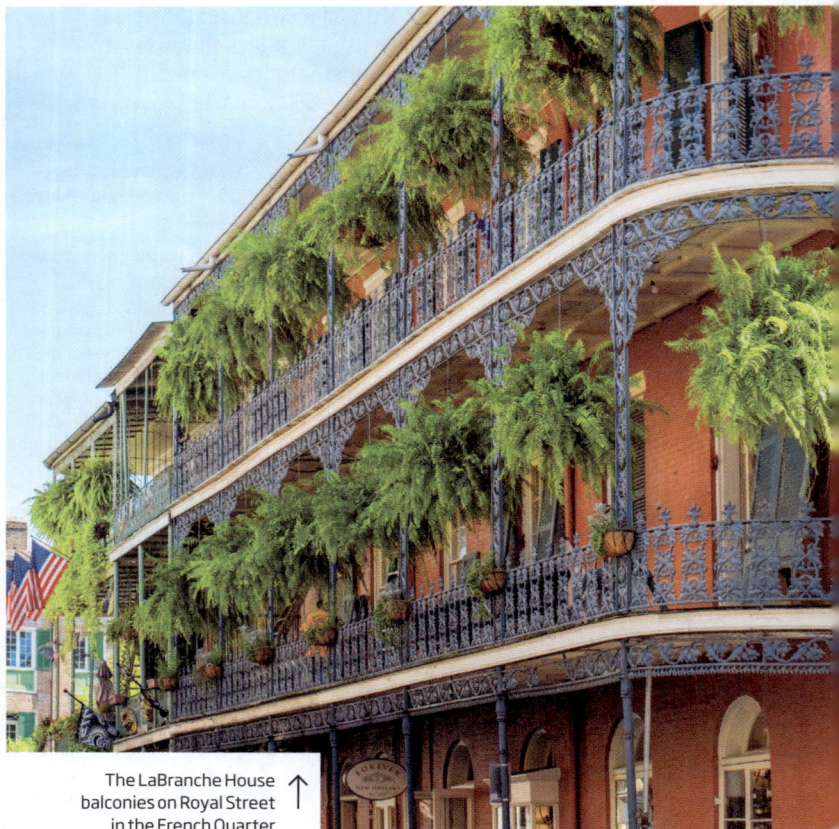

The LaBranche House
balconies on Royal Street
in the French Quarter ↑

NEW ORLEANS IRONWORK

The shadows cast by New Orleans ironwork add a romantic touch to the city. Lacy galleries and artfully decorated gates are scattered across New Orleans' neighborhoods. The French Quarter is a particular focus for handmade Creole wrought iron, while the Garden District brims with sumptuous examples of cast iron.

WROUGHT IRON

Wrought iron came to the city before cast iron, in the early 19th century. Fashioned by hand into beautiful, fluid shapes by German, Irish, and Creole artisans, wrought ironing contains a purer metal, and is stronger than cast iron. The signature of New Orleans is its beautifully wrought Creole ironwork, which appears in many forms, including fences, gates, window grilles, balconies, hinges, doorknobs, and lanterns. It is particularly common in the French Quarter, where delicate ironwork balconies with unique designs and patterns were added to many buildings in the 1850s, influenced by the lacy galleries of Spanish architecture.

Wrought-iron balconies depicting oak leaves and acorns can be seen on the LaBranche House on Royal Street (p70).

Fashioned by hand into beautiful, fluid shapes by German, Irish, and Creole artisans, wrought ironing contains a purer metal, and is stronger than cast iron.

CORNSTALK FENCES

New Orleans has three "cornstalk" fences, so-called because of their decorative cast-iron motifs featuring ears of corn, along with swirls of morning glory, swans, and pumpkins. Each of these fences are designs by the Wood & Perot foundry. One is at 915 Royal Street's Cornstalk Hotel, another at Colonel Short's Villa in the Garden District (p150), and a third is at the Dufour-Plassan house on the corner of White and Bell streets in Faubourg St. John.

CAST IRON

Cast iron was poured into wooden molds and allowed to set – as a result, it has a solid, fixed appearance. However the material's greater plasticity meant that it could be shaped into ornate, raised relief designs, like the many found adorning homes in the Garden District. Favored as superior to wood as they with-stood humidity, cast-iron designs could also be reproduced on a mass scale. The Pontalba Buildings, commissioned by Baroness Pontalba, spurred on the craze for ironwork (p77) in the 1850s, with some of the patterns designed by the Baroness's son.

IRONWORK MOTIFS

In the 1850s, Philadelphia ironmongers Wood & Perot opened a branch office in New Orleans. Offering hundreds of patterns specially designed for the city, the company quickly grew. Its motifs, including abstracts, acorns, fruits, cherubs, vines, and animals, were soon seen in railings throughout the city.

↑ Typical lacy ironwork motifs

→ Cast-iron emblem of Baroness Pontalba in the grillwork of the Pontalba Buildings

15

Payne-Strachan House

📍 G10 🏠 1134 First St
🚋 St. Charles 🚌 11, 27
🚫 To the public

This grand Neo-Classical home was built in the 1850s by Judge Jacob U. Payne, who brought enslaved workers from his plantation in Kentucky and had them construct it by hand. The two-story Greek Revival residence has Ionic columns on the first gallery and Corinthian on the second. The house passed to Payne's son-in-law, Charles Erasmus Fenner, a close friend of Jefferson Davis, the controversial United States senator and president of the Confederacy. Davis died here on December 6, 1889, in the first-floor guest room.

A striking aspect of the house is the sky-blue ceiling in the gallery, the color having

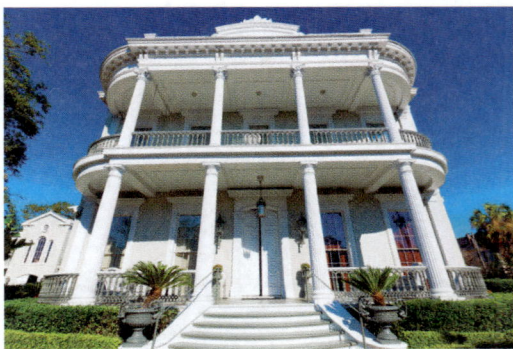

↑ Neo-Classical Payne-Strachan House, where Jefferson Davis spent his last days

been chosen in the belief that it would keep winged insects from nesting there and would also ward off evil spirits. In fact, many homes in the neighborhood follow this superstition.

↓ Loyola University's Marquette Hall with the Holy Name of Jesus church

16

Loyola University

📍 C9 🏠 6363 St. Charles Ave 🚋 St. Charles 🚌 15
🌐 loyno.edu

The Jesuit Order established the College of the Immaculate Conception downtown in 1840. It merged with Loyola College, becoming Loyola University in 1912. The Tudor-Gothic buildings house the largest Catholic university in the South. The three buildings facing St. Charles Avenue are Marquette Hall, the oldest building on campus; the adjacent Thomas Hall, a former residence and chapel for the Jesuits; and the Holy Name of Jesus Roman Catholic church, whose design was inspired by Canterbury Cathedral in the UK.

Notable Loyola alumni include former NASA administrator Sean O'Keefe, longtime *Simpsons* voice actor and Spinal Tap bassist Harry Shearer, and singer Harry Connick, Jr. The statue of Jesus with uplifted arms in front of Marquette Hall is referred to locally as "Touchdown Jesus," for obvious reasons.

18,000
—
undergraduate and postgraduate students attend the Tulane and Loyola universities.

18

Amistad Research Center

B9 Tilton Hall, Tulane University St. Charles 15 10am-3:30pm Mon-Fri, 10am-2pm Sat amistadresearch center.org

This research center is named for the famous mutiny aboard the Cuban slave ship *Amistad* in 1839. After a trial in Hartford, Connecticut, the enslaved passengers were acquitted and allowed to return home.

The American Missionary Association, an organization formed to defend the enslaved mutineers, established the center's archive, which moved to New Orleans in 1969. It consists of documents, photos, pamphlets, and oral records that trace the history of slavery, race relations, African American community development, and the civil rights movement. A small gallery showcases artists including such names as Henry O. Tanner and Elizabeth Catlett.

17 Ⓜ

Tulane University

C8 6823 St. Charles Ave St. Charles 15 tulane.edu

Founded in 1834 as a medical college, the precursor of Tulane University was given its new name in 1882 after receiving a substantial gift from Paul Tulane, a native of Princeton, New Jersey. He made a fortune from running a merchandising business, which he launched in New Orleans in 1822. Tulane's School of Business is the oldest college of commerce in the United States.

The university moved to its current location in 1894. The 110-acre (45-hectare) campus has 79 buildings in a variety of styles. The Howard Tilton Memorial Library houses the Hogan Jazz Archive, plus other special collections.

SHOP

Hazelnut
This store has a great selection of home goods and gifts, and is owned by Bryan Batt, who famously played Salvatore Romano in the TV show *Mad Men*.

C11 5525 Magazine St hazelnut neworleans.com

Trashy Diva
A homegrown success story, this women's fashion store specializes in retro patterns, and elegant dresses and lingerie.

H10 2048 Magazine St trashydiva.com

Uptown Costume and Dancewear
Locals come here for last-minute costume inspiration. Perfect for Mardi Gras or Halloween.

E11 4326 Magazine St 895-7969

19

Newcomb Art Museum

B8 Tulane University St. Charles 15 Hours vary, check website Public hols and summer months newcombart museum.tulane.edu

In 1886 Josephine Le Monnier Newcomb founded a women's college that was allied with Tulane University. Initially, she donated $100,000 in memory of her daughter Harriot Sophie Newcomb, who died at age 15 in 1870. When Josephine herself died, she left an estate of over $2.5 million to the college.

The Woldenberg Art Center houses the Newcomb Art Museum and a smaller space to display student and faculty works. The Newcomb Museum focuses on traveling shows and curates its own exhibitions.

The name of Newcomb is more familiarly associated with the arts-and-crafts style of pottery that was made at the Newcomb College of Art from 1895 to 1940. The gallery has some typical pieces on display.

20

Audubon Park

B10 6500 Magazine St St. Charles 11 audubon institute.org

This park was carved out of the plantations owned by the Foucher and Boré families in 1871. In 1884 the World's Industrial and Cotton Exposition was held here, helping to boost the city's morale at a time when New Orleans was still recovering from the double devastations of the Civil War and Reconstruction *(p52)*. The exposition's main building alone covered almost four times the surface of the Superdome *(p132)*, and it was here that the first streetcar was introduced to the city. During the festivities, the Mardi Gras Krewe of Rex *(p66)* arrived aboard a yacht, establishing a tradition that survives to this day.

↑ Audubon Park fountain, and *(inset)* an egret nesting on one of the park's many ponds

PICTURE PERFECT
Say "Trees"

Deep within Audubon Park is the ancient Étienne de Boré Oak, or "Tree of Life," a southern live oak tree thought to be around 500 years old. The tree's gnarled trunk, rippling roots, and vast canopy make it a popular spot for wedding ceremonies and set the backdrop for the perfect snap.

In the park there are several ponds which host myriad bird species, along with recreation areas, sports facilities, and Audubon Zoo. With the Zoo, Aquarium *(p135)*, and the Butterfly Garden and Insectarium, the park forms part of the Audubon Nature Institute, named for naturalist John James Audubon, whose statue stands in its grounds. Audubon, the artist of *Birds of America*, was born in the West Indies. He came to New Orleans and rented his first studio in 1821 at 706 Barracks Street. He stayed only four months before taking off for a brief sojourn as tutor at Oakley Plantation in West Feliciana Parish. Here, in this rich ornithological environment, he began many of his renowned bird portraits, but due to a dispute with his employer, quickly returned to New Orleans and took up residence at another studio at 505 Dauphine Street.

21 🚲 🎿 🖥 🎁

Audubon Zoo

📍A10 🏠6500 Magazine St 🚃St. Charles 🚌11 🕐10am–5pm daily 🚫First Fri in May, Thanksgiving, Dec 24–25, Mardi Gras 🌐audubon natureinstitute.org/zoo

Part of the highly respected Audubon Nature Institute, along with the Audubon Aquarium, this world-class establishment traces its history back to the 19th century. Audubon Zoo is home to many rare and endangered creatures, and its ethos centers around conservation and protecting natural habitats.

Landscaped with fountains and water gardens, this attractive 58-acre (23-hectare) zoo is located in Audubon Park, and can be toured easily in a few hours. It opened in 1938 but was redesigned in the 1980s; today, the animals live in open paddocks that replicate their natural habitats. Only a few of the 1930s buildings remain. The award-winning Louisiana Swamp exhibit is one of the most engaging, showcasing Cajun culture and music alongside rare white alligators, who bask along the banks or float like logs in the muddy lagoon. Meanwhile, in the African Savanna exhibit, rhinos, zebras, and white pelicans all live together with a host of opportunistic visitors such as ibis, heron, and egrets.

22

Riverbend

📍A8 🏠Riverfront of St. Charles Ave 🚃St. Charles 🚌34

With more than 300 billion gallons of water flowing by the city each day, New Orleans lives under the constant threat of flood. A system of spillways, pumps, and levees, like this one along the riverfront of St. Charles Avenue, forms a line of defense against the temperamental Mississippi. Still, certain sections of the city are prone to flooding, particularly after heavy rains. The pumping system was installed soon after 1927 when the city was so threatened that the authorities cut the levee below the city in St. Bernard Parish to forestall urban flooding. This part of the levee has been adapted as a recreation area, where visitors can enjoy a beautiful view of the river. The charming Riverbend neighborhood, dotted with locally owned restaurants, cafés, and shops, is perfect for an unhurried stroll. Browse through vintage boutiques on Maple Street or peruse second-hand books on Oak Street.

DRINK

Avenue Pub

Avenue always has around 40 excellent beers on tap, rotated often enough to keep you coming back. The kitchen, which serves up everything from burgers to bruschetta, won't disappoint either.

📍G8 🏠1732 St. Charles Ave 🌐theavenue pub.com

Cure

New Orleans is the spiritual home of the cocktail, and they don't get better than at this chic craft cocktail bar. Peruse the innovative menu or let the skilled mixologists guide you.

📍D9 🏠4905 Freret St 🌐curenola.com

Courtyard Brewery

Microbreweries are sprouting up across the city, and this Garden District venture is one of the best, serving up its own tasty brews. A range of rotating street food trucks complement the drinks.

📍H8 🏠1160 Camp St 🌐courtyardbrewery. square.site

A SHORT WALK
GARDEN DISTRICT

Distance 0.4 miles (0.6 km) **Time** 10 minutes
Nearest Streetcar St. Charles Ave

Historically, this neighborhood consisted of huge plantation houses surrounded by even bigger gardens. Eventually, as the area became more urban, those large plots of land were subdivided into smaller residential parcels – hence the name, "Garden District." Today, this area is a residential neighborhood, home to the great, Gothic Lafayette Cemetery No. 1, and filled with grand Victorian mansions built by wealthy city merchants and planters. The gardens, planted with magnolia, camellia, sweet olive, jasmine, and azalea, are as stunning as the residences themselves.

Confederate General Harry T. Hays and Samuel Jarvis Peters, a wealthy 19th-century developer of the Garden District, are buried in **Lafayette Cemetery No. 1** *(p144).*

FINISH

WASHINGTON AVENUE

COLISEUM STREET

4TH STREET

Excellent Creole food is the specialty at this landmark restaurant, **Commander's Palace** *(p145).*

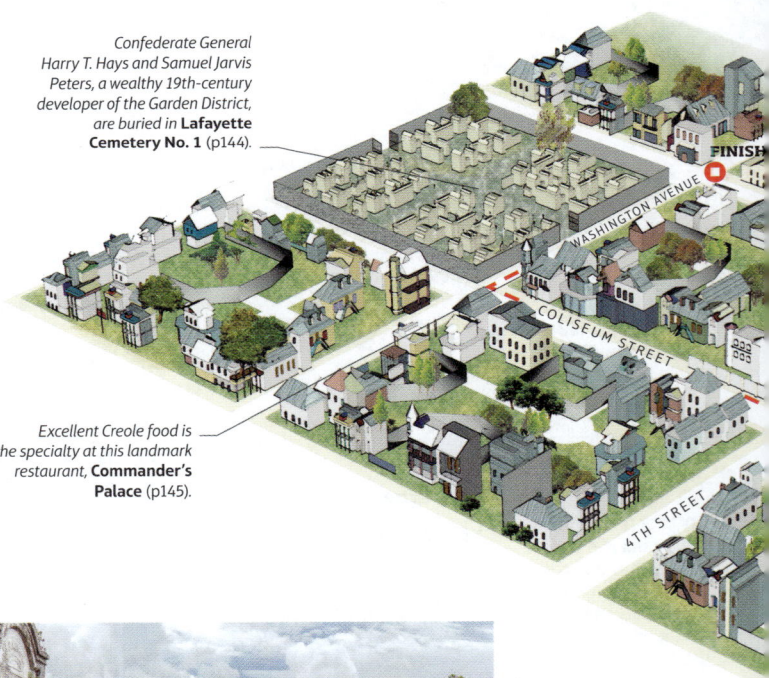

0 meters   50   N
0 yards   50

← Historic tombs lining the paths of Lafayette Cemetery No.1

Tourists admiring the Gothic Briggs-Staub House surrounded by greenery

Locator Map
For more detail see p140

GARDEN DISTRICT AND UPTOWN

Garden District

Built in 1859 for Colonel Robert Short of Kentucky and designed by Henry Howard, **Colonel Short's Villa** (p150) is known for its exquisite cornstalk fence (p153).

The handsome Gothic Revival **Briggs-Staub House** (p145) was designed by James Gallier, Sr. in 1849.

Claiborne Cottage was built in 1857 for the daughter of the first American governor of Louisiana (p144).

ST. CHARLES AVENUE

PRYTANIA STREET

START

3RD STREET

Musson-Bell House was the home of Michel Musson, uncle of artist Edgar Degas (p150). Its lacy galleries were added by a later owner, an iron merchant.

One of the Garden District's grandest residences, **Robinson House** was built between 1859 and 1865 for Virginia tobacco merchant Walter Robinson (p145).

A SHORT WALK
LOWER GARDEN DISTRICT

Distance 1.75 miles (2.8 km) **Time** 30 minutes
Nearest Streetcar St. Charles Ave

With its mix of mansions, markets, boutiques, and cafés, the Lower Garden District offers visitors a sample of the influences at play in the city through the last two centuries. Although this area is not as opulent as the neighboring Garden District, it has seen tremendous revitalization since the 1990s. This walk takes you along wide, shaded avenues past historic buildings, ornate churches, an antebellum mansion, and a cut-down version of the Eiffel Tower.

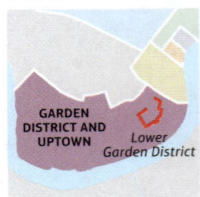

GARDEN DISTRICT AND UPTOWN
Lower Garden District

Locator Map
For more detail see p140

0 meters 300
0 yards 300
N

At the end of this walk, on the corner of **St. Andrew Street,** *is a streetcar stop for the return trip downtown on the St. Charles Avenue streetcar line.*

At No. 2040 you'll find the striking **Nieux** *building, formed from pieces of the Eiffel Tower restaurant in Paris that were removed during its 1981 renovation and shipped here.*

CARONDELET

CHARLES

BRAINARD STREET

PHILIP STREET

ST. ANDREW

FINISH

ST.

Nieux

JOSEPHINE STREET

At No. 2220 St. Charles Avenue is the **House of Broel,** *an antebellum and High Victorian mansion open to the public for tours.*

CARONDELET

JACKSON

House of Broel

Louise S. McGehee School

St. Charles Avenue is the main route for Mardi Gras parades (p66): look up and you might spot carnival beads tangled in the branches of the oaks along the street.

1ST STREET

2ND STREET

PHILIP STREET

AVENUE

Toby's Corner

Women's Opera Guild House

Carroll Crawford House

Robinson House

3RD STREET

Brevard-Wisdom-Rice House

At No. 1239 is **Brevard-Wisdom-Rice House** *(p150), a private home previously owned by novelist Anne Rice and the setting for her book The Witching Hour.*

Payne-Strachan House

MAGAZINE ST

CONSTANCE

LAUREL

At No. 1134 1st Street is the privately owned **Payne-Strachan House** *(p154), where Jefferson Davis, president of the American Confederacy, died in 1889.*

↑ The 1850s Greek Revival-style Brevard-Wisdom-Rice House

Strolling down Magazine Street, with its boutiques and vintage stores

Begin at the streetcar stop at **St. Charles Avenue** and Melpomene Street, which is one of a collection of parallel streets in the area named for the Nine Muses of Greek mythology.

START

Head toward the river to **Coliseum Park**. Laid out in 1806, the park's name refers to an outdoor arena that was planned here but never realized. Continue along Camp Street beneath shady oak trees.

Dominating this corner of Magazine Street is **Hotel Saint Vincent**, with its fanciful wrought-iron balconies. The inn was originally built as an orphanage in 1861 during epidemics of yellow fever.

Continue up **Magazine Street**, where homes give way to rows of boutiques and restaurants with large balconies shading the sidewalks beneath.

Constance Street is home to two historic Catholic churches built in the mid-19th century. The first, the Irish **St. Alphonsus**, is now an arts and cultural center with tours available.

The second of Constance Street's churches is **St. Mary's Assumption**. Much of the ornate interior decoration of this German Baroque Revival church was imported from Munich.

↑ St. Mary's Assumption, a German Catholic church

MID-CITY

Extending from the French Quarter toward Lake Pontchartrain, Mid-City is the greenest part of New Orleans. Because it stands on low-lying terrain once known as the "backswamp," this was one of the last neighborhoods to be developed in the late 19th and early 20th centuries. A great swath of this district is occupied by City Park. Carved out of the former Allard Plantation, the land was purchased in 1845 by bank director John McDonogh from the bankrupt Allard family. Upon McDonogh's death in 1850, the land was donated to the city, on the proviso that the funds from its sale be used for public schools. Instead, the city bent the rules a little and created a park. NOMA, the city's oldest fine arts institution, was established here in 1911 by Isaac Delgado, a wealthy sugar broker. The other green areas in Mid-City are given over to cemeteries such as Greenwood, Metairie, St. Louis Cemetery #3, and Cypress Grove. Laid out in the mid-19th century, ornate, above-ground tombs and mausoleums became the final resting places of prominent New Orleanians.

Architecturally and culturally diverse, today Mid-City runs the gamut from characterful bars and restaurants to colorful shotgun houses and stately homes.

B   C   D   E

ACADEMY ROAD
Outfall Canal
HOMEDALE STREET
Metairie Relief Canal
NARCISSUS ST
Pumping Station
Metairie Cemetery 6
PONTCHARTRAIN
Greenwood Cemetery
NAVARRE STREET
GENERAL DIAZ STREET
MARSHALL FOCH ST
CANAL BOULEVARD
Tad Gormley Stadium
ROOSEVELT MALL
Storyland and Carousel Gardens
New Orleans Botanical Garden
Peristyle
Delgado Community College
Holt Cemetery
CITY PARK

2

VINCENT STREET
LAKE AVENUE
METAIRIE ROAD
City Park Avenue
Masonic Cemetery
Hurricane Katrina Memorial 10
Cypress Grove Cemetery 8
TOULOUSE STREET
N PATRICK ST
BIENVILLE ST
CONTI STREET
ALEXANDER ST
ORLEANS STREET
IBERVILLE STREET
NORTH
Canal Streetcar

New Orleans Country Club
EXPRESSWAY
Longue Vue House and Gardens 9
BAMBOO RD
ORPHEUM AVE
PALMETTO STREET
HOLLY GROVE ST
CANAL STREET
Canal Streetcar
PALMYRA STREET
S ST PATRICK ST
BANKS STREET
S ALEXANDER ST
N PIERCE ST
2

3

AVENUE
PALMETTO STREET
PEACH STREET
BAUDIN STREET
D'HEMECOURT STREET
SOUTH ALEXANDER STREET
SOUTH CARROLLTON AVE
S PIERCE STREET
S CORTEZ STREET
GENOIS STREET
BANKS STREET
NORTH
4

4
AIRLINE HIGHWAY
FORSHAY STREET
MISTLETOE STREET
EAGLE STREET
MONTICELLO AVENUE
TULANE AVENUE
S CORTEZ STREET
BAUDIN STREET
Comiskey Park
3

5

PERDIDO
PONTCHARTRAIN
EARHART
SOUTH
MARTIN

MID-CITY

Must See
1 City Park

Experience More
2 St. Louis Cemetery #3
3 Free People of Color Museum
4 Pitot House
5 Bayou St. John
6 Metairie Cemetery
7 Degas House
8 Cypress Grove Cemetery
9 Longue Vue House and Gardens
10 Hurricane Katrina Memorial

Eat
1 Dooky Chase Restaurant
2 Angelo Brocato

Drink
3 Twelve Mile Limit
4 Finn McCool's Irish Pub
5 Bayou Beer Garden

E

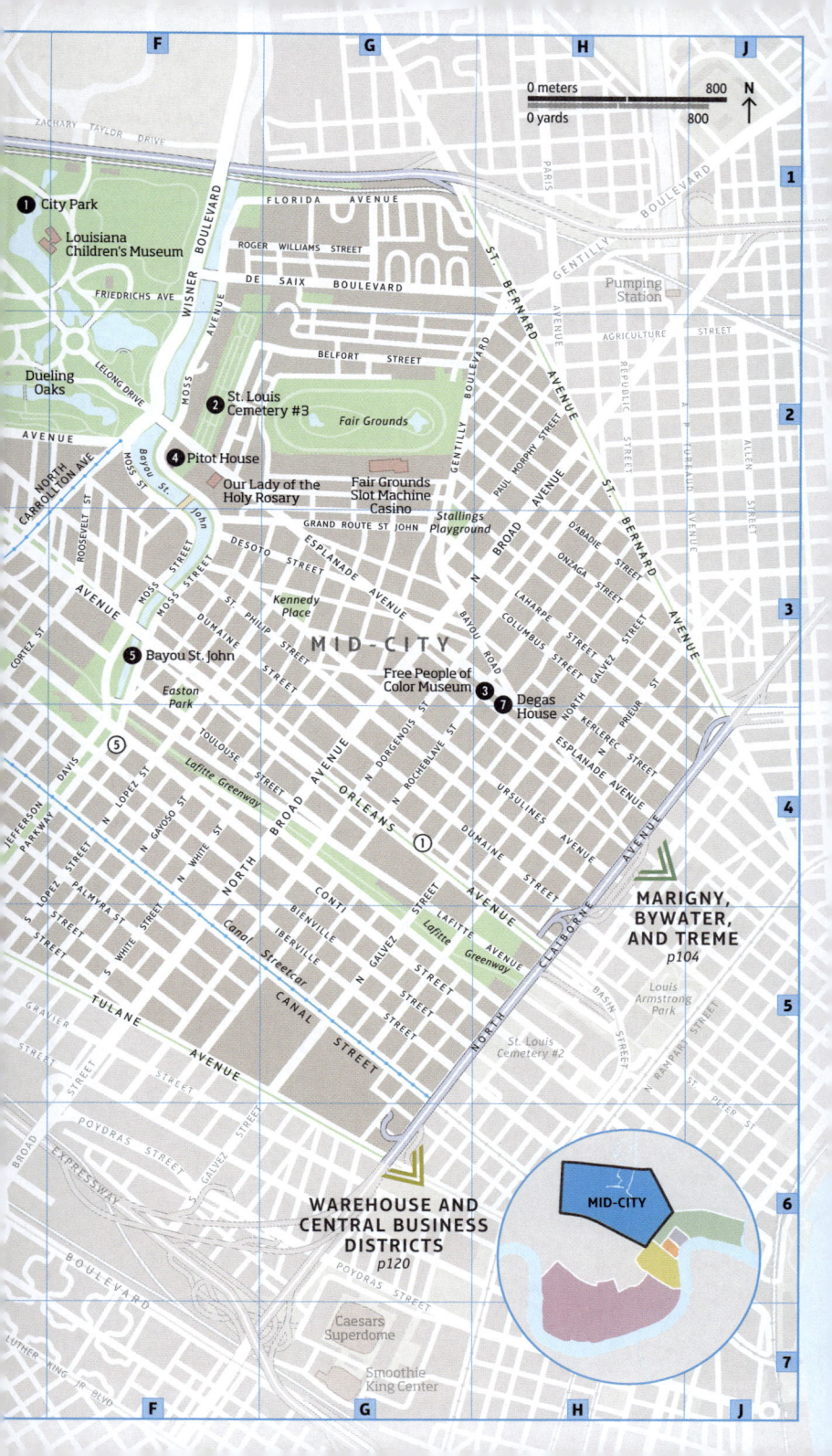

0 meters 800

0 yards 800

N

ZACHARY TAYLOR DRIVE

1 City Park

Louisiana
Children's Museum

FLORIDA AVENUE

ROGER WILLIAMS STREET

DE SAIX BOULEVARD

FRIEDRICHS AVE

WISNER BOULEVARD

MOSS AVENUE

PARIS AVENUE

GENTILLY

Pumping
Station

AGRICULTURE STREET

REPUBLIC STREET

BELFORT STREET

Dueling
Oaks

LELONG DRIVE

2 St. Louis
Cemetery #3

Fair Grounds

ST. BERNARD AVENUE

PAUL MURPHY STREET

DABADIE STREET

URBAN STREET

ALLEN STREET

AVENUE

NORTH CARROLLTON AVE

Bayou St.
John

MOSS ST.

4 Pitot House

Our Lady of the
Holy Rosary

Fair Grounds
Slot Machine
Casino

Stallings
Playground

GRAND ROUTE ST JOHN

GENTILLY BOULEVARD

BROAD AVENUE

ST. BERNARD AVENUE

AVENUE

ROOSEVELT ST.

MOSS STREET

DESOTO STREET

ESPLANADE AVENUE

LAHARPE STREET

ONZAGA STREET

CORTEZ ST.

MOSS STREET

ST. PHILIP STREET

DUMAINE STREET

Kennedy
Place

MID-CITY

BAYOU ROAD

COLUMBUS STREET

N. GALVEZ STREET

N. JOHNSON STREET

PRIEUR ST.

5 Bayou St. John

Easton
Park

Free People of
Color Museum **3 7** Degas
House

ESPLANADE AVENUE

KERLEREC STREET

5

DAVIS

N. LOPEZ ST.

Lafitte Greenway

TOULOUSE STREET

BROAD AVENUE

ORLEANS AVENUE

N. DORGENOIS ST.

N. ROCHEBLAVE ST.

URSULINES AVENUE

CLAIBORNE AVENUE

JEFFERSON PARKWAY

N. GAYOSO ST.

N. WHITE ST.

DUMAINE STREET

DUMAINE STREET

1

AVENUE

**MARIGNY,
BYWATER,
AND TREME**
p104

S. LOPEZ STREET

PALMYRA ST.

N. WHITE STREET

CONTI STREET

BIENVILLE STREET

IBERVILLE STREET

N. GALVEZ STREET

Lafitte
Greenway

LAFITTE AVENUE

BASIN STREET

Louis
Armstrong
Park

S. WHITE STREET

Canal Streetcar

CANAL STREET

N. RAMPART STREET

ST. PETER ST.

St. Louis
Cemetery #2

GRAVIER STREET

TULANE AVENUE

STREET

**WAREHOUSE AND
CENTRAL BUSINESS
DISTRICTS**
p120

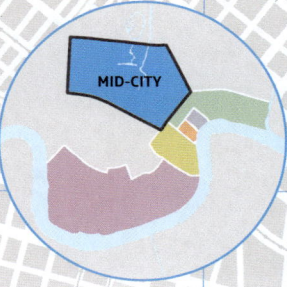

MID-CITY

BROAD STREET

POYDRAS STREET

POYDRAS EXPRESSWAY

S. GALVEZ STREET

POYDRAS STREET

BOULEVARD

Caesars
Superdome

Smoothie
King Center

LUTHER KING JR BLVD

CITY PARK

📍 E1, E2, F1, & F2 🏠 Adm Building: 1 Palm Dr 🕐 Sunrise-sunset daily 🌐 neworleanscitypark.org

Built on the site of the former Allard Plantation beside Bayou St. John, New Orleans City Park has grown vastly since its inception, and today is one of the largest urban parks in the U.S, at 1,300 acres (530 hectares). Home to incredible natural beauty and an exciting range of activities, it's an oasis of calm in the heart of the city.

💬 INSIDER TIP
Let There Be Light

Each December, City Park hosts the month-long Celebration in the Oaks Festival. Food and entertainment tents are set up and impressive light displays illuminate the park.

① Dueling Oaks

📍 F2 🏠 City Park 🚋 Canal 🚌 46, 48, 90

To the left of the Lelong Drive entrance to City Park is a rather grand, solitary oak. This magnificent gnarled tree is still called the Dueling Oaks, despite the fact that there is now only one. Its fellow was destroyed in a hurricane in 1949 (the park then lost another 2,000 trees during Hurricane Katrina).

Many duels were fought in New Orleans, and most of these took place in the shady acres of what is now City Park. Under the massive branches of the live oaks, as many as ten duels a day were fought. Reports indicate that one particular dueler insisted on using whaling harpoons to settle the dispute, after which the offended party decided he wasn't so offended after all. The last duel was fought in 1939. The owner of the original plantation from which City Park was carved, Louis Allard, is rumored to be buried at the foot of the oaks.

② Storyland and Carousel Gardens

📍 E1 🏠 5 Victory Ave, City Park 🚋 Canal 🚌 46, 48, 90 🕐 Storyland: 10am–4:30pm Tue-Sun; Carousel Gardens: 11am–6pm Sat & Sun 🚫 Dec 25 🌐 neworleanscitypark.com

Storyland, a whimsical theme park for children, is filled with all kinds of entertainments derived from traditional folk tales and well-known nursery rhymes. Kids can enjoy Jack and Jill's slide, climb around Miss Muffet's spider web, or bravely challenge Captain Hook to a duel. Along the way, they may also encounter fairytale characters such as Jack (of the Beanstalk), Puss in Boots, Rapunzel, and many others. There is also story reading, puppet shows in the Puppet Castle, and face painting.

The carousel, situated in the adjacent Carousel Gardens Amusement Park, was built in 1906 and is one of the few antique wooden carousels left in the U.S. Nearby, visitors can climb aboard a miniature train (11am–4:30pm Wednesday–Friday), which has run around the park since 1896. A large Ferris wheel offers a bird's-eye view of the park.

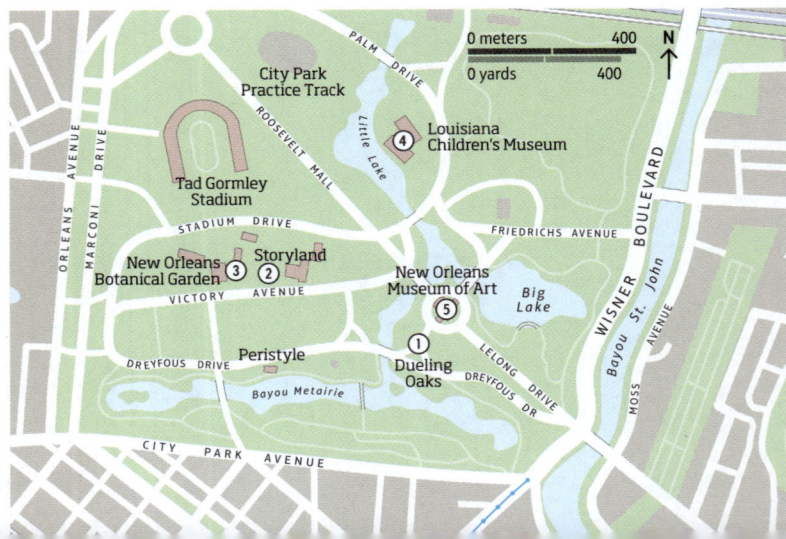

↑ The Botanical Garden's lily pond and Pavilion of the Two Sisters, and *(inset)* seasonal displays

3 (icons)

New Orleans Botanical Garden

E2 ⚐ Victory Ave, City Park 🚋 Canal St - City Park/Museum 🚌 90, 91 🕐 10am–4:30pm Tue-Sat 🚫 Jan 1, Dec 25, Mardi Gras 🌐 new orleanscitypark.com

This 10-acre (4-hectare) public garden was created in the 1930s. Back then, it was mainly a rose garden, but today there are more than 2,000 varieties of plants from around the world, with aquatics, native and tropical plants, ornamental trees, shrubs, perennials, and much more inside various theme gardens.

The Garden Study Center and the Pavilion of the Two Sisters are reminiscent of European garden architecture. The Conservatory houses orchids and two major fascinating exhibits: Living Fossils, showcasing fossilized plants that grew on the earth before flowering plants, and the impressive Tropical Rainforest exhibit, with educational displays of geckos, tree frogs, and snakes.

The Enrique Alférez Sculpture Garden features several works by the beloved Mexican-American artist surrounded by ornate shrubs, vibrant cherry blossoms, and an ancient live oak tree, including his *Women in Huipil* and *The Flute Player*.

One of the park's unique treasures is the Historic New Orleans Train Garden, a miniature railway featuring streetcars and trains from the late 1800s to the early 1900s.

4 (icons)

Louisiana Children's Museum

F1 ⚐ 15 Henry Thomas Dr 🚋 St. Charles Canal St - City Park/Museum 🚌 90, 91 🕐 9:30am–4:30pm Wed-Sat, 11:30am–4:30pm Sun 🚫 Public hols 🌐 lcm.org

This activity-oriented museum allows children to entertain themselves with a variety of role-playing games, plus other interactive exhibits. The museum relocated to City Park in mid-2019. Its lagoon-side site encompasses play areas, nature exhibits, and galleries where kids can explore the journey of food from field to fork, along with a literacy center, two cafés, and sensory and edible gardens.

TOP 4 **CITY PARK SPORTS**

Tennis
City Park Tennis Center has 26 floodlit courts that can be reserved in advance.

Golf
The Bayou Oaks complex has a 67-bay lighted driving range and two 18-hole golf courses with water features.

Boating
The park's 8 miles (13 km) of lagoons provide ample opportunities for boating, and bass and trout fishing.

Horse Riding
City Park's Equest Farm offers riding lessons and trail rides.

⑤ 🪚 ⚡ 🍴 💻 🛍️

NEW ORLEANS MUSEUM OF ART

📍F2 🏛️1 Collins Diboll Circle, City Park 🚋Canal St - City Park/Museum 🚌90, 91
🕐Museum: 10am-5pm Tue & Thu-Sun, noon-7pm Wed; Besthoff Sculpture Garden: 10am-6pm daily (Oct-Mar: to 5pm) 🚫Public hols 🌐noma.org

Together, the New Orleans Museum of Art (NOMA) and the adjacent Sydney and Walda Besthoff Sculpture Garden comprise one of the most important cultural destinations in the Gulf South. Housed in a grand Neo-Classical building in New Orleans City Park, NOMA's collection includes art from the Renaissance to the modern era.

For over a century, NOMA has been the city's principle fine arts institution. Its impressive permanent collections and rotating exhibits rival those found in the best museums in the country. Visitors to NOMA can view works by Picasso, Degas, Miró, Rodin, and Pollock; a 10,000-piece photography collection; and Asian, African, and American art. In a beautiful 11-acre (4.5-hectare) site, the sculpture garden showcases pieces by world-renowned artists, such as those by Henry Moore and Barbara Hepworth.

💬 INSIDER TIP
Garden Yoga

Yoga classes are held in the soothing surrounds of the Besthoff Sculpture Garden every Saturday morning – check the museum website for details.

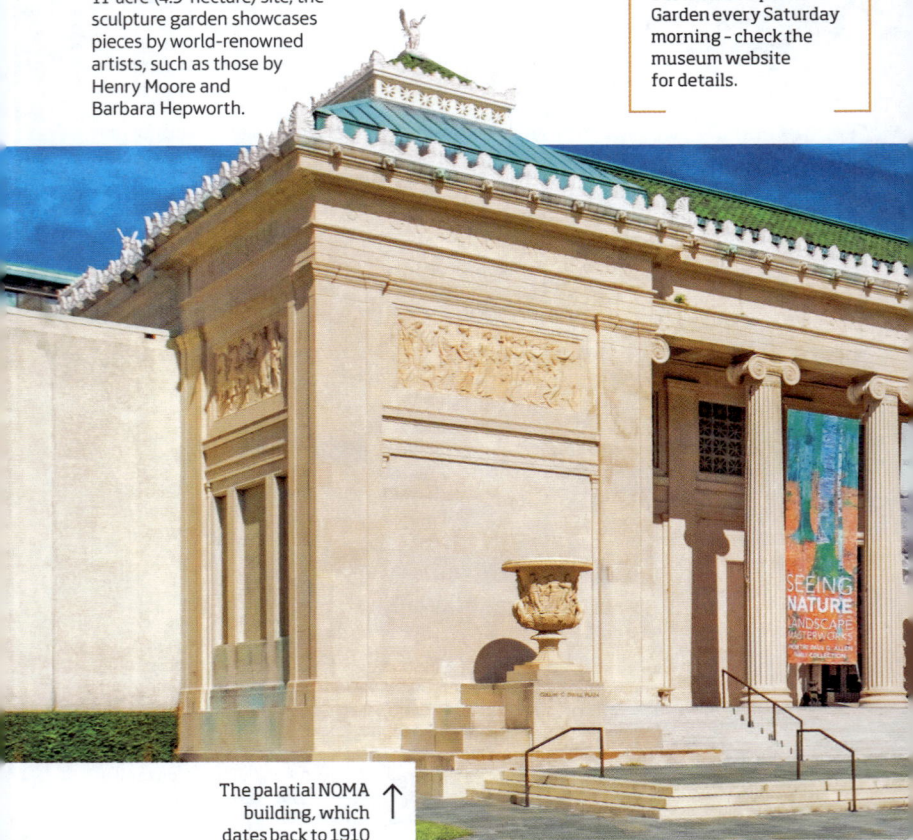

The palatial NOMA building, which dates back to 1910 ↑

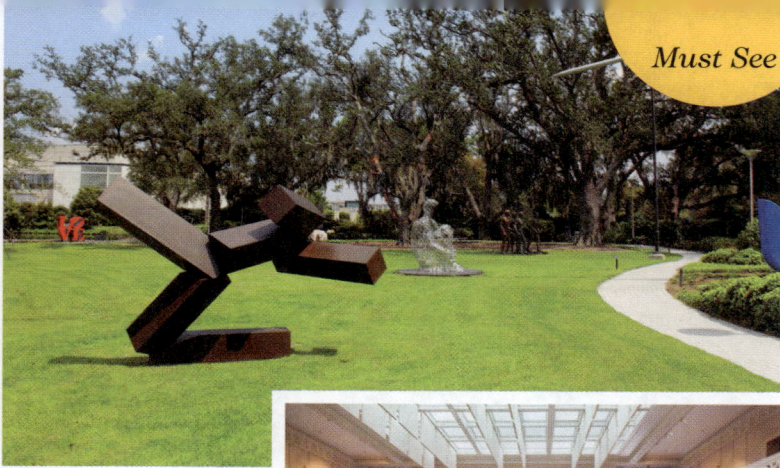

Joel Shapiro's bronze *Untitled* (1991) on display in the Besthoff Sculpture Garden

→

The resplendent lobby at NOMA, with its art-lined walls, Classical columns, and decorative balcony

THE BESTHOFF SCULPTURE GARDEN

The dynamic sculptures of Henry Moore, Barbara Hepworth, Louise Bourgeois, George Segal, and other renowned artists are displayed among the ancient oaks, magnolias, and tranquil lagoons of the Sydney and Walda Besthoff Sculpture Garden. It is home to 90 works displayed over 11 acres, an amphitheater, and a 70 ft (21 m) glass bridge with swirling, multi-colored lines reflecting the meandering path of a river. Visitors can wander around the park for free, or join one of the daily tours.

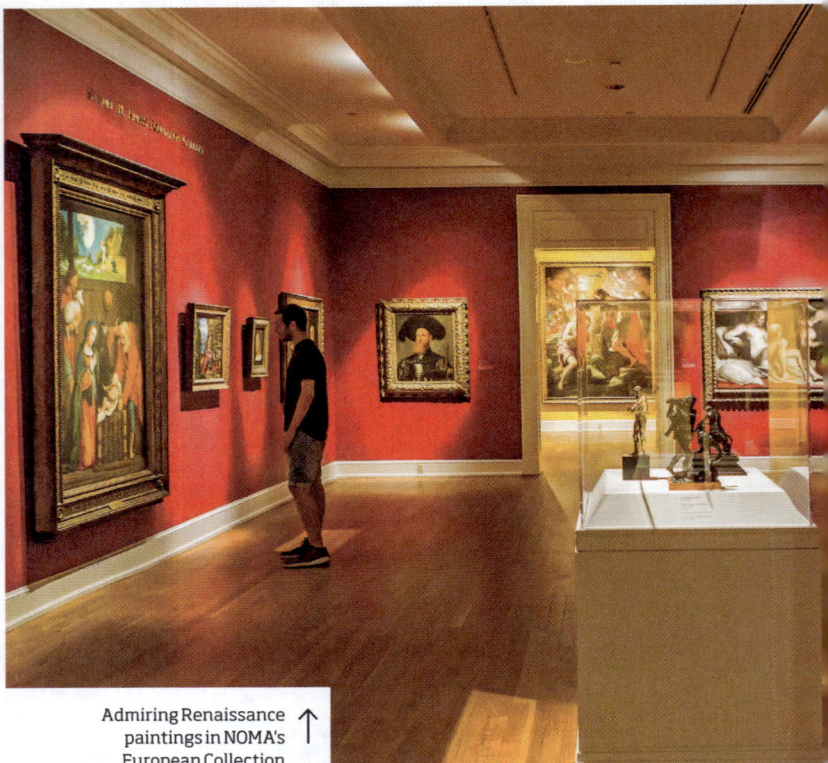

↑ Admiring Renaissance paintings in NOMA's European Collection

↑ *Portrait of a Young Woman* (1918) by Amedeo Modigliani, displayed in one of the first-floor European galleries

Exploring the New Orleans Museum of Art

The museum has expanded from exhibiting just nine pieces of art when it opened in 1911 to displaying almost 50,000 works over three floors today. Major collections in NOMA's 46 galleries include a vast selection of works of European art, which is spread across the first and second floors, from 12th-century Italian Florentine to 20th-century French and Spanish works. There are specialized collections of Latin American and Prehispanic art; Indigenous works; arts of Africa and Asia; photography; and decorative arts, on the second and third floors. Modern art enthusiasts are catered for in a display located on the second floor, which covers all the major 20th-century American and European movements.

> The museum has expanded from exhibiting just nine pieces of art when it opened in 1911 to displaying almost 50,000 works over three floors today.

African Art

▷ This is one of the finest African art collections in the country. It features figures, sculptures, ancient terracottas, textiles, furniture, masks, costumes, marionettes, and musical instruments. A highlight is a rare palace veranda post carved in the shape of an equestrian warrior figure.

Oceanic Art

This gallery showcases art from across the Pacific islands, including canoes carved into the form of crocodiles, surreal masks from Papua New Guinea, and Polynesian clubs.

Art of the Americas

North, Central, and South American art are the focus here, with works spanning Latin America, and the U.S. Works range from Mayan artifacts and pre-Columbian artworks, right through to the Spanish colonial period. It also has fine examples of early American artists, a collection of Louisiana paintings, and Indigenous art from ancient times to the present day.

Contemporary Art

◁ A variety of sculpture, paintings, and mixed-media works are part of the Contemporary Art collection, including contemporary European art and the American art exhibits.

Asian Art

NOMA began its collection of Asian art in 1914 with a selection of Chinese jade and stone carvings. The Asian Art galleries contain a fine collection of Edo paintings from Japan. All the major Japanese schools are represented, particularly the Nanga, Zenga, and Maruyama-Shijo schools. The collection also includes a wide variety of ceramics, lacquer, textiles, prints, and photographs.

Decorative Arts

▷ More than 15,000 works comprise this distinctive collection, which includes more than 6,000 glass items, furniture, and miniature portraits. The pottery collection features pieces from New Orleans' own Newcomb Pottery and a rare collection of "Old Paris" porcelain.

European Art

The European collection spans a period of 600 years and features examples from the major national schools. The Kress Collection includes sublime Italian Old Master paintings from the early Renaissance to the 18th century. Dutch, Flemish, and Impressionist works are also showcased, with French art well represented in the form of works from the 17th to the 20th centuries. Among them are paintings by Impressionist Edgar Degas, who visited New Orleans in the 1870s.

Photography, Prints, and Drawings

These rotating collections consist of more than 20,000 objects including prints, books, and unique works on paper that are displayed in a special suite of galleries. This department has two exhibitions a year. Highlights of the collection include works by French artist Henri Matisse.

TOP 3 COLLECTION HIGHLIGHTS

Mounted Warrior Veranda Post (c. 1910-14)
A rare carving by Yoruba artist Olowe of Ise, on the third floor.

Standing Ganesha (12th-13th century)
A beautiful Indian stone carving of the Hindu elephant-headed god, on the third floor.

Portrait of Marie Antoinette (c. 1788)
One of Vigée Le Brun's sympathetic portraits of Marie Antoinette, on the second floor.

A SHORT WALK
CITY PARK

Distance 1.1 miles (1.8 km) **Time** 20 minutes
Nearest Streetcar Canal

The many pristine paths make for an ideal walk through the City Park, which has a history of about 170 years. Despite Hurricane Katrina causing $43 million worth of damage to the grounds and facilities, the park was repaired, improved, and is now thriving. Visitors flock to the spectacular Botanical Garden and the New Orleans Museum of Art, while Storyland, a theme park with rides and fairy-tale exhibits, is a great spot for kids. Eight miles (12 km) of lagoons allow for fishing and boating, and ancient trees amid lush planting grant ample dappled shade for picnics post a stroll.

Storyland and Carousel Gardens *are the main attractions in the amusement park (p166).*

The landscaped **Goldring/Woldenberg Great Lawn** *hosts many concerts and events.*

VICTORY AVENUE

DREYFOUS DRIVE

CITY PARK AVENUE

Did You Know?

The vast City Park is 50 per cent larger than Central Park in New York City.

Situated beside a pretty lagoon, the **Peristyle** *has been a popular gathering spot for more than a century.*

Playgrounds surround **Popp's Bandstand**, *which is named after lumber magnate John Popp.*

↑ Strolling in the cool
shade of the Dueling Oaks

Exhibits of the **New Orleans Botanical Garden** *cover 10 acres (4 hectares) of the park (p167). Statues by artist Enrique Alferez stand among the trees.*

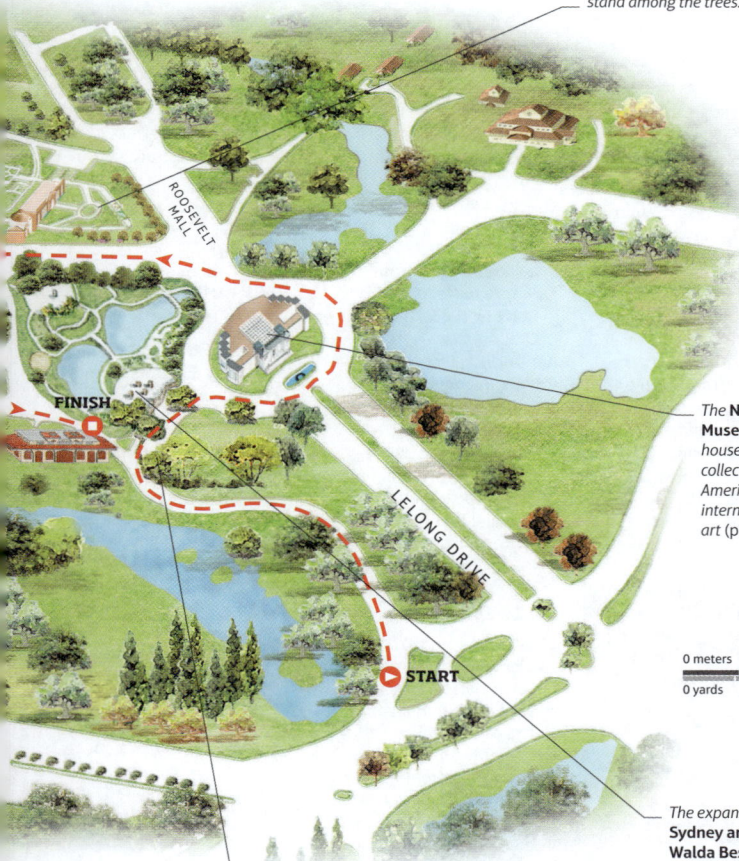

ROOSEVELT MALL

LELONG DRIVE

FINISH

The **New Orleans Museum of Art** *houses a fine collection of American and international art (p168).*

0 meters 100
0 yards 100

N
↑

▶ **START**

The expansive **Sydney and Walda Besthoff Sculpture Garden** *(p169).*

As many as ten duels a day were once fought under the **Dueling Oaks** *(p166). The last one was a challenge with sabers that took place in 1939.*

→ Wandering St. Louis Cemetery #3, one of the city's largest graveyards

EXPERIENCE MORE

2

St. Louis Cemetery #3

📍F2 🏠3421 Esplanade Ave 🚌90, 91 🕐8am–4:30pm Mon–Sat, 8am–4pm Sun 🚫Mardi Gras 🌐nola catholiccemeteries.org

This pristine cemetery, with its beautiful wrought-iron gates was established in 1854. Among the notable figures buried here is Antoine Michoud, the original owner of a plantation which is now the site of the NASA Michoud Assembly Facility where the Saturn rocket booster was constructed

in the 1960s. There is also a memorial to architect James Gallier, Sr. *(p132)* and his wife, who are buried in Metairie Cemetery *(p176)*. Both were tragically killed when the steamer *Evening Star* sank en route from New York to New Orleans in October 1866.

Other famous figures here include Father Rouquette, missionary to the Choctaw, and Black Creole philanthropist Thomy Lafon, the owner of the old Orleans Ballroom who also sponsored an orphanage for African American children.

JAZZ FEST

What started in 1970 as a local celebration in Louis Armstrong Park, the New Orleans Jazz and Heritage Festival, or Jazz Fest, is now a major player on the international festival circuit. Today it attracts hundreds of thousands to hear world-class jazz and pop music acts, from Herbie Hancock to Elton John *(nojazzfest.com)*.

Less visited than #1, St. Louis Cemetery #3 is perfect for taking a quiet stroll and gathering your thoughts.

3 ♿ 🚫

Free People of Color Museum

📍H3 🏠2336 Esplanade Ave 🚌91 🕐Tours: 1pm Fri & 11am Sat 🌐lemusee defpc.com

Dedicated to chronicling the rich history of the city's free Black population before the Civil War, this fascinating museum is housed in a beautiful Greek Revival home built in 1859. Documented as early as 1722, an astounding 18,000 free people of color owned and paid taxes on property worth $15 million in the city. Guides share the stories of some remarkable members of this community, highlighting objects related to them, such as old documents, paintings, and photos that were collected by museum founders, Beverly Stanton McKenna and Dr. Dwight McKenna. Note, the museum is only open for

guided tours, which last for 45 minutes and need to be booked in advance.

4

Pitot House

F2 1440 Moss St
Canal 10am–3pm Wed–Fri Public hols
pitothouse.org

This Creole colonial-style raised house was built in 1799, on the banks of Bayou St. John. Once a working plantation, it was carefully moved by a block in the 1960s to this location. In 1810, the house was purchased by James Pitot, who had been the mayor of the city five years earlier. He had arrived from Haiti in 1796 after the uprising of enslaved workers led by Toussaint L'Ouverture. Pitot went on to direct a bank and run the New Orleans Navigation Company before being appointed a probate judge of the Territory of Orleans.

In 1904 Pitot House was bought by Mother Cabrini, who would later become America's first saint, and converted into a convent. It is now a museum containing original antiques and furnishings from the house.

5

Bayou St. John

F3 Canal 46, 48, 90

The French recognized this bayou – utilized by Indigenous peoples as a navigable waterway – as an asset, providing access to the Gulf of Mexico via Lake Pontchartrain. As New Orleans grew, so did plantations along the bayou, and a canal was dug, linking it to downtown, ending in Basin Street at Congo Square. The canal was eventually filled in and became a railroad. It has since been redeveloped as the Lafitte Greenway *(p116)*, a 2.6-mile (4.2-km) pedestrian path running from Basin Street up to Bayou St. John, whose grassy banks are perfect for settling down with a picnic and watching the sun set.

DRINK

Twelve Mile Limit

This neighborhood bar has a wonderful secret – its cocktail menu, designed by the owner, one of the city's best mixologists. It's the perfect spot to chill and sip a sundowner.

E4 500 South Telemachus St
twelvemilelimit.com

Finn McCool's Irish Pub

The city has a good number of Irish bars, but this one is a favorite among locals as it is one of the few places showing live soccer matches from around the world.

E4 3701 Banks St
finnmccools.com

Bayou Beer Garden

Come for the beer and stay for the garden, a lovely hangout for eating and drinking when the weather is in those sweet spots just before or just after summer.

F4 326 North Jefferson Davis Pkwy
bayoubeergarden.com

↓ Gazing out at the peaceful waters of Bayou St. John at sunset

6

Metairie Cemetery

⬛ C2 **🏠 5100 Pontchartrain Blvd** **🚌 45, 91** **🕐 7:30am–5:30pm daily**

This is the most attractively landscaped cemetery in New Orleans, and the final resting place of many of its blue-bloods. In the 19th century, the city was the premier venue for horseracing, and the Metairie Racetrack was the most famous. After the Civil War, mismanagement afforded entrepreneur Charles T. Howard the opportunity to take revenge on the racetrack members who had refused him admission. He purchased it in 1872 and converted it into a cemetery. The oval racecourse became the cemetery's main drive.

Many tombs are located here, and near the entrance stands the 85-ft- (26-m-) high Moriarty monument, which required the laying of a special railroad to bring it into the cemetery. Daniel Moriarty was a 19th-century Irish immigrant and saloon-keeper who

↑ A marble Angel of Grief draped over a tomb in Metairie Cemetery

succeeded financially but was shunned by the city's tight-knit elite for his background. He was determined to avenge his wife, Mary, and designed this tomb so that in death she could look down on all those who had snubbed her.

The tomb of the legendary Josie Arlington bears a bas-relief of a young girl knocking on a door. Orphaned at the age of four, as a teenager Arlington engaged in sex work to support her family with her earnings. Notorious for her temper, she once bit off half an ear and the lower lip of a rival.

A large bell from his boat *America* marks the grave of Captain Cooley, who ran several steamboats until his death in 1931. Other denizens include William C. C. Claiborne, the first governor of Louisiana, and P. B. S. Pinchback, a free man of color who became the state's only Black governor in 1872–3. In 2022, beloved author Anne Rice, along with her husband, was laid to rest in the Rice Family Mausoleum.

7

Degas House

⬛ H3 **🏠 2306 Esplanade Ave** **🚌 91** **🕐 Tours: 10:30am & 1:45pm daily (by reservation only)** **🌐 degashouse.com**

Calling himself "almost a son of Louisiana," Impressionist painter Edgar Degas (1834–1917) visited his uncle, Michel Musson (*p150*), at this house from October 1872 until March 1873. Degas was charmed by America and especially New

1873

The Musée des Beaux Arts in Pau, France, bought *A Cotton Office in New Orleans*, Degas' first museum sale.

Orleans. Several important paintings evolved from his sojourn here, despite the fact that he did not venture far from the house for fear of the intense New Orleans sun affecting his eyesight. *A Cotton Office in New Orleans* (1873) shows his uncle with several members of his family, including the artist's own brothers René and Achille, who both worked in the cotton business.

The Esplanade house, which dates from 1854, has Greek Revival details and cast-iron balconies. The house has been restored with gorgeous period furnishings and reproductions of Degas' work on display, and visitors are welcomed every day for guided tours with one of Degas' descendants (reservations are required).

↑ An alley of oaks lining the drive of Longue Vue House, and (inset) the pristine rear gardens and fountain

tomb, which features a broken column, was designed by famous architect J. N. B. de Pouilly (p114).

8
Cypress Grove Cemetery

📍 D3 🏠 120 City Park Ave ⏰ 8:30am–4:30pm daily 🌐 greenwoodnola.com/cypress-grove

This cemetery, established by the Firemen's Charitable and Benevolent Association, was laid out in 1841, and the decision was made to move the remains of firemen who had been buried in other cemeteries in New Orleans and reinter them here. The impressive Egyptian-style gate leads into a graveyard filled with handsome memorials. Many of the tombs are dedicated to individual firefighters, such as Irad Ferry, who lost their lives in the line of duty. Ferry's

9
Longue Vue House and Gardens

📍 B3 🏠 7 Bamboo Rd ⏰ 9:30am–5pm daily; tours start on the half hour 📍 Public hols 🌐 longuevue.com

Cotton broker Edgar Stern and his wife Edith Rosenwald, heiress to the Sears fortune, built this estate between 1939 and 1942. When the couple finally moved into their new home, the sizable alley of oaks that line the drive was already established, made possible by installing 20-year-old live oaks rather than saplings. The lavish interiors are decorated with antiques,

carpets, and fine art, including works by Jean Arp, Pablo Picasso, and Barbara Hepworth. The gardens, which contain no fewer than 23 fountains, created by Ellen Biddle, are exceptional examples of landscape design. The largest garden is modeled on the 14th-century Alhambra Gardens in Spain; others are inspired by French and English designs. Aimed at younger visitors, the Discovery Garden is an educational and interactive environment for children.

10
Hurricane Katrina Memorial

📍 D3 🏠 5056 Canal S 🚇 Canal

This poignant memorial commemorates the 86 unclaimed and unidentified New Orleanians killed in the devastating storm of 2005. The memorial and garden designed in 2008 evoke the spiral shape of a hurricane from space, creating a contemplative labyrinth. Nearby, the historic Charity Hospital Cemetery was selected to hold the remains (in five simple columbaria).

A LONG WALK

FAUBOURG ST. JOHN

Distance 2 miles (3.2 km) **Time** 40 minutes
Nearest Streetcar Canal

This walk circles a portion of Bayou St. John, the natural waterway that drains into Lake Pontchartrain, visited by kayakers, picnickers, and the occasional pelican. The bayou is a historically strategic waterway, where some of the city's earliest colonial development took place: it is surrounded by original Creole mansions and the distinctive above-ground St. Louis Cemetery #3. The area is easily accessible from downtown via the Canal streetcar and is not far from the attractions in City Park *(p166)*.

↑ Pitot House, built for the third
mayor of New Orleans, James Pitot

Locator Map
For more detail see p164

Begin this walk at North
Carrollton Avenue. Cross
Esplanade Avenue bridge
and follow the grassy
footpath around **Bayou
St. John** (p175).

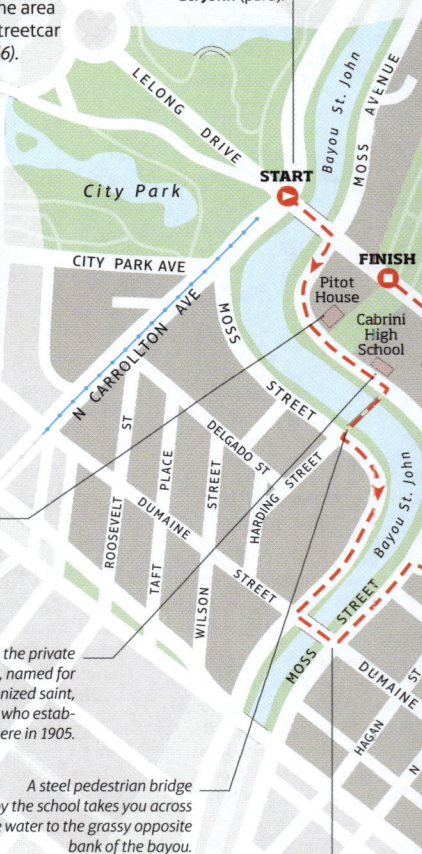

You'll soon reach **Pitot House**,
an outstanding example of the Creole
architecture built in this area in the
18th and early 19th centuries (p175).

Beside Pitot House is the private
Cabrini High School, named for
America's first canonized saint,
Mother Frances Cabrini, who estab-
lished an orphanage here in 1905.

A steel pedestrian bridge
by the school takes you across
the water to the grassy opposite
bank of the bayou.

At the next bridge at **Dumaine
Street,** cross back to the west side of
the bayou, where embankments and
steps provide good spots to sit and
admire the wildlife and views.

Did You Know?

Invasive Asian swamp
eels have made the
bayou their home, but
how they got there
is a mystery.

Our Lady of the
Holy Rosary Church,
visible from the bayou

0 meters 300 N
0 yards 300

Towards the end of this
walk, you'll pass the lovely
**Our Lady of the Holy
Rosary**, a Catholic church
built in 1925 with Classical
columns and a dome.

BELFORT STREET

Each spring, the New Orleans
Jazz and Heritage Fest, or
Jazz Fest, is held at the
Fair Grounds (p174).

*Fair Grounds
Race Course*

VERNA STREET

MYSTERY STREET

ESPLANADE AVE

GENTILLY BOULEVARD

Fair Grounds
Slot Machine Casino

Our Lady
of the Holy
Rosary

FORTIN STREET

MAUREPAS STREET

PONCE DE LEON STREET

GRAND ROUTE ST. JOHN

On **Ponce de Leon
Street** there are clusters
of charming restaurants,
cafés, and small boutiques
to explore.

DESOTO

N LOPEZ STREET

STREET

From Ursulines, with its Victorian houses
and cottages trimmed with gingerbread
woodwork, head towards **Esplanade
Avenue**, where you'll spot impressive
19th- and 20th-century mansions (p97).

BELL STREET

N DUPRE STREET

Kennedy
Place

URSULINES AVE

ST PHILIP ST

RENDON ST

N LOPEZ STREET

N SALCEDO ST

N GAYOSO ST

ORLEANS
AVENUE

Ursulines Avenue,
named for the French
nuns (p92), was laid
out around 1860
after the marshy
lands around the
bayou were drained.

↑ Ursulines Avenue comes alive
with street musicians

BEYOND NEW ORLEANS

In the countryside surrounding New Orleans, the Mississippi meanders west through marsh and swampland. This is where the Acadians arrived from Nova Scotia in 1764, to settle around the bayous and prairies now known as Cajun Country. Today, towns such as Lafayette, Opelousas, and Eunice showcase the region's rich Cajun history and culture.

Baton Rouge lies northwest of New Orleans. Today an oil-refining center, the city was established as a French fort in 1719. Following a century of secession and seizure, it became the Louisiana state capital in 1849. In the 18th and 19th centuries, the fertile river banks from New Orleans to Baton Rouge were lined with hundreds of plantations, where cash crops like sugarcane and indigo were cultivated to be shipped around the world. By 1850, two-thirds of America's millionaires lived in vast mansions along this stretch, the River Road, along with the thousands of enslaved people who worked and resided on the plantations. Today, some of the antebellum estates that remain have been revitalized as museums. The Whitney is a particularly poignant example – its tours and exhibits explore the experience of life on the plantation, from the perspective of the enslaved.

Pollock

167

84

Natchez

28

167

15

61

33

Alexandria

Red

Lake
Mary

Marksville

Woodville

2a

Lecompte

49

Simmesport

Tunica Hills

Jackson

19

165

Cocodrie
Lake

167

Bunkie

71

107

1

Cat Island
National Wildlife Refuge

Audubon State
Historic Park

ST. FRANCISVILLE **4**

61

Turkey Creek

10

13

29

49

Lebeau

71

10

Morganza

Mississippi

Zachary

Ville Platte

167

Port Barre

190

1

61

Mamou

OPELOUSAS **8**

9 EUNICE   Creole Heritage
Folklife Center

190

49

BATON ROUGE **3**

L O U I S I A N A

Church
Point

182

31

10

Plaquemine

1

13

Carencro

Breaux Bridge

Atchafalaya

10

Rayne

Cypress Island
Nature Preserve

75

90

Crowley

LAFAYETTE **2**

31

White Castle

13

Broussard

ST. MARTINVILLE **5**

Youngsville

90

Cossinade

167

14

7 NEW IBERIA

Abbeville

Rip Van Winkle
Gardens

14

182

Jeanerette

Six Mile
Lake

Lake
Verret

73

AVERY
ISLAND **7**

Baldwin

82

Esther

90

White
Lake

Vermilion
Bay

West Coast
Blanche
Bay

Morgan City

Pecan
Island

Marsh
Island

Atchafalaya
Bay

0 kilometers   25

0 miles   25

N

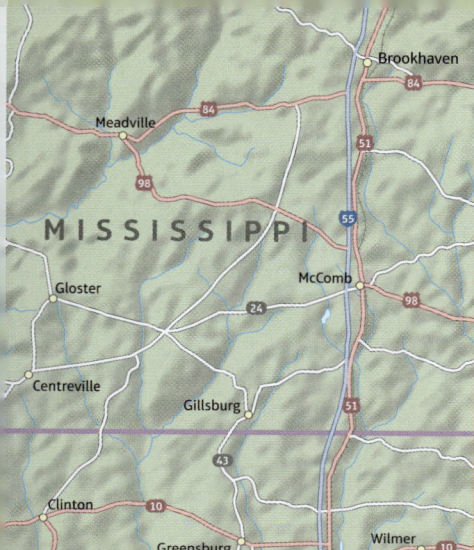

BEYOND NEW ORLEANS

Must Sees
1. River Road Plantations
2. Lafayette
3. Baton Rouge

Experience More
4. St. Francisville
5. St. Martinville
6. Jean Lafitte National Historical Park and Preserve
7. New Iberia and Avery Island
8. Opelousas
9. Eunice
10. Chalmette Battlefield

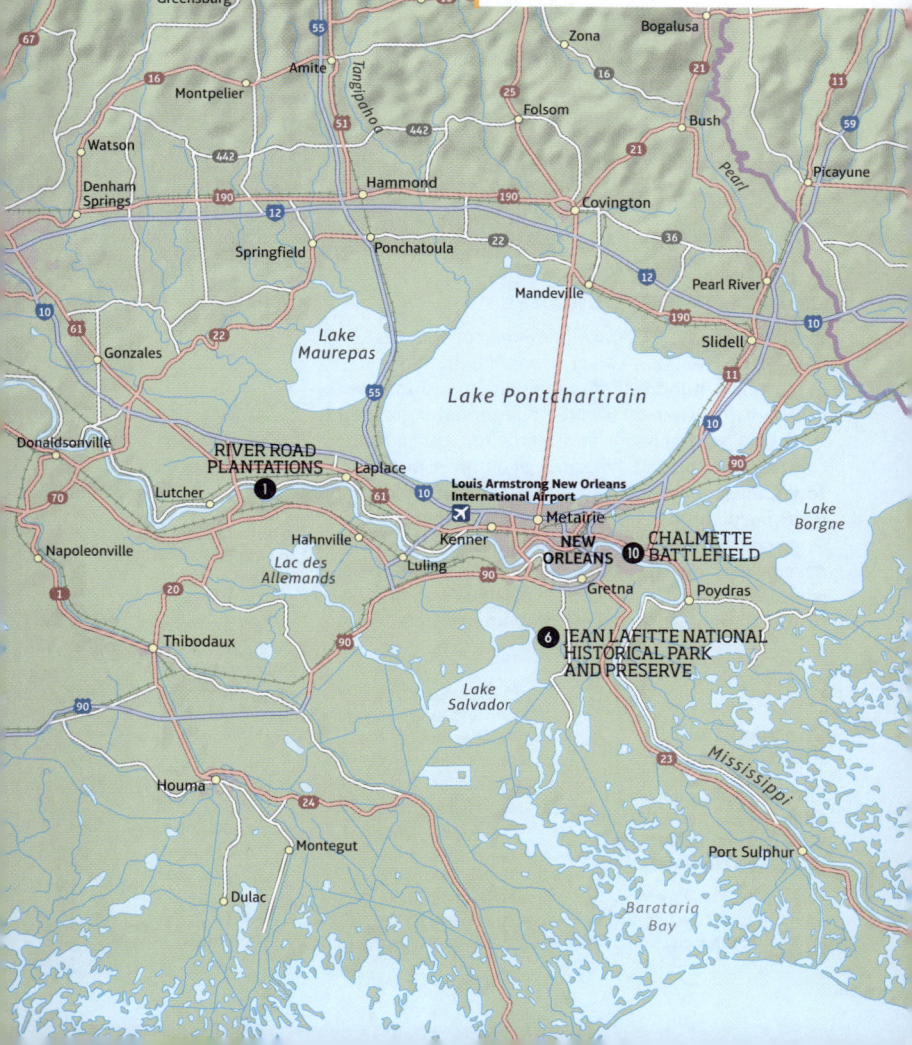

MISSISSIPPI

Brookhaven

Meadville

Gloster

McComb

Centreville

Gillsburg

Clinton

Greensburg

Wilmer

Zona

Bogalusa

Amite

Montpelier

Folsom

Bush

Watson

Picayune

Denham Springs

Hammond

Covington

Springfield

Ponchatoula

Mandeville

Pearl River

Slidell

Lake Maurepas

Lake Pontchartrain

Gonzales

Donaldsonville

RIVER ROAD PLANTATIONS

Laplace

Louis Armstrong New Orleans International Airport

Metairie

Lake Borgne

Lutcher

Napoleonville

Hahnville

Kenner

NEW ORLEANS

CHALMETTE BATTLEFIELD

Lac des Allemands

Luling

Gretna

Poydras

Thibodaux

JEAN LAFITTE NATIONAL HISTORICAL PARK AND PRESERVE

Lake Salvador

Houma

Montegut

Port Sulphur

Dulac

Barataria Bay

Tangipahoa

Pearl

Mississippi

EXPERIENCE Beyond New Orleans

❶

RIVER ROAD PLANTATIONS

⌂ 50 miles (80 km) NW of New Orleans

The River Road is a 70-mile (130-km) corridor that follows the Mississippi River towards Baton Rouge. In the 1850s, hundreds of antebellum mansions lined this stretch, owned by wealthy planters who profited from trading sugarcane, a cash crop processed by a captive labor force of thousands of enslaved people. Today, the road meanders past petrochemical plants and surviving plantation houses, a few still surrounded by living quarters and sugar mills. Some of these residences have been given a new lease on life as small museums, where visitors can learn about Louisiana's plantation history and the enslaved people who once lived here.

💬 INSIDER TIP
Plantation Tours

At the Whitney, the only plantation to focus mostly on the perspective of those enslaved, guided walking tours of the site offer a unique insight into plantation life. Tours last 90 minutes, and should be booked in advance.

① ⚐ Ⓜ
The Whitney Plantation

⌂ 5099 Louisiana Hwy 18, Edgard ⌚ 9:30am-4:30pm Wed-Mon (last adm: 3pm) 🌐 whitneyplantation.com

Located near Wallace in St. John the Baptist Parish, the Whitney Plantation Historic District stretches across some 2,000 acres (800 hectares) and is now an exceptional museum dedicated to those enslaved at the plantation. The original plantation dates back to 1752, though the main part of the house, built in a French-Creole raised style, was built in 1803. Curated by a Senegalese historian specializing in the history of the slave trade, the museum opened its doors in 2014 after 15 years of preparation.

Visitors can read the oral histories of some of the last survivors of slavery, recorded by the Federal Writers Project in the 1920s, and see Woodrow Nash's sculptures of these last survivors, who were children at the time of

→

Sculpture of a formerly enslaved young girl at the Whitney Plantation

↑ The tunnel of trees leading to Oak Alley plantation house

plantation. They were planted over 300 years ago, before the house was built by enslaved laborers for Creole planter Jacques Telesphore Roman III in 1837. Oak Alley was established as a sugarcane plantation, but pecans were also harvested here: Antoine, an enslaved gardener, developed the first commercial variety of pecan nut, the "Paper Shell," on the property.

There are exhibits on the process of sugar production and slavery, and visitors can wander the plantation's striking main house and grounds, which have been used as the location for several movies.

③ 🔲 🔲
Laura

🏠 2247 Hwy 18, Vacherie
🕐 10am–4pm daily
🚫 Public hols 🔲 laura plantation.com

Revolutionary War veteran Guillame Duparc was given a large land grant, and built this French Creole plantation house in 1805. After he died, four generations of women ran the sugar plantation.

Laura gained notoriety for the stories told by the French-speaking enslaved people, later tenant farmers, living there. Folklorist Alcée Fortier first translated these

Senegalese stories of central folk character Br'er Rabbit.

Guided tours of the main house and surviving outbuildings explore the history of the plantation; it is highly recommended that you book in advance. A permanent exhibition is dedicated to telling the story of the enslaved community who lived and worked at this Creole farm.

GRINDING SEASON

Processing sugarcane, the primary crop grown along the River Road, was a brutal endeavor. In the early 19th century, grinding season (from mid-October) saw enslaved workers toil around the clock to harvest the mature canes. The canes were ground in sugar mills, and the resulting pulp boiled in huge sugar kettles known as "Jamaica Trains." The labor was relentless and the conditions perilous – workers sustained machete wounds while harvesting in the dark and terrible burns while cooking the sugar over an open flame, and fatalities were common.

emancipation. There are poignant memorials listing names of the people enslaved here, and specially commissioned works of art. Original slave cabins and many of the outbuildings still survive.

② 🔲 🔲
Oak Alley

🏠 3645 Hwy 18, Vacherie
🕐 8:30am–5pm daily
🔲 oakalleyplantation.com

Oak Alley's name comes from the 28 live oaks that line the entrance to this former sugar

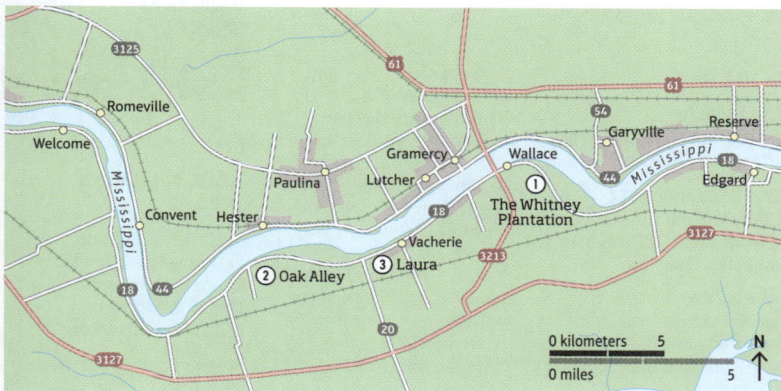

185

2

LAFAYETTE

🏛 135 miles (217 km) W of New Orleans ✈ 2 miles (3.2 km) SE 🚌 100 Lee Ave 🛈 1400 NW Evangeline Throughway; lafayettetravel.com

When the first Acadians arrived in this area, they settled along the bayous and in the prairies west of New Orleans. These rural people – whose name would eventually Anglicize from "les Cadiens" into "Cajuns" – worked as farmers and made a living from the swamps. Lafayette is now Cajun Country's largest city. Community centers, restaurants, several detailed reconstructions of Cajun villages, and a distinct local architectural style have imprinted this city with a truly unique atmosphere.

① ⟳ Ⓜ

Lafayette Museum/Alexandre Mouton House

🏛 1122 Lafayette St
🕐 10am–4pm Tue–Sat
🚫 Public hols 🖥 lafayette museum.com

Jean Mouton, founder of Lafayette, built the original house around 1800. He, his wife Marie, and their 12 children used it only on Sundays, when they came from their plantation in Carencro to attend church and socialize. In 1825, the sixth son, Alexandre, moved his family and law practice into the house. He later became a United States senator and governor of Louisiana. The house contains furnishings, paintings, maps, and documents relating to the city's history, plus some glittering Mardi Gras costumes and regalia.

THE ACADIANS

Driven by the British from Acadia in Nova Scotia, Canada, French-Canadian Acadians (or "Cajuns") settled in Louisiana from 1764. Disparaged for long, the Acadians have survived numerous threats to their Francophone culture. Today, their unique Cajun cuisine and music is highly acclaimed.

② ⟳ Ⓜ 🏛

LARC's Acadian Village

🏛 200 Greenleaf Dr
🕐 10am–4pm Mon–Sat
🚫 Jan 1, Thanksgiving, Dec 25, Mardi Gras
🖥 acadianvillage.org

At this version of a re-created 19th-century Cajun village,

Did You Know?

Today, Cajun Country is the largest French-speaking community in the United States.

←

Traditional Cajun buildings at the LARC's Acadian Village, a living history museum in Lafayette

most of the buildings are original, although they have been moved here from other locations. The houses are furnished with typical Cajun furniture and tools, and are tended by costumed guides who demonstrate a variety of traditional skills such as spinning, weaving, and blacksmithing.

③

Acadian Cultural Center

🏠 501 Fisher Rd
🕐 Hours vary, check website Ⓦ nps.gov/jela

The informative exhibits of photographs and artifacts here focus on Acadian culture, including language, music, architecture, religion, cuisine, the Cajun Mardi Gras, and handicrafts. A film dramatizes the British deportation of the Acadian population from Canada, charting their diaspora to France and to places along the east coast of North America, before their final arrival in Louisiana.

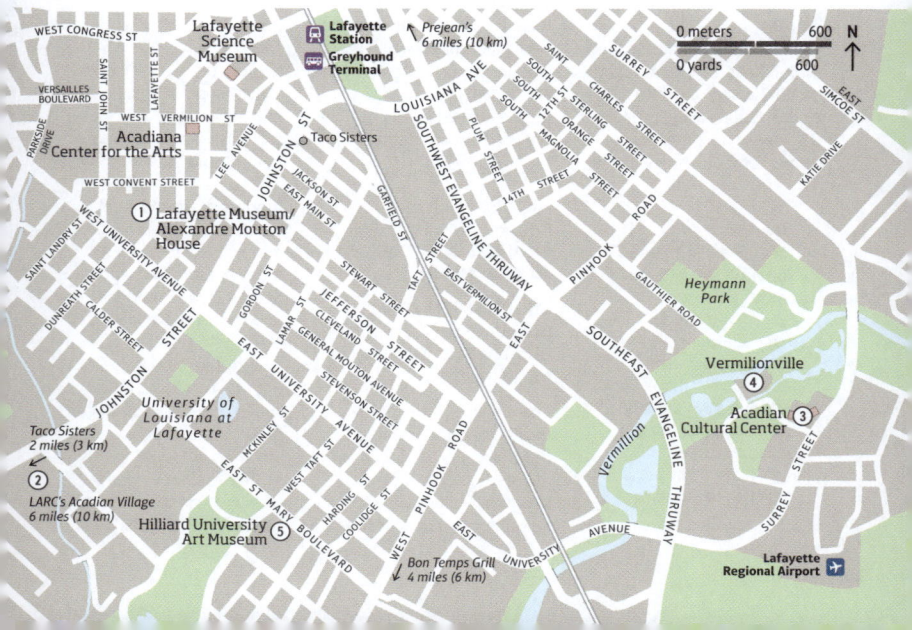

↑ A craftsperson using a wheel to spin cotton at Vermilionville, a living re-creation of Cajun life

④ 🖼 🖼 🍴 🛍

Vermilionville

🏠 300 Fisher Rd 🕐 10am–4pm Tue–Sun (last adm 3pm) 🚫 Public hols 🌐 bayouvermiliondistrict.org/vermilionville

This fascinating living-history museum features a collection of buildings dating from 1790 to 1890 assembled into a typical Cajun village over 23 acres (9 hectares). Its name, Vermilionville, was the original name for the city of Lafayette. Costumed artisans demonstrate the skills that were needed to survive in 18th- and 19th-century Louisiana: woodworking, blacksmithing, spinning, weaving, and cooking. Wandering from building to building, visitors can imagine what traditional Cajun life was like. A performance hall, where Cajun bands regularly entertain, is open in the afternoon.

💬 INSIDER TIP
Special Sausage

You can't leave Cajun Country without tasting the *boudin,* a regional specialty sausage made from pork blood and rice. Look out for tasty variations like deep-fried *boudin* balls, or different fillings, from shrimp and crawfish to alligator.

⑤ 🖼

Hilliard University Art Museum

🏠 710 E St. Mary Blvd 🕐 10am–5pm Tue–Sat 🚫 Public hols 🌐 hilliardmuseum.org

This small art museum is located on the campus of the University of Louisiana at Lafayette. The museum was founded in 1968 and has a permanent collection of more than 2,000 works including paintings, sculpture, folk art, and textiles. The emphasis is on the cultural heritage of Louisiana. The museum is housed in a modern glass and steel building with state-of-the-art exhibition spaces. Its many outstanding works of art include European and American art from the 18th, 19th, and 20th centuries, 2nd century BCE Egyptian artifacts, and a superb collection of African American folk art. Diverse architectural drawings, as well as student works, are displayed along with temporary exhibits all year long.

EAT

Bon Temps Grill

Meat is cooked on a mesquite wood grill at this elevated "swamp edge" Cajun and Creole neighborhood diner.

🏠 1211 W Pinhook Rd
🌐 bontempsgrill.com

$$$ (one dimmed)

Taco Sisters

Sample zesty fresh fish and sumptuous brisket tacos at the outdoor picnic tables beside this trendy food stand.

🏠 3902 Johnston St
🌐 tacosisters.com

$$$ (two dimmed)

Prejean's

A Lafayette institution since 1980, this award-winning restaurant serves Cajun classics including crawfish étouffée.

🏠 3480 NE Evangeline Throughway
🌐 prejeans.com

$$$ (one dimmed)

MUSIC IN CAJUN COUNTRY

Cajuns have a strong musical tradition, rooted in the folk music that the French-Canadian settlers brought with them in the 19th century. Cajun music's catchy dance numbers and soulful ballads are closely related to Zydeco music, which you'll also hear a lot of in Louisiana.

CAJUN MUSIC

As the Acadians traveled to the South they brought what musical instruments they could carry, and kept their folk music alive. Down in Louisiana, they were influenced by Jamaican and Haitian sounds, and European accordion music. Styles of Cajun music range from traditional (with lively accordion, fiddle, and triangle playing), through Texas swing (with piano and swung rhythms), to contemporary (rock and R&B influenced), but all forms of Cajun music are catchy and up-tempo.

ZYDECO MUSIC

Zydeco shares many elements with Cajun music, but is known as the music of Louisiana Creoles. Zydeco combines traditional R&B, blues, jazz, gospel, and Cajun dance music, and features call and response patterns from African folk music. Fast-tempo Zydeco dance pieces incorporate the accordion, guitar, drums and fiddle, along with the *vest froittoir* or Zydeco rubboard – a percussion instrument made from corrugated steel.

↑ Dancing the Cajun two-step

→ Accordion player Anthony Dopsie performing

CAJUN DANCE PARTIES

At traditional Cajun dance parties, or *fais do-dos*, dancehall Cajun music is performed to accompany two-step, the Cajun Jitterbug and the waltz (three-step). Roughly translating as "go to sleep," the phrase *fais do-do* would have been said to children who would sleep while their parents danced the night away.

↑ Zydeco musician Geno Delafose entertaining dancers in Breaux Bridge

3

BATON ROUGE

🚗 90 miles (144 km) NW of New Orleans ✈ 9430 Jackie
Cochran Dr 🚌 Greyhound Bus Lines, 1001 Loyola Ave
ℹ 359 3rd St; visitbatonrouge.com

In 1721 the French established Baton Rouge as a fort
designed to control access to the Mississippi and the
interior. In 1763 they ceded it to the British. Then,
during the American Revolution, the Spanish seized
the garrison, which remained under their control until
1810, when the local American population proclaimed
it the Republic of West Florida. The area was incorporated into the Union in 1817 as part of Louisiana, and
has been the state capital since 1849.

①

Louisiana State University (LSU)

🚗 Nicholson Dr between
Highland Rd and
W Chimes St 🌐 lsu.edu

With its 41,000 students,
LSU is the state's flagship
university. The campus is
attractively landscaped and
has some unique features.
In the northwest corner, for
example, two mounds rise
some 20 ft (6 m) high.
Archaeologists believe that
they are 5,000-year-old
Indigenous ceremonial
mounds, the oldest in the
country, built even before
the first Egyptian pyramids.

There are two cutting-edge
research facilities on site:
the Pennington Biomedical
Research Center, devoted to
nutritional medicine; and the
Center for Microstructures and
Devices. The collection at the
Museum of Natural Science
in Foster Hall is also worth
seeing. The visitor information
center is at Dalrymple Drive
and Highland Road.

Louisiana State's sports
team games are some of
the hottest tickets in college
sports. In baseball, the Tigers
are consistently a force to
be reckoned with, and the
enthusiasm generated by
the football team is legendary.

②

Old Governor's Mansion

🚗 502 North Blvd
🕐 9am–4pm Mon–Fri
(tours hourly) 🚫 Public
hols 🌐 laogm.org

Louisiana Governor Huey
Long had this mansion built
in 1930. He modeled it on the
White House, even down to
the office, which is a smaller
version of the Oval Office.
The building has been
carefully restored, and the

DRINK

Hayride Scandal
This classy cocktail joint
has the air of a seasoned
speakeasy, with plush
decor and a well-
stocked bar. Stop
by to sip whiskey and
bourbon craft cocktails
and enjoy a taste of
Southern hospitality.

🚗 5110 Corporate
Blvd 🌐 hayride
scandal.com

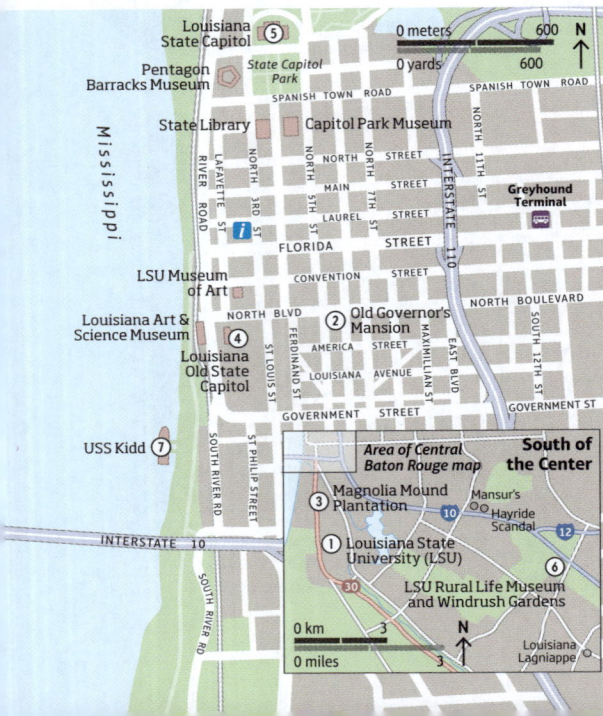

Louisiana
State Capitol ⑤

Pentagon
Barracks Museum

State Capitol
Park

State Library

Capitol Park Museum

SPANISH TOWN ROAD

0 meters   600
0 yards   600
N

Mississippi

NORTH STREET

LSU Museum
of Art

Louisiana Art &
Science Museum

Louisiana
Old State
Capitol ④

USS Kidd ⑦

Old Governor's
Mansion ②

NORTH BLVD

SOUTH BOULEVARD

GOVERNMENT ST

Greyhound
Terminal

**South of
the Center**

Area of Central
Baton Rouge map

Magnolia Mound ③
Plantation

Mansur's

Hayride
Scandal

① Louisiana State
University (LSU)

LSU Rural Life Museum ⑥
and Windrush Gardens

Louisiana
Lagniappe

0 km   3
0 miles 3

INTERSTATE 10

The winding staircase of the Old State Capitol's rotunda, and *(inset)* its fortress-like exterior

rooms have even been repainted in their original colors, some of which are outlandish; Huey Long apparently loved hot pinks, purples, and greens, which appear in several bathrooms. Many of the furnishings in the library and the master bedroom are original to the house. There is also memorabilia from other governors, including the singing governor Jimmie Davis, who wrote the famous song *You Are my Sunshine*.

③ ♦ ⚡ 📷

Magnolia Mound Plantation

📍 2161 Nicholson Dr
🕐 10am–4pm Mon–Sat, 1–4pm Sun 🗓 Public hols
🌐 brec.org/facility/ magnoliamound

John Joyce had this plantation home built in 1791. In the 19th century, it stood at the center of a 900-acre (360-hectare) farm, where crops, including tobacco and sugarcane, were cultivated by enslaved workers until the 1860s. Purchased by the City of Baton Rouge in 1966, the building has been restored to reflect the ante-

bellum era. The main house holds a small museum, and visitors can explore the former slave quarters and open-hearth kitchen.

④ 📷 📷

Louisiana Old State Capitol

📍 100 North Blvd 🕐 10am–4pm Tue–Fri, 9am–3pm Sat
🗓 Public hols 🌐 louisiana oldstatecapitol.org

James Harrison Dakin designed this striking castle-like building in 1847. William Freret conceived the soaring

iron spiral staircase, installed during a renovation in 1882, which winds from the foyer toward the stained-glass dome. In 1861 it was here, in the House Chamber, that Louisiana's state representatives voted to secede from the Union. Seven decades later, in 1929, impeachment proceedings were begun here against Huey "Kingfish" Long. Today, this magnificent building serves as the state's Museum of Political History. Visitors can see the "The Ghost of the Castle" show, an immersive 4D experience featuring the resident ghost from the Civil War era, Sarah Morgan.

> **In 1861 it was here, in the Old State Capitol's House Chamber, that Louisiana's state representatives voted to secede from the Union.**

HIDDEN GEM
Highland Park Road Observatory

On the southern edge of Baton Rouge, just a 20-minute drive from the city center, this lovely observatory (run by LSU) hosts scientific lectures and sky viewings (bro.lsu.edu).

⑤ 🏛 Ⓜ 🏬

Louisiana State Capitol

🏛 State Capitol Dr at 900 N 3rd St ⏰ 8am–4:30pm daily 📅 Jan 1, Easter Sunday, Thanksgiving, Dec 24 & 25 🌐 crt.state.la.us/tourism/welcome-centers/state-capitol

The 40th Louisiana governor, Huey Long, worked hard to persuade legislators to approve the $5 million funding for this Modernist 34-story building, erected in 1932. It is the tallest capitol in the United States. Both the House and Senate chambers are impressive, as are the murals in Memorial Hall.

Still visible are the bullet holes in the marble walls of the first-floor executive corridor, where Long was assassinated on September 8, 1935, by Dr. Carl A. Weiss, the son-in-law of a political enemy, Judge Benjamin Pavy. The grounds of the Capitol are home to Long's grave in a sunken memorial garden, presided over by a statue of the governor.

Visitors can enjoy excellent views of the Mississippi river and the city from the Capitol's 27th-floor observation deck.

⑥ 🏛 🏬

LSU Rural Life Museum and Windrush Gardens

🏛 4560 Essen Lane at I-10 ⏰ 8am–5pm daily 📅 Jan 1, Easter Sunday, Thanksgiving, Dec 24 & 25 🌐 lsu.edu/rurallife

Ione Burden and her brother, Steele, who landscaped Louisiana State University, assembled this collection of buildings and 19th-century tools and artifacts. Each building is filled with fascinating objects, including a washing machine dating from 1900, pirogues (a type of boat used on the bayous), and a tobacco press. Steele Burden's paintings and ceramic figures are also displayed. Steele also rescued all the buildings from nearby Welham Plantation and re-erected them in a typical plantation layout. Here, exhibits and restored plantation buildings provide an insight into how such a plantation functioned as a self-contained community.

⑦ 🏛 Ⓜ 🏬

USS Kidd

🏛 305 S River Rd ⏰ 9:30am–3:30pm daily 📅 Thanksgiving, Dec 25 🌐 usskidd.com

Commissioned in 1943, this World War II destroyer saw action in the Pacific, where it suffered a kamikaze attack by Japanese forces on April 11, 1945, and 38 members of the crew were killed. The ship was also deployed in the Korean War and other missions until 1964, when it was decommissioned. Guided tours explore the cramped quarters shared by the 330-man crew below decks, and visitors can view the anti-aircraft guns and other military paraphernalia. There is even the option for small parties to stay the night and camp on board the ship.

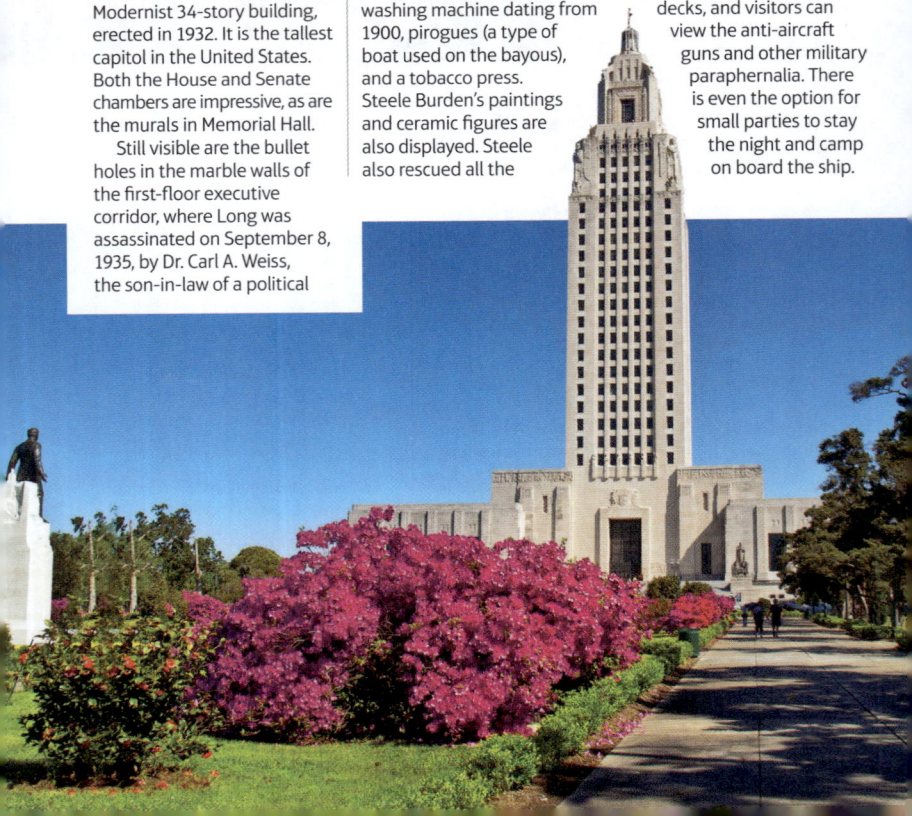

EAT

Mansur's

At this sophisticated restaurant, one of the city's upscale options for Creole dining, seafood features heavily on the menu. The shrimp and grits dish is an exercise in decadence.

🅟 5720 Corporate Blvd A
Ⓦ mansursonthe boulevard.com

$$$

Louisiana Lagniappe

The seafood specialists here vow to serve only the freshest crawfish, crab, and oysters. A house favorite is the gulf fish with shrimp and crab, served *en papillote* (wrapped in paper).

🅟 9990 Perkins Rd
Ⓦ louisianalagniappe restaurant.com

$$$

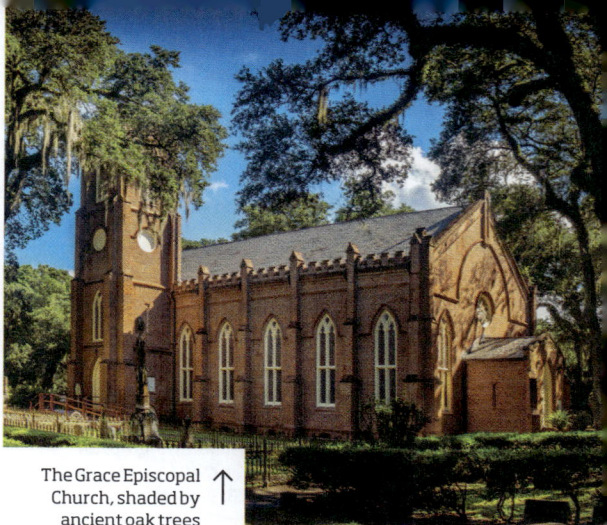

The Grace Episcopal Church, shaded by ancient oak trees ↑

← The towering Louisiana State Capitol, the seat of the state's government

EXPERIENCE MORE

④

St. Francisville

🅟 112 miles (180 km) NW of New Orleans ℹ West Feliciana Tourist Office, 11757 Ferdinand St; visit stfrancisvillela.com

Dating back to 1809, the secluded St. Francisville has long been known as "the town two miles long and two yards wide," due to its location on a narrow ridge overlooking the Mississippi. In the early 19th century, it was an important port and briefly served as the capital of the Republic of West Florida. Today, the town has a population of less than 2,000, but many buildings put up during its heyday survive. The historic downtown has several 19th-century churches, the oldest of which is the **Grace Episcopal Church** (1827). The **West Feliciana Historical Society & Museum** is likewise housed in a 19th-century building and covers the cultural and architectural history of the area. Minutes away, **Audubon State Historic Site** was where famous ornithologist John James Audubon spent much of his time (p156). Explore the great outdoors at the **Cat Island National Wildlife Refuge**, host to many species in its wetland habitats, or hike and camp in the vast forests of **Tunica Hills**.

Grace Episcopal Church

🅟 11621 Ferdinand St
Ⓦ gracechurchwfp.org

West Feliciana Historical Society & Museum

🕐 🅟 11757 Ferdinand St
🕘 9am–5pm daily Ⓦ west felicianamuseum.org

Audubon State Historic Site

♿ 🅟 11788 Hwy-965
🕘 9am–5pm daily 🗓 Jan 1, Thanksgiving & Dec 25
Ⓦ lastateparks.com/historic-sites/audubon-state-historic-site

Cat Island National Wildlife Refuge

🅟 Creek Rd 🕘 Seasonally
ℹ West Feliciana Tourist Office; 11757 Ferdinand St; fws.gov/refuge/cat_island

Tunica Hills

🅟 Hwy-66, St. Francisville
Ⓦ wlf.louisiana.gov/page/tunica-hills

5

St. Martinville

⌂ **138 miles (222 km) NW of New Orleans**
ⓦ **stmartinville.org**

This small town on a natural levee of the Bayou Teche was founded in 1765 as a military outpost. It became known as "Petit Paris" after many French noblemen settled here having fled the French Revolution. In the main square, the **Acadian Memorial** houses *The Arrival of the Acadians in Louisiana*, a mural by Robert Dafford, who modeled some of the portraits on contemporary descendants. Opposite the painting, the Wall of Names lists some 3,000 Acadians deported from Canada by the British in the 1750s. Behind the memorial, an eternal flame burns in a courtyard garden above Bayou Teche. The building next door houses two small museums: the **Museum of the Acadian Memorial** charts Acadian history in southern Louisiana, while the **African American Museum** commemorates Black history in the state from the early 1700s.

Nearby, the Evangeline Oak marks the spot where the two famous Acadian lovers, Gabriel and Evangeline, of poet Henry Wadsworth Longfellow's epic *Evangeline, A Tale of Acadie*, supposedly met.

Established in 1765 by French missionaries, **St. Martin de Tours Church** was the first church to serve the Acadian community. The grave of Evangeline Labiche (mythologized in Longfellow's *Evangeline*) and a bronze statue of her are located in the garden. Stretched along Bayou Teche, the **Longfellow-Evangeline State Historic Site** offers picnicking and walking trails among 300-year-

→

Observation platform on Avery Island giving a view of snowy rows of nesting egrets

old oaks. At the center of the park stands the Maison Olivier, a plantation house from the 1810s, a classic example of a raised Creole cottage. There's also a reconstruction of Acadian Farmstead.

A 15-minute drive from St. Martinville is Lake Martin, set between Lafayette and Breaux Bridge, where the **Cypress Island Nature Preserve** is a stunning example of Louisiana swampland.

Museum of the Acadian Memorial

♿ ⌂ 121 S New Market St
🕐 10am–4:30pm Tue-Sat, noon–4pm Sun ⊘ Public hols
ⓦ acadianmemorial.org

African American Museum

♿ ⌂ 125 S New Market St
🕐 10am–4:30pm Tue-Sat, noon–4pm Sun ☎ (337) 394-2250

St. Martin de Tours Church

⌂ 133 S Main St 🕐 8am–6pm daily ⓦ stmartindetours.org

Longfellow-Evangeline State Historic Site

♿ ⌂ 1200 N Main St
☎ (337) 394-3754
🕐 9am–5pm daily ⊘ Jan 1, Thanksgiving & Dec 25

💬 INSIDER TIP
Completely Swamped

Visit Louisiana's stunning swamps on a guided boat tour – Jean Lafitte Swamp Tours (*jeanlafitte swamptour.com*) and Bayou Swamp Tours (*bayouswamp tours.com*) are some of the best, with pickups from New Orleans city.

Cypress Island Nature Preserve

⌂ 1264 Prairie Hwy, St. Martinville ⓦ nature.org

6

Jean Lafitte National Historical Park and Preserve

⌂ 6588 Barataria Blvd, Marrero 🕐 9:30am–4:30pm Wed-Sun (trails open daily)
ⓦ nps.gov/jela

In the early 19th century, legend has it that the pirate Jean Lafitte used the lands around here to hide treasure. Whatever the truth may be, this national historic park, found just

25 miles (40 km) south of New Orleans, is well worth hunting down. The Marrero section of the park opened in 1978, incorporating the existing Barataria Preserve into the network of sites. The park has a total of six sites across the state, but this one covers about 26,000 acres (10,500 hectares) of bayous, forests, and swamps. The nature trails offer the chance to see local wildlife, from alligators and beaver-like nutria to over 200 bird species. There's a visitor's center with exhibits on the ecological significance of the wetlands and their impact on Louisiana culture.

7

New Iberia and Avery Island

⌂ 133 miles (214 km) W of New Orleans 🚍 1103 E Main St 🚃 2513 Hwy 14; iberiatravel.com

New Iberia is notable for its sugarcane plantations. The area also owes its wealth to salt mining. In fact, the "islands" here, such as Avery and Jefferson, are domes sitting atop salt mines.

At the plantation home known as **Shadows-on-the-Teche**, a cache of more than

720

Drops of Tabasco® hot sauce fill each bottle of Avery Island's classic spicy condiment.

17,000 letters, photographs, receipts, and papers relating to the plantation owners and enslaved workers that lived here was found. This is used as background for the tour of the house. The **Tabasco Brand Factory Tour & Museum** on Avery Island is the source of the famous condiment, an essential ingredient in Bloody Marys and in local cuisine. Some 75 acres (30 hectares) of pepper plants blaze red here from August to November, and visitors can tour the factory.

The founder considered himself a botanist-naturalist and the Jungle Gardens that he assembled are spectacular. In addition to abundant plant life, the gardens shelter a diverse population of egrets, herons, and peacocks, as well as nutria. Wildfowl stop here in winter. The **Rip Van Winkle Gardens** are located on the Jefferson

Island salt dome. It was built by actor Joseph Jefferson in 1870 and named after the role he played 4,500 times. An architectural hodgepodge of Moorish, Steamboat Gothic, and Victorian, the Joseph Jefferson Mansion is surrounded by beautiful gardens, which are on the banks of Lake Peigneur.

After Joseph Jefferson died in 1905, J. Lyle Bayless of the Salt Island Mining Company purchased the house. Shortly afterward, oil was discovered on the property. It was soon producing up to 250,000 barrels of oil a week from 30 wells. Keep an eye out for a Buddha statue and shrine, which is a focal point for visitors and is used as an active worship site by local Buddhists.

Shadows-on-the-Teche
♿ ⌂ 320 E Main St, New Iberia ⌚ 10am–4pm Thu–Sat 🚫 Public hols 🌐 shadows ontheteche.org

Tabasco Brand Factory Tour & Museum
♿ 🅿 🚻 🍴 ⌂ Hwy 329, Avery Island ⌚ Factory: 9am–4pm daily; gardens: 9am–5pm daily 🚫 Public hols 🌐 tabasco.com

Rip Van Winkle Gardens
♿ 🅿 🚻 🍴 ⌂ 5505 Rip Van Winkle Rd, Jefferson Island ⌚ 9am–5pm daily 🚫 Public hols 🌐 ripvanwinkle gardens.com

Moss-wreathed cypresses on Lake Martin, St. Martinsville

EAT

Soileau's Dinner Club
This second-generation Cajun restaurant is famed for its oysters and shrimp. Try the crawfish if they're in season, and the gumbo any time.

⌂ 1618 N Main St, Opelousas
🌐 soileaus.com

💲💲💲

The St. John Restaurant

This unassuming wooden building houses an inventive kitchen that prides itself on its Cajun classics, such as frog's legs, fried alligator, and sautéed crab fingers.

⌂ 203 N New Market St, St. Martinville 🌐 thestjohnrestaurant.com

💲💲💲

8

Opelousas

⌂ 138 miles (222 km) NW of New Orleans 🚌 Greyhound Bus Lines, 1001 Loyola Ave 🛈 828 E Landry St; cityof opelousas.com

The capital of Confederate Louisiana during the Civil War, and the state's third-oldest city, Opelousas was named after the Indigenous community that lived in this area before the Europeans arrived. The current city was founded as a French trading post during the 1700s, and is now one of the liveliest towns in this district, thanks to its cuisine and music.

Opelousas is the ideal place to explore on foot, with clusters of antebellum, Victorian,

↑ Trees lining Court Street in the center of the historic old town of Opelousas

and early-20th-century buildings spread around town. The major collections of the **Opelousas Museum and Interpretive Center** focus on local culture and history. The museum's two main exhibit areas are devoted to the prehistory of the area, its agricultural and commercial development, and the people of different races and religions who have contributed to the region's culture. One room contains Civil War memorabilia, while another houses a collection of more than 400 dolls. The museum also holds the Louisiana Video Library and the archives of the Southwest Louisiana Zydeco Festival.

A slice of Opelousas life is on view at **Le Vieux Village**, a historical park and museum with a collection of buildings from the 1700s, including a church, a schoolhouse, and a doctor's office, that offers visitors an opportunity to appreciate the historic local architecture. A tourist information center is also located here, as well as a small museum devoted to Jim Bowie, who was one of the Alamo defenders and the namesake of the well-known frontier knife.

Just around the corner from the tourist center, visitors can explore a little-known part of history at the **Louisiana Orphan Train Museum**. This small museum is dedicated to preserving the personal belongings saved by orphans sent from New York to Louisiana as part of the

Orphan Train movement. This relocation program saw over 2,000 trains arrive in Louisiana between 1873 and 1929. The exhibits showcase a variety of original documents, clothing, and images, and many of the volunteers are descendants of orphans who arrived on these trains. A short documentary offers an introductory overview of the orphan trains.

To the west of the town is the **Creole Heritage Folklife Center** run by local folklorist Rebecca Henry. It explores local Creole culture through traditional uses of herbs, folk medicine, and work tools, and displays on home life and folk art. Note, tours need to be booked in advance.

Opelousas Museum and Interpretive Center
♿ ⌂ 315 N Main St 📞 (337) 948-2589 ⏰ 8am–4:30pm Mon–Fri 🚫 Public hols

Le Vieux Village
♿ ⌂ 28 E Landry St 📞 (337) 948-6263 ⏰ 10am–2pm Tue–Fri 🚫 Public hols

Louisiana Orphan Train Museum
⌂ 223 S Academy St ⏰ 10am–3pm Tue–Fri, by appt Sat 🌐 laorphantrainmuseum.com

Creole Heritage Folklife Center
♿ ⌂ 1113 W Vine St ⏰ Noon–4pm Tue–Fri, 1–4pm Sat 🌐 cajun travel.com/things/creole-heritage-folklife-center

9
Eunice

🏠 158 miles (254 km) NW of New Orleans ℹ️ 200 South CC Duson Dr; eunice-la.com

Every weekend is a celebration of Cajun music in this Louisiana town, founded in 1893 by C. C. Duson, who named it in honor of his wife. The **Liberty Theater** is the Grand Ole Opry of Cajun music, open since the 1920s. Every Saturday from 6pm to 8pm, it hosts a live broadcast of the *Rendez-Vous des Cajuns* radio show, filled with Cajun and Zydeco music *(p189)* and good Cajun humor. Located nearby, the **Cajun Music Hall of Fame and Museum** honors the originators of Cajun music and the artists who have kept the tradition alive *(p189)*. It displays memorabilia, photos, instruments, and biographies of the 80 or so inductees. These include early legends such as Amédé Ardoin, Alphé Bergeron, Dennis McGee, Joe Falcon, Amédé Breaux, Iry Lejeune, and Lawrence Walker, and more recent stars, such as Michael Doucet, Zachary Richard, and Wayne Toups. On the way from Eunice to

Opelousas along Highway 190, the **Savoy Music Center** is owned by accordion-maker and musician Marc Savoy and his wife, Ann. It sells musical instruments, records, and books on Cajun culture and music. On Saturday mornings, local musicians assemble in the front of the store for a jam session around the upright piano.

Liberty Theater

♿ 🏠 200 Park Ave 🕐 For renovation 🌐 eunice libertycenter.org

Cajun Music Hall of Fame and Museum

🏠 240 South CC Duson Dr
📞 (337) 457-6534
🕐 Summer: 9am–5pm Wed-Sat; winter: 8:30am–4:30pm Wed-Sat 🚫 Public hols

Savoy Music Center

🏠 4413 Hwy 190 East, Savoy
📞 (337) 457-9563 🕐 1:30–4pm Wed-Fri, 9am–noon Sat
🚫 Public hols

> Other displays highlight aspects of Acadian culture, including the *Courir*. Literally "to run," this is the Cajun, and distinctly medieval, version of Mardi Gras.

10
Chalmette Battlefield

🏠 1 Battlefield Rd, Chalmette 🚢 Creole Queen 🕐 9am–4:30pm daily 🚫 Public hols
🌐 nps.gov/jela

Part of the Jean Lafitte National Historical Park and Preserve, located just down the Mississippi from the city, this was the site of Andrew Jackson's famous victory at the Battle of New Orleans in 1815. Today it includes the 100 ft- (30 m-) high Chalmette Monument, a reconstructed American rampart, and the visitor center. Here, films and exhibits add context about the largely forgotten War of 1812 between the U.S. and Great Britain. Nearby, the Chalmette National Cemetery holds over 14,000 graves of soldiers from the War of 1812 up to the Vietnam War.

↑ Musicians at the grave site of legendary Cajun fiddler Dennis McGee

NEED TO KNOW

BEFORE
YOU GO

Things change, so plan ahead to make the most of your trip. Be prepared for all eventualities by considering the following points before you travel.

AT A GLANCE

CURRENCY
Dollar (USD)

AVERAGE DAILY SPEND

SAVE	SPEND	SPLURGE
$100	$250	$400

BOTTLED WATER	COFFEE	BEER	DINNER FOR TWO
$2.00	$3.50	$6.00	$75

CLIMATE

Hours of sunshine average around 8.5 in summer and 6 in winter.

Temperatures average 82°F (28°C) in summer and 36°F (13°C) in winter.

June has the heaviest rainfall. Hurricane season is from June to November.

ELECTRICITY SUPPLY

The standard U.S. electric current is 110 volts and 60 Hz. Power sockets are type A and B, fitting plugs with two flat pins.

Passports and Visas

For entry requirements, including visas, consult your nearest U.S. embassy or check the **U.S. Department of State** website. Canadian visitors require a valid passport to enter the U.S. Citizens of Australia, New Zealand, the UK, and the EU do not need a visa, but must apply in advance for the Electronic System for Travel Authorization **(ESTA)** and have a valid passport to enter. All other visitors will need a passport and tourist visa to enter, and will be photographed and have their fingerprints checked. A return airline ticket is required to enter the U.S. Be sure to allow plenty of time for the U.S. border agency's thorough passport and visa checks at the airport.
ESTA
w esta.cbp.dhs.gov/esta
U.S. Department of State
w travel.state.gov

Government Advice

Now more than ever, it is important to consult both your and the U.S. government's advice before travelling. The U.S. Department of State, the **UK Foreign, Commonwealth & Development Office (FCDO)**, and the **Australian Department of Foreign Affairs and Trade** offer the latest information on security, health, and local regulations. The **National Hurricane Center** has a useful page for hurricane information and safety precautions.
Australian Department of Foreign Affairs and Trade
w smartraveller.gov.au
National Hurricane Center
w nhc.noaa.gov
UK Foreign, Commonwealth & Development Office (FCDO)
w gov.uk/foreign-travel-advice

Customs Information

You can find information on laws relating to goods and currency taken in or out of the U.S. on the **Customs and Border Protection Agency** website.
Customs and Border Protection Agency
w cbp.gov/travel

Insurance

We recommend that you buy a comprehensive insurance policy, covering theft, loss of belongings, medical care, cancellations, and delays, and read the small print carefully. There is no universal healthcare in the U.S. for citizens or visitors and healthcare is very expensive, so it is particularly important to take out comprehensive medical insurance.

Vaccinations

No inoculations are required to visit New Orleans.

Money

Most establishments accept major credit, debit, and prepaid currency cards. Contactless payments are becoming increasingly common, but cash is usually required by smaller shops and businesses, street vendors, and on buses. ATMs are available at most banks and street corners.

Tipping is customary in the U.S. In restaurants it is normal to tip 15–20 per cent of the total bill. Allow for a tip of 15 per cent for taxi drivers and bar staff. Hotel porters and housekeeping expect $1–$2 per bag or day.

Booking Accommodations

New Orleans offers a good choice of accommodations. The city's top hotels can be expensive, but there are also many budget and mid-priced hotels, family-run B&Bs, and hostels. Hotels are busiest mid-week when business travelers are in the city, and during major festivals such as Mardi Gras. Rates are subject to an additional 15–17 per cent room tax, plus a $1-2 room fee per night.

Travelers with Specific Requirements

Ramps, elevators, and special parking spaces can be found around the city. However, few of the historic buildings have these facilities, nor do most restaurants and bars. Always check mobility restrictions before visiting. Outside of the French Quarter and downtown areas, sidewalks may be in a state of disrepair and not suitable for wheelchairs. On public transport, both the Canal and Riverfront streetcar routes and all RTA buses have wheelchair ramps.

The **Disability Rights Louisiana** provides advice and services for people with specific requirements in the state of Louisiana.
Disability Rights Louisiana
🅦 disabilityrightsla.org

Language

Louisiana's rich cultural heritage means that a variety of languages are spoken in New Orleans. French, Spanish, Cajun, Creole, German, and Indigenous words have also been mixed together into a New Orleans patois (p220).

Opening Hours

> Situations can change quickly and unexpectedly. Always check before visiting attractions and hospitality venues for up-to-date opening hours and booking requirements.

Mondays and Tuesdays Museums and many restaurants close.
Sundays Most banks and smaller businesses close for the day.
Federal and State Holidays Museums, attractions, and many businesses close.

FEDERAL HOLIDAYS

Jan 1	New Year's Day
3rd Mon in Jan	Martin Luther King, Jr. Day
3rd Mon in Feb	President's Day
Last Mon in May	Memorial Day
Jun 19	Juneteenth
July 4	Independence Day
Sep 2	Labor Day
4th Thu in Nov	Thanksgiving Day
Dec 25	Christmas Day

GETTING AROUND

Whether exploring New Orleans on foot or by public transportation, here is all you'll need to navigate the city like a pro.

AT A GLANCE

PUBLIC TRANSPORT COSTS

SINGLE BUS OR STREETCAR JOURNEY

$1.25

(plus 25 cents to transfer)

ONE DAY JAZZY PASS

$3

Unlimited bus and streetcar journeys

SEVEN DAY JAZZY PASS

$15

Unlimited bus and streetcar journeys

SPEED LIMIT

RURAL FREEWAYS

70 mph
113 km/h

URBAN FREEWAYS

60 mph
(96 km/h)

URBAN AREAS

30 mph
(48 km/h)

NEIGHBORHOOD SLOW ZONE

20 mph
(32 km/h)

Arriving by Air

Located about 15 miles (24 km) from downtown New Orleans, the **Louis Armstrong International Airport** is the city's main airport. All the major U.S. airlines, including American Airlines, Southwest Airlines, United Airlines, and Delta Air Lines, have scheduled services to Louis Armstrong International Airport. Most of them also service international flights, but these will usually entail a connection at another U.S. airport en route. Air Canada offers scheduled flights direct from Toronto to New Orleans. British Airways has a direct route from London Heathrow.
Louis Armstrong International Airport
w flymsy.com

Domestic Train Travel

Amtrak, the U.S. passenger rail service, offers routes to New Orleans from a number of cities across the country. Visitors traveling to New Orleans by train arrive at Amtrak's Union Passenger Terminal on Loyola Avenue, at the edge of the Central Business District (CBD), near the Superdome. All long-distance Amtrak trains have a full complement of refreshment facilities and sleeping accommodations. At peak times, passengers are advised to reserve seats in advance on many services. Amtrak offers a range of special deals and packages, including 5-, 15-, and 30-day passes that allow unlimited travel. Note that these are available only for international travelers.
Amtrak
w amtrak.com

Long-Distance Bus Travel

Long-distance coach services are operated by **Greyhound Bus Lines** and arrive at Union Passenger Terminal. This terminal, which is shared with Amtrak, provides full baggage, ticketing, and package express services throughout the day and into the early hours of the morning. Greyhound buses are modern, clean, and safe. Some services are express, with few stops

GETTING TO AND FROM THE AIRPORT

Airport	Transport	Price	Journey time
Louis Armstrong International Airport	Taxi	$36	25 minutes
	City Bus (202)	$1.25	45 minutes

between major destinations, while others serve a greater number of cities. If you are planning to break your journey several times along the way, or you wish to tour the country, there are various packages designed to suit your requirements. Overseas visitors should also note that passes may be less expensive if you buy them from a Greyhound agent outside the U.S.

Greyhound Bus Lines
🅦 greyhound.com

Public Transportation

The New Orleans Regional Transport Authority (**RTA**) is New Orleans' main public transport authority. Safety and hygiene measures, time-tables, ticket information, transport maps, and more can be obtained from the RTA website.

RTA runs an efficient public transportation system. Bus routes crisscross the city, but no visitor should miss the opportunity to travel on the oldest streetcar in the nation – the St. Charles Avenue Streetcar (*p142*). Ferries are a pleasant way to cross and travel along the Mississippi River. Note that most of the city's popular tourist sights in and near the French Quarter are easily accessible on foot.

RTA
🅦 norta.com

Planning Your Journey

Buses are busiest during the rush hours: 7–9am and 4:30–6pm. Streetcars can be packed throughout the day, and are especially busy during major festivals such as Mardi Gras and Jazz Fest. Note that public transportation runs a reduced service during major holidays. The RTA's Le Pass smartphone app provides live transport information.

Tickets

The RTA offers one-way and express fares as well as a variety of Jazzy Pass options for the bus, streetcar, and ferry network; 1-, 3-, 7-, and 31-day passes are available. They can be purchased online from the RTA website and Le Pass app, or from various vendors across New Orleans, such as the ticket vending machines (cash only) along the Canal Streetcar line. Fares and passes are only applicable on the New Orleans RTA system.

On buses, streetcars, and ferries, one-way tickets and one-day passes can be purchased directly from your bus driver or a streetcar operator, with cash only.

Buses

Bus stops are indicated by white and yellow signs displaying the RTA logo. The route numbers of the buses stopping there are usually listed at the bottom of the sign. Buses stop only at desig-nated bus stops, which are located every two or three blocks, depending on the area of the city.

Buses in New Orleans are less frequent and less reliable than in many major U.S. cities, so be sure to check schedules, especially outside of peak hours. All New Orleans buses are accessible to travelers with specific needs, and guide dogs are allowed on board. Front seats are reserved for senior citizens and disabled passengers. Buses have bike racks that can accommodate up to two bicycles on board.

On boarding the bus, put the exact change in the fare box, swipe your Jazzy Pass, or tap your phone's Le Pass app. Smoking, drinking, eating, and playing music are all prohibited on buses.

Ferries

The **Canal Street Ferry** (RTA) crosses the river daily, carrying pedestrians and vehicles from the Central Business District to Algiers Point, on the West Bank. The ferry departs roughly every 15 minutes from 6am to 8:45pm daily and costs $2.

Canal Street Ferry
🅦 neworleans.com/plan/transportation/algiers-ferry

Streetcars

New Orleans' streetcars makes a pleasant way to get around the city, moving at a moderate pace and stopping frequently around major sights. There are five streetcar lines in New Orleans, all operated by the RTA.

The Riverfront Streetcar line travels a distance of 1.5 miles (2.4 km) along the Mississippi Riverfront, from Esplanade Avenue, at the far side of the French Quarter, to Julia Street (near the cruise terminal). The streetcar runs approximately every 30 minutes, 6am to 11:45pm daily.

The first stop for the St. Charles Streetcar is at the corner of Canal and Carondelet streets. The streetcar turns onto Canal Street, then back around on St. Charles Avenue for the trip uptown. It travels the length of St. Charles Avenue, turning on to Carrollton Avenue at the Riverbend, and terminating at Claiborne Avenue. The return trip is the reverse of the outbound trip until Lee Circle, where it turns onto Carondelet Street to get to Canal Street. This line operates 24 hours a day and runs every 12 minutes, but is less frequent off peak.

The Canal Streetcar route starts at the Riverfront, at the foot of Canal Street, and runs to City Park Avenue. It runs approximately every 20–30 minutes 24 hours a day. There is also a spur line along North Carrollton Avenue, linking Canal Street to the New Orleans Museum of Art and City Park at Beauregard Circle. It runs approximately every 30–40 minutes.

The Rampart/UPT Streetcar line runs from Union Station to Elysian Fields Avenue along Loyola Avenue, Rampart Street and St. Claude Avenue. This line operates between approximately 5:30am to midnight, and runs every 30 minutes.

When you board the streetcar, pay the driver in cash (with the exact fare) or swipe your Jazzy Pass or Le Pass app. You will need to pull the cord to indicate that you want to disembark. You can exit from either the front of the car or the back, depending on how crowded the streetcar is. Each streetcar displays its destination on the front.

Bus Tours

One of the most popular ways to see the sights is aboard a hop-on-hop-off bus tour. Get off wherever you like, and catch another bus when you are ready. **City Sightseeing New Orleans** offers such tours aboard double-decker buses.

City Sightseeing New Orleans
W citysightseeingneworleans.com

Taxis

The city's taxis are affordable, convenient, and highly recommended for trips after dark to areas outside the French Quarter. Cabs are easily found at airports, bus and train stations, all major hotels, and regular taxi stands. For time-sensitive journeys, pre-book a taxi; **United Cabs** is recommended. Arrange a pickup at a definite time and place. All fares should be metered according to the distance traveled. All taxis have a light on their windshield to indicate when they are available. **Uber** and **Lyft** also operate in New Orleans.

Lyft
W lyft.com
Uber
W uber.com
United Cabs
C (504) 522-9771
W unitedcabs.com/home

Driving

The good public transportation network and short distances between sights make driving in central New Orleans largely unnecessary, but a car is convenient if you wish to visit the smaller towns and plantations beyond the cities of Baton Rouge and Lafayette.

Driving in the city takes patience, good skills, and the ability to read the road and the street signs quickly. In central New Orleans, be prepared for heavy traffic and a severe shortage of parking facilities, especially in the French Quarter.

New Orleans is notorious for large potholes; drive carefully and make sure there is paved road ahead. Frequent heavy downpours can cause street flooding. Make sure to drive slowly through standing water, or if possible find another route.

Car Rental

Rental car companies can be found at the airport and other locations in the city. To rent a car in the US you must be at least 21 years old with a valid driving license and a clean record – drivers under 25 will usually pay extra and may have their choice of car restricted. All agencies require a major credit card.

Damage and liability insurance is recommended just in case something unexpected should happen. It is advisable always to return the car with a full tank of gas; otherwise you will be required to pay the inflated fuel prices charged by the rental agencies. Be sure to check for any pre-existing damage to the car and note this on your contract before you leave the rental lot.

Parking

If you do decide to drive in the city, check with your hotel to see if they offer parking; this will usually add at least $25 per night to your bill. In the French Quarter, valet parking (often the only option) can add $45–50 per night to your bill. Otherwise, there are meters across the city, charging $3 per hour in Marigny, CBD and the Warehouse District, and $2 per hour elsewhere. Meters do not have to be paid between 7pm and

8am, or on Sundays. Use the **ParkMobile** app to avoid having to return to your car every one or two hours to feed the meter; a parking fine will set you back $30. Avoid parking in the French Quarter, where the narrow streets are frequently cleaned, meaning that cars must be moved or face being towed away (see street signs). Parking on any major city street or thoroughfare is forbidden during Mardi Gras. The city's tow-away crew is very active.

ParkMobile
🅦 parkmobile.io

Rules of the Road
All drivers are legally required to carry a valid driver's license and must be able to produce registration and insurance documents. Most foreign licenses are valid, but if your license is not in English, or does not have a photo ID, apply for an International Driving Permit.

In private vehicles, seat belts are compulsory in front seats and are suggested in the back. In cabs, seat belts must be worn at all times in both the front and back seats. Children under three years old must ride in a child seat in the back.

Traffic drives on the right-hand side of the road, and the speed limit is usually 35 mph (56 km/h) unless otherwise stated. When it is safe to do so you may turn right on a red light. If a school bus stops to let passengers off, all traffic from both sides must stop and wait for the bus to drive off.

Drinking and Driving
A limit of 0.08 per cent blood alcohol is strictly enforced at all times. For drivers under the age of 21 there is a zero tolerance policy for drink-driving – driving while intoxicated is a punishable offense that incurs heavy fines or even a jail sentence.

Breakdown Assistance
In the event of an accident or breakdown, drivers of rental cars should contact their car rental company first. Members of the American Automobile Association (**AAA**) can have their vehicle towed to the nearest service station to be fixed. For simple problems like a flat tire or a dead battery, the AAA will fix it or install a new battery on site for a fee.

AAA
🅦 aaa.com

Walking
The city is made up of distinct neighborhoods and it is often simplest to take public transportation to a particular area and then explore on foot. The French Quarter, for example, is particularly compact and easily strolled around. A variety of guided and unguided walking tours are available. **Friends of the Cabildo** conduct daily tours of the historic French Quarter. Tours start outside the 1850 House at 10:30am and 1:30pm. Tickets can be reserved online in advance. **Two Chicks Walking Tours** lead groups around the French Quarter, Garden District, and the city's cemeteries, with tours focusing on quirky and unexpected aspects of history.

Wear comfortable shoes; some sidewalks and streets in New Orleans are very old and uneven. Parts of Mid-City, Uptown, and the Bywater are best avoided at night, but it is wise to be cautious at all times in all areas of New Orleans.

Friends of the Cabildo
🅦 friendsofthecabildo.org
Two Chicks Walking Tours
🅦 twochickswalkingtours.com

Cycling

Cycling in New Orleans is easy and convenient thanks to the city's flat, gridded network of streets and bike-friendly initiatives. It's a leisurely way to experience the charm of its historic neighborhoods. All city buses are equipped with bike racks, allowing you to combine modes of transport. Be sure to lock your bike securely when you park it, as bicycle thefts are common. **Bicycle Michael's** and **American Bicycle Rental Co** offer rental services, as well as guided tours. The city's bike-sharing scheme, **Blue Bikes**, has stations around the city. It can be used by registering online and then paying with a credit card.

The **Lafitte Greenway** is a 2.6-mile- (4.2-km-) long pedestrian and cycle trail. A pleasant, tree-lined stretch, the Greenway links Armstrong Park to City Park, where there are more cycle paths to explore.

Bicycle Michael's
🅦 bicyclemichaels.com
Blue Bikes
🅦 bluebikesnola.com
American Bicycle Rental Co
🅦 bikerentalneworleans.com
Lafitte Greenway
🅦 lafittegreenway.org

Boats Trips

Traditional riverboats offer tours stopping at popular destinations. The *Creole Queen* runs two cruises: a day trip to the Chalmette Battlefield, where the Battle of New Orleans took place, and a night cruise that includes dinner accompanied by live jazz. The **Steamboat** *Natchez* (p74) offers a two-hour tour in the morning and a night cruise with an excellent buffet and live jazz.

Creole Queen
🅦 creolequeen.com
Steamboat *Natchez*
🅦 steamboatnatchez.com

PRACTICAL
INFORMATION

A little local know-how goes a long way in New Orleans. Here you will find all the essential advice and information you will need during your stay.

EMERGENCY NUMBERS

GENERAL EMERGENCY

911

TIME ZONE
CST/CDT (Central Daylight Time)
PST +3
UTC/GMT -6
AEDT +15

TAP WATER
Unless otherwise stated, tap water in New Orleans is safe to drink.

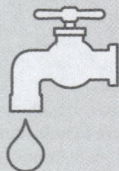

WEBSITES AND APPS
New Orleans
Visit the city's official tourist information website at *neworleans.com.*

NORTA Le Pass App
New Orleans' RTA public transport app for tracking streetcars, buses, and ferries in real time, at *norta.com/ride-with-us/how-to-pay/lepass.*

Mardi Gras Parade Tracker
The best app for information about the dozens of carnival parades, at *mardigrasparadetracker.com.*

Personal Security

Although much of New Orleans is safe for visitors, there are areas, as in any city, that may not be especially tourist friendly, and things can change on a block by block basis. Use your common sense and be alert to your surroundings, and you should enjoy a trouble-free trip.

If you are mugged, do not challenge the thief – hand over your phone or your money instead. If you have anything stolen, report the crime within 24 hours to the nearest police station and take ID with you. Get a copy of the crime report in order to claim on your insurance. Contact your embassy if you have your passport stolen, or in the event of a serious crime or accident.

As a rule, New Orleanians are very accepting of all people, regardless of their race, gender or sexuality. The city celebrates its multicultural heritage, which includes French, Spanish, Cajun, Creole, German, and Indigenous influences. While New Orleans champions its LGBTQ+ communities (and was one of the first cities in the country to pass an ordinance prohibiting discrimination based on sexual orientation), the state of Louisiana remains conservative; homosexuality was only legalized in 2003 (via a Supreme Court ruling), with same-sex marriage following in 2015. Women might experience catcalls in some parts of the French Quarter, especially around Bourbon Street, a well-known party spot.

Health

The U.S. has a world-class healthcare system. However, there is no universal healthcare available and costs for medical and dental care can be high. Comprehensive medical insurance is therefore highly recommended for international travelers to the U.S.

It is possible to visit a doctor or dentist in New Orleans without being registered, but you will be asked to pay in advance. Keep receipts to make a claim on your insurance later. There are plenty of walk-in medical clinics, emergency rooms, and 24-hour pharmacies. **CrescentCare** offers

convenient walk-in or by-appointment services at locations around the city. Hospital emergency treatment is available 24 hours a day. If you are able, call the number on your insurance policy first, and check which hospitals your insurance company deals with. For emergency treatment, call an ambulance.

CrescentCare
ⓦ crescentcare.org

Smoking, Alcohol, and Drugs

Smoking is prohibited in all public buildings, bars, restaurants, and stores. Cigarettes can be purchased by those over 18 years old; proof of age will be required.

The legal minimum age for drinking alcohol in the U.S. is 21, and you will need photo ID as proof of age in order to purchase alcohol and be allowed into bars. In New Orleans, it is legal to drink alcohol in public (in a can or sealed container) but it is illegal to carry an open container of alcohol in your car, and penalties for driving under the influence of alcohol are severe.

Possession of illegal drugs is prohibited and could result in a prison sentence.

ID

It is not compulsory to carry ID at all times in New Orleans. If you are asked by police to show your ID, a photocopy of your passport photo page (and visa if applicable) should suffice. You may be asked to present the original document within 12 or 24 hours.

Responsible Travel

New Orleans is committed to becoming carbon neutral by 2050. Do your part by recycling, carrying reusable bottles and bags, and taking public transportation. Streetcars in New Orleans are fully electric and provide an easy and economical way to get around town.

Visiting Churches, Cathedrals, and Synagogues

Dress respectfully when visiting religious buildings: cover your torso and upper arms, and ensure shorts or skirts cover your knees.

Cell Phones and Wi-Fi

Cafés and restaurants will usually permit the use of their Wi-Fi on the condition that you make a purchase.

Cell phone service in New Orleans is generally excellent but if you are visiting from overseas and want to guarantee that your cell phone will work, make sure you have a quad-band phone. In order to use your phone abroad you may need to activate the "roaming" facility. Other options include buying a prepaid cell phone in the U.S. or a SIM chip for a U.S. carrier.

Mail

Stamps can be purchased from post offices and drugstores. On-street mailboxes are usually blue, and are for letters only. Small packages must be taken to a post office. The city's main **General Post Office** is open from 9am to 5pm Monday to Friday. Mail can take from one to five days to arrive at its destination.

General Post Office
ⓦ usps.com

Taxes and Refunds

Taxes will be added to hotel and restaurant charges, theater tickets, some grocery and store sales, and most other purchases. Always check if tax is included in the price displayed. Sales tax is around 10 per cent, and hotel tax is around 15–17 per cent.

When tipping in a restaurant, it is the norm to include tax in your calculation. A quick way to calculate restaurant tips is simply to double the tax, which adds up to 20 per cent. Tax-free shopping is available at participating stores to foreign visitors who are staying in the U.S. for fewer than 90 days.

Discount Cards

The **Go New Orleans Pass** offers entry to some of the city's top sights and experiences, including museums and tours. These digital passes, covering one, two, three, or five days, are available to purchase online and from participating tourist offices.

Go New Orleans Pass
ⓦ gocity.com/en/new-orleans

INDEX

PHRASE BOOK

South Louisiana has a rich heritage of blending its disparate cultures, and New Orleans is no exception. French, Spanish, Cajun French, Creole French, English, German, and some Indigenous words have all been mixed together into a New Orleans patois. The following is a list of the most frequently used words and phrases, plus a guide to correct pronunciation.

WORDS AND PHRASES

armoire	(arm-wah) **cupboard or wardrobe**
arpent	**measure of 180 ft (55 m)**
au dit	(oh-dee) **ditto or "the same"**
aw-right	**accepted greeting or acclamation on meeting friend s or acquaintances**
banquette	(ban-ket) **sidewalk**
baptiser	(bap-tee-zay) **to give a name to something**
bateau	**boat**
bayou	(bay-you or bye'o) **a waterway or creek**
boeuf	(berf) **cow, meat, steak**
Bouree	**Cajun card game**
bousillage	(boor-sill-arge) **mixture of Spanish moss and mud, used to insulate walls**
brulé	(bru-lay) **burned, toasted (as in café brulé)**
cabinette	**outhouse**
cocodrie	**alligator**
Cajun	**descendants of the Acadians who settled in South Louisiana in the 18th century**
charivari	(shi-va-ree) **noisy mock serenade to a newly married older couple**
chaudron	**a cauldron or large kettle**
cher	(share) **widespread term of endearment in Cajun French**
cold drink	**soda with ice**
coulée	(cool-ay) **ravine or gully**
Creole	**descendant of original French or Spanish settlers**
Creole of color	**descendant of French or Spanish settlers with African blood**
doubloons	**aluminum coins thrown to Mardi Gras crowds**
dressin' room	**polite term for the bathroom**
fais-do-do	(fay-doh-doh) **literally "go to sleep"; Cajun term for a community dance where parents bring their children, who often fall asleep to the music**
fourche	**the fork of a creek (as in Bayou Lafourche)**
gallery	**balcony or porch**
gris-gris	(gree-gree) **voodoo charm**
Guignolée	**New Year's Eve celebration**
jour de l'An	**New Year's Day**
krewe	**private club that sponsors a parade and a ball during Mardi Gras**
lagniappe	(lan-yap) **"something extra" at no cost**
levee	**embankment for flood control or riverside landing**
neutral ground	**the median of a large avenue or street (the St. Charles Avenue streetcar runs on the neutral ground)**
nonc	**uncle**
nutria	**South American rodent imported to Louisiana in the late 18th century. The nutria is an important part of the fur industry**
ouaouaron	(wah-wah-rohn) **bullfrog**
parish	**civil and political division in Louisiana (like a county)**
patois	(pat-wah) **dialect: different Cajun communities speak their own patois**
pirogue	(pee-row) **long, shallow canoe**
praline	(praw-LEEN) **candy made with sugar, cream, and pecans, very popular in New Orleans**
rat de bois	(rat-de-bwah) **opossum**
shotgun house	**long, narrow house**
T or Ti	**petite, junior, a nickname (T-frere = baby brother)**
Vieux Carré	(voo-cah-RAY) **literally "Old Square", the French Quarter**
ward	**political division of New Orleans**
where y'at?	**how are you?**

STREET AND TOWN NAMES

Atchafalaya	(chaf-fly) **large (800,000 acres/ 320,000 hectares) swampy wilderness area in South Louisiana**
Tchoupitoulas St	(chop-a-TOOL-us)
Burgundy St	(bur-GUN-dy)
Chartres St	(CHART-ers)
Euterpe St	(YOU-terp)

Melpomene Ave	(MEL-pom-meen)
Metairie	(MET'ry) **suburb of New Orleans**
Terpsichore St	(TERP-si-core)
Opelousas Ave	(opp-a-LOO-sas)
Lafayette	(laugh-e-YET) **unofficial capital of Cajun Country**
Plaquemine	(PLACK-a-meen) **town and parish south of Baton Rouge**
Baton Rouge	(bat'n ROOZH) **capital of Louisiana**
Thibodeaux	(TIBB-a-doh) **common surname, also a town in Cajun Country**
Natchitoches	(NACK-uh-dish) **oldest town in the Louisiana Purchase area**
Ponchatoula	(ponch-a TOOL-ah) **town on the north shore of Lake Pontchartrain**

CAJUN AND CREOLE COOKING

andouille	**pork and garlic sausage**
beignet	**square, deep-fried doughnut, dusted with powdered sugar**
boudin	**spicy pork, rice, and onion sausage**
bread pudding	**French bread soaked in milk and egg, baked, and served with whiskey sauce**
bouillabaisse	**French seafood stew**
café au lait	**dark roast coffee served with steamed milk**
chicory	**coffee additive, made of roasted, ground roots**
crawfish	(cray-fish) **often called "mudbugs," a delicious, small, lobster-like crustacean found in the creeks and bayous in Louisiana**
dirty rice	**rice mixed with chicken gizzards and livers, green pepper, onions, and spices**
etouffée	**method of cooking crawfish or shrimp, simmered with vegetables**
filé	**ground sassafras leaves, used to thicken gumbo**
grillades	**meat smothered with thick tomato gravy, always served with grits**
grits	**ground, hulled corn, cooked with butter, salt, and pepper**

gumbo	**spicy soup with okra, tomatoes, and seafood, served over rice**
jambalaya	**thick stew of rice, sausage, seafood, vegetables, and spices**
muffuletta	**huge sandwich of cold cuts, cheese, and olive salad, served on Italian bread**
okra	**pod vegetable, usually served in gumbo**
oysters Rockefeller	**oysters on the half shell, covered with a creamy spinach sauce, and baked on a bed of salt**
po'boy	**sandwich of fried seafood, roast beef, ham, or a mixture, served on French bread**
remoulade	**spicy mayonnaise-based seafood sauce**
roux	**mixture of butter and flour, mixed with water and seasonings; used as a base for many soups, gravies, and sauces**
shrimp Creole	**shrimp cooked with tomato sauce and seasoned with onions, green pepper, celery, and garlic**
Tabasco®	**hot, red pepper sauce made only at Avery Island; often used for any brand of pepper sauce, of which there are hundreds available**
tasso	**local highly seasoned smoked ham**

ACKNOWLEDGMENTS

This edition updated by

Contributor Stephen Keeling
Senior Editors Dipika Dasgupta, Keith Drew
Senior Art Editors Stuti Tiwari,
Vinita Venugopal
Project Editor Anuroop Sanwalia
Editors Catrina Conway, Manjari Thakur
Assistant Picture Research Administrator
Manpreet Kaur
Rights & Permissions Specialist Vagisha Pushp
Deputy Picture Research Manager
Virien Chopra
Publishing Assistant Simona Velkova
Senior Cartographer Mohammed Hassan
Cartography Manager Suresh Kumar
Pre Production Coordinator Tanveer Zaidi
Production Controller Kariss Ainsworth
Deputy Managing Editor Dharini Ganesh
Managing Editor Beverly Smart
Managing Art Editor Gemma Doyle
Senior Managing Art Editor Priyanka Thakur
Editorial Director Hollie Teague
Art Director Maxine Pedliham
Publishing Director Georgina Dee

DK would like to thank the following for their
contributions to the previous edition: Donna
Dailey, Susanne Hillen, Ian McNulty, Sarah
O'Kelley, Paul Oswell, Helen Peters, Peter
Reichard, Harriet Swift, Marilyn Wood

The publisher would like to thank the following
for their kind permission to reproduce their
photographs:

Key: a-above; b-below/bottom; c-centre; f-far;
l-left; r-right; t-top

123RF.com: Fotoluminate 100-1t; Imagecom
16c, 58-9; Andrei Ivanov 33clb; Michael
Rosebrock 8cla.

4Corners: Massimo Borchi 68-9b, 70-1t.

akg-images: National Gallery of Art,
Washington / *Chief of the Taensa Indians
Receiving La Salle March 20, 1682* (1847/1848)
by George Catlin 49tl.

Alamy Stock Photo: A.F. ARCHIVE 110clb,
116bl; Irene Abdou 167t; Rubens Alarcon,
79b; 91cra, 98b, 103tl, 173tl, 178cl; American
Photo Archive 126bc; Archive Images 50-1t;
BHammond 17t, 86; Andriy Blokhin 8cl; Kristina
Blokhin 80bl; age fotostock / Massimo Borchi
83tl, 90-1b; Eric Brown 54clb; Ron S Buskirk
99br, 179br; Cavan / Joseph De Sciose 29br;
Charles O. Cecil 153br, 154-5b; Naum Chayer

75cra; Patrick Civello 151b; Jeff Compasso
177cla; Richard Cummins 131cra; Ian Dagnall
77bl; Danita Delimont / Cindy Miller Hopkins
101br, / Jamie & Judy Wild 114b; dbimages /
Jeremy Graham 30-1b,112-3b, / Roy Johnson
24-5t, 28cb; Sean Drakes 115t; Richard Ellis
199b; Everyday Artistry Photography 91tr, 177t;
FineArt 51clb; Geopix 55bc; GJGK Photography
39crb; Glasshouse Images / Circa Images 52cr;
Tim Graham 13br, 17bl, 104-5, 154tr, 188tl;
Granger Historical Picture Archive 50tl,110bc;
Leigh Green 113tl; Steve Hamblin 101cr, 126cb;
hemis.fr / Patrick Frilet 137tr, 186crb, 189b;
Cindy Hopkins 41cla; Ian Dagnall Commercial
Collection 198tr; Images-USA 96cla, 109br,
160bl, / *Statue of Louis Armstrong "Satchmo"*
by Elizabteh Catlett © Catlett Mora Family
Trust / VAGA at ARS; NY and DACS; London
2019 109cra; jejim120 125crb; Jon Arnold
Images Ltd / John Coletti 136bl; Inge Johnsson
176bl; Brenda Kean 19t, 162-3; Daniel
Korzeniewski 91tl; James Houser New Orleans
118-9t; Jason Langley 168-9b; Simon Leigh
85br, 184br; Chon Kit Leong 150tl; Andy Levin
91br, 175b; Melvyn Longhurst 99tl; Martin
Thomas Photography 94tr; Masterpics 49cb;
Ninette Maumus 10-1b, 35clb, 38tl, 76t; Nitu
Mistry 113cla; William Morgan 24cra, 132t,
159tl; Nature and Science 54bc; Niday Picture
Library 49bl; Nikreates 144–45t, 145bl;
Nathaniel Noir 22crb; North Wind Picture
Archives 48bc, 50cla, 51cr; Panther Media
Global / Joerg Hackemann / meinzahn 158bl;
The Picture Art Collection 51br; The Print
Collector / Heritage Images 49tr; Laura Prieto
94-5b, 97br; The Protected Art Archive 142br;
Tom Pumphret 47clb; Reciprocity Images 39tl,
161tr; Golden Richard 111bc; Khristina Ripak
22t; RM USA 114crb, 153cr; robertharding
128br, / Ken Gillham 153crb; Stephen Saks
Photography 194-5b; Trinity Mirror / Mirrorpix
110cra; UPI / A.J. Sisco 55cb, 189crb; Francis
Vachon 48crb; Vespasian 100br; Jim West 46cl,
167cla; Jennifer Wright 130bl, 132bl, 151crb;
ZUMA Press; Inc. 80-1t, / Daniel DeSlover 8clb.

Audubon Nature Institute: 40-1t, 134-35t,
144-5t, 145cra, 145clb, 145br; Digital Roux
Photography LLC / Susan Poag 135c.

AWL Images: Patrick Frilet 12-3b; Marco
Gaiotti 196-7; Christian Heeb 10ca; Jason
Langley 18tr, 120-1, 152-3t.

Bella Blue: Roy Guste 45bl.

Blue Bikes New Orleans: 35tr.

Bridgeman Images: Davis Museum and
Cultural Center, Wellesley College, MA, USA -
Museum purchase with funds provided by

Wellesley College Friends of Art *Storyville Portrait, c.1912* (gelatin silver printing-out print) by E. J. Bellocq 52br; Granger / *1803 American cartoon, c. 1900, on the purchase of Louisiana by the United States from France* 50clb.

Brustman Carrino Public Relations: Hot Tin / Randy Schmidt 10clb, / Sienna Viette 25tl.

Cochon - Link Restaurant Group: Chris Granger 137br.

© DACS 2019: *Statue of Louis Armstrong "Satchmo"* by Elizabteh Catlett / © Catlett Mora Family Trust / VAGA at ARS, NY and DACS, London 2019 109cra; *Untitled,1991, Bronze, ed. 4 / 4* by Joel Shapiro © ARS, NY and DACS, London 2019 New Orleans Museum of Art purchase, Sydney and Walda Besthoff Foundation Fund, 98.213 169t.

Dorling Kindersley: William Reavell 27tr; Helena Smith 179tr.

Dreamstime.com: Joe Benning 174-5t; Crackerclips 52-53t; F11photo 42-3b; Fotoluminate 156-7t; Roberto Galan 4; Legacy1995 147tr; Maomaotou 161br; Meinzahn 12clb, 24tl, 38br, 44tl, 63, 143; Alexander Mychko 27cl; Sean Pavone 6-7, 184-5t, 200-1; William Perry 148-49; Photofires 62c; Anne Power 46cla; Terryfultineer 81cla; Lawrence Weslowski Jr 85tl.

The Ehrhardt Group - Compère Lapin: Dominique Ellis 26b.

French Quarter Festival, Inc presented by Chevron: Zac Smith 47tr.

Getty Images: 500Px Unreleased Plus / Steve Tosterud 93br; AFP 55t; AFP / Claire Bangser 56-57; Archive Photos / Charles Peterson 110-1t, / P. L. Sperr 142cb; Bettmann 43tl, 51tr; Bloomberg 39tr; Canopy / Robert Mullan 100crb; Cavan Images 34tr; Christian Science Monitor 43cl, 54cr; AWL Images / John Coletti 108-9t; John Coletti 25cla; Corbis Documentary / Atlantide Phototravel 126-7, 169cra, 170-1t, / VCG / Robert Holmes 102bl; Corbis Historical / Stefano Bianchetti 110crb; Corbis NX / Richard T. Nowitz 116-7t; De Agostini 50br, / Biblioteca Ambrosiana 52tl; FilmMagic / Josh Brasted 53br, / Erika Goldring 31tr; Cheryl Gerber 66-7b; Sean Gardner 67clb; Erika Goldring 11cr, 12t, 28-9t, 46cra, 66bc, 67cla, 67cl, 109cb,133bl, 174bl; Tim Graham 11br; Icon Sportswire 46clb; The Image Bank / Anne Rippy 192-3b; In Pictures / Barry Lewis 29cla; Tyler Kaufman 47cla, 53tr; The LIFE Picture Collection / Mansell 142clb;

Lonely Planet Images 93tc, / Judy Bellah 40br, / Richard Cummins 191tl, 191tr, / Ray Laskowitz 34-5b, / Kylie McLaughlin 11t, 47cra, 101tr, / Stephen Saks 186-7t; MediaNews Group / Pasadena Star-News / Keith Birmingham 53clb; Michael Ochs Archives 111clb; Moment Open / Gerard Plauche 156c; Tim Mosenfelder 45crb; MPI / Archive Photos 49cla; Photolibrary / Marianna Massey 20crb; Redferns / Frank Hoensch 111crb, / David Redfern 110br; Michael Serna 8-9b; Mario Tama 92br; Universal Images Group / Education Images 78tr, 146b, / Encyclopaedia Britannica 48t, / Marka 75t, / Photo 12 52cla; The Washington Post 36bl; WireImage / Skip Bolen 189cra / Erika Goldring 27br.

Getty Images / iStock: Melissa Burovac 18bl, 138-139; Geoff Eccles 193tr; grandriver 2-3, 128-9t; Jenniveve84 66cra; Pgiam 96-97t; Renphoto 71cb; SeanXu 62cra; sfe-co2 131t; wynnter 52clb.

HiHo Lounge: Nkechi Chibueze 44br.

The Historic New Orleans Collection: 72cra, 72-3b, 73tr, 73cla; *Portrait of Lydia Brown (1922–28)* by Josephine Marien -Gift of Laura Simon Nelson 73cra; Gift of Harold F. Naquet and Cheron Bryiski, 2016.0172.3.43 113br; Gift of Mr. G. William Nott, 1974.61.1 113cra.

Krewe of Armeinius: Barrett DeLong 67bl.

LeMieux Galleries: *Corner Bar* by David Lambert 37cl.

Louisiana State Museum: Jay Rosenblatt 65clb; Mark J Sindler 64bl, 64-5t, 65crb, 65bl, 68cra.

Mardi Gras World: 41br.

Napolean House: 30tl.

Courtesy of The National WWII Museum: Jeffery Johnston 126clb.

courtesy of the New Orleans Museum of Art: 170bl, 171tr, 171crb, / *Untitled,1991, Bronze, ed. 4 / 4* by Joel Shapiro © ARS, NY and DACS, London 2019 purchase, *Sydney and Walda Besthoff Foundation Fund, 98.213* 169t, / *Looking Through the Doomsday Fog, 1990, paper maché on wood with ink notations* by Clyde Connell - *Gift of Jack Sullivan in loving memory of Christopher Karnes, 2000.5.1* 171cla.

New Orleans and Company: 26tl; Paul Broussard 13t, 25tr, 46cr, 47crb; LA Gourmetreise 2010 45tl; Zac Smith 31br; Travelling Newlyweds 31cl.

New Orleans Glassworks: 37br.

New Orleans Historic Voodoo Museum:
Charles M. Gandolfo 113cb.

Ogden Museum of Southern Art: Ryan Hogdson
/ *Stormy 2015, Stoneware and acrylic paint* by
Mapo Kinnord 36-7t; Ryan Hodgson-Rigsbee /
Eating Cake (2008) - Mixed media Gift of the Artist
by Shawne Major 124-25t

Picfair.com: Andrew Areoff 20cr.

Ralph's on the Park: Chris Granger 22cr.

Reuters: Jonathan Bachman 67tl.

Robert Harding Picture Library: Jason
Langley 13cr.

**Sazerac Bar at Roosevelt / Waldorf Astoria
Hotels & Resorts:** Brian F Huff 32tl.

Shutterstock.com: Bruce Alan Bennett 46crb;
Elliott Cowand Jr 92-3t; f11photo 20bl; JustPixs
22bl; William A. Morgan 82bl; Page Light Studios
112cl; Micha Weber 20t.

SuperStock: Richard Cummins 19cb, 180-1.

**Tales of the Cocktail - Foxglove
Communications:** Cory James Photo 32-3b.

**Tennessee Williams & New Orleans Literary
Festival:** Ride Hamilton 42tl, 47tl.

The Ashima Group: Christian Horan 33tr.

Front flap: Alamy Stock Photo: BHammond
cra; **AWL Images:** ClickAlps br; **Dreamstime.
com:** F11photo bl; **Getty Images:** John Coletti
cla; **Getty Images / iStock:** grandriver t;
Picfair.com: Marco Montenegro.

Sheet map cover: Shutterstock.com:
GTS Productions.

Cover images:
Front and Spine: **Shutterstock.com:**
GTS Productions.
Back: **Dreamstime.com:** Sean Pavone cla;
Getty Images: Lonely Planet Images / Ray
Laskowitz tr; **Shutterstock:** f11photo c;
GTS Productions b.

Illustrators:
Ricardo Almazan, Ricardo Almazan Jr.

DK | Penguin Random House

First edition 2002
Published in Great Britain by Dorling Kindersley Limited,
20 Vauxhall Bridge Road,
London SW1V 2SA

The authorised representative in the EEA is
Dorling Kindersley Verlag GmbH. Arnulfstr.
124, 80636 Munich, Germany

Published in the United States by DK Publishing,
1745 Broadway, 20th Floor, New York, NY 10019

Copyright © 2002, 2026 Dorling Kindersley Limited
A Penguin Random House Company

25 26 27 28 10 9 8 7 6 5 4 3 2 1

The publishers cannot accept responsibility for any
consequences arising from the use of this book,
nor for any material on third party websites, and
cannot guarantee that any website address in this
book will be a suitable source of travel information.

A CIP catalog record for this book
is available from the British Library.

A catalog record for this book is available
from the Library of Congress.

ISSN: 1542 1554
ISBN: 978 0 2417 8373 3

Printed and bound in China.

www.dk.com

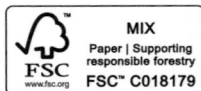

A NOTE FROM DK

The rate at which the world is changing is constantly
keeping the DK travel team on our toes. While we've
worked hard to ensure that this edition of New
Orleans is accurate and up-to-date, we know that
opening hours alter, standards shift, prices fluctuate,
places close and new ones pop up in their stead.
So, if you notice we've got something wrong or
left something out, we want to hear about it.
Please get in touch at travelguides@dk.com